Gaudry, Eric.
Anxiety and educational achievement.

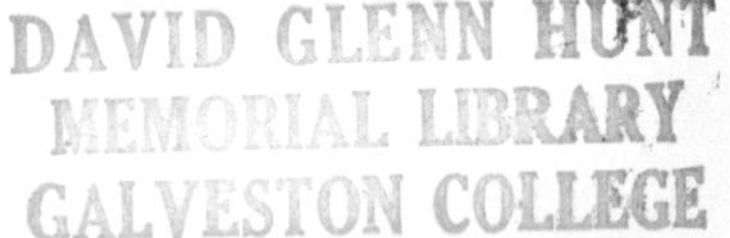

ANXIETY AND EDUCATIONAL ACHIEVEMENT

Anxiety and Educational Achievement

Eric Gaudry
University of Melbourne

Charles D. Spielberger
Florida State University

John Wiley & Sons Australasia Pty Ltd
SYDNEY New York London Toronto

ISBN and National Library of Australia Card Number:
Cloth: 0 471 29289-3
Paper: 0 471 29290-7
Library of Congress Catalog Card Number: 76-171907

Registered at the General Post Office, Sydney, for transmission through the post as a book.

Printed at The Griffin Press, Adelaide, South Australia

Contents

Preface

In recent years, there has come to be a gradual recognition of the fact that personality and motivational variables are important correlates of scholastic achievement in the same way that intellectual aptitudes have long been regarded as being important. With the increasing demands to individualise instruction to suit the abilities, capacities and personalities of each child, the need to bring together the rather voluminous research on anxiety and achievement has become apparent. The questions of how anxiety level is related to performance in various settings and how the learning situation might be structured to allow both the low- and the high-anxious students to realise their full potential are taken up in this book.

The book is designed to overcome the objection frequently raised by students taking courses in Educational Psychology that the content of their courses is too academic and too far removed from the teaching-learning situation. By anchoring the book to achievement in school and college settings, it is expected that this volume will offer an original review and enquiry which will link relevant aspects of psychological theory to what must surely be an area of major concern to teachers and potential teachers: achievement in the classroom.

The studies reviewed are taken from American, English and Australian settings. A set of readings is provided in the second part of the book to facilitate reference to some of the investigations under review. This volume does not require any previous knowledge of psychology for effective reading, and a deliberate attempt has been made to keep it as free as possible of technical terminology. At the same time, it is hoped that the several psychological theories which are introduced, without, we hope, any serious distortion, will stimulate the reader's interest in the source discipline of psychology.

We are especially grateful to F. D. Naylor for his detailed and constructive criticism of the manuscript. Grateful acknowledgement is also made to the following individuals and organisations for their kind permission to reproduce tables, figures and the articles selected for reading: G. D. Bradshaw, E. L. Cowen, F. N. Cox, D. Fitzgerald, S. B. Hammond, D. N. Hansen, W. F. Hodges, L. D. Izzo, H. R. Kight, R. Klein, H. F. O'Neil, J. M. Sassenrath, K. E. Sinclair, M. A. Trost, M. Zax, *Australian Journal of Education*, *Australian Journal of Psychology*, *British Journal of Educational Psychology*, *Child Development*,

Journal of Abnormal and Social Psychology, Journal of Educational Psychology, Journal of Educational Research, Journal of Personality and Social Psychology, Mental Hygiene, Psychophysiology.

ERIC GAUDRY and CHARLES D. SPIELBERGER

September, 1971

Part One

Chapter I

Introduction

Over the last two decades, there has been an ever increasing number of reports on the effects of anxiety on learning and retention. This area of research has been of considerable interest to teachers who have observed that some children appear to perform below their best in situations characterised by a high degree of stress. It is a common occurrence to hear teachers comment that a certain student gets so upset that he "falls to pieces" or "chokes up" during an examination, and fails to live up to the promise shown in his class work. Somewhat less commonly, and seemingly less directly related to anxiety, teachers comment about students with little motivation who, they feel, could do much better "if I only could stir him up".

The major aim of this book is to examine the relationship between anxiety and school attainment, and to discuss this relationship in the context of important educational issues, such as streaming by ability or ability grouping. A second goal is to examine the relationship betweeen anxiety and performance with modern techniques of instruction, such as programmed learning and computer-based instruction. The text is based on empirical research rather than speculative opinion, and most of the inferences drawn here are derived from experimental studies rather than from the opinion of "experts". Since these studies are found under the general heading of the psychology of learning, a brief survey of two fundamental sources of data on learning will be given.

Basic Research on Learning

Faced with the apparently bewildering complexity of the learning process, many psychologists have made a deliberate decision to retreat to the laboratory, where it is much easier to exercise experimental control over the conditions under which learning occurs than it is in the classroom or in individual study. The question of experimental control has four facets: the first is concerned with stimulus conditions, the second with organismic conditions, the third with response conditions, and the fourth with events which follow the response.

Much of the basic research on learning has been concerned with the study of the acquisition of a simple response under laboratory conditions. For example, an investigator may decide to study the acquisition of a response, such as an animal learning to run down a straight runway to obtain some food. The stimulus conditions include all aspects of the environment to which the animal can respond: the door which opens to let him into the runway, the walls, the wire top, and so on. Organismic conditions would include the animal's state of hunger and its previous experience with similar situations. Response conditions refer to the entire range of responses that can be made—for example, not moving, going to sleep, running down the alley, or biting the roof. The consequence of the response on a successful run might be the delivery of a pellet of food, or the omission of reinforcement if the animal does not run fast enough.

In the runway situation described in the previous paragraph, considerable experimental control may be exercised. The stimulus conditions are fairly simple, the hours without food can be regulated, and the previous history of the animal can be controlled and specified within limits. The number of possible responses is also limited, and precise control can be exercised over the events following a response. By manipulating food deprivation, the experimenter can study the effect of motivation (organismic condition) on performance. Similarly, other factors, such as amount of reinforcement, can be varied and studied by manipulating the conditions of reward.

By observing the development of a variety of responses in simple situations, psychologists with a basic research orientation hope to evolve a theory of learning that is trans-situational. The attempt is then made to extend the theory to more complex situations. Basic research on learning has been criticised, however, by those whose main interest is in education. The two main criticisms are: the relevance of the problems that are investigated, and the allied question of generalising from the laboratory to the classroom. More specifically the attack is focused on four major issues: the type of experimental subjects, the nature of the tasks, the past experience of the subjects, and the effects of social variables.

SUBJECTS

Animals are frequently used as subjects in learning experiments. When human subjects are used, they are often college or university students who are not representative of the general population because most college students have been relatively successful in coping with the demands imposed by the educational system. The significant question is whether it is possible to generalise from animal studies, or from college students learning a list of nonsense syllables, to the average high school student trying to master French or Mathematics.

THE NATURE OF THE TASK

The tasks used in basic research on learning tend to be relatively simple, and bear little resemblance to classroom tasks. It is quite possible that the laws governing the learning of simple tasks are not adequate for a description or explanation of the learning process that governs the mastery of more complex material. In addition, laboratory learning tasks are usually relatively brief in duration. Many of them are completed in less than half an hour, and the majority in under an hour. It may not be possible to extrapolate from such brief learning experiences to learning tasks which are cumulative in nature, and where knowledge and understanding is built up over a period of years.

The criterion of learning used in many studies is typically set at a fairly low level. In one type of experiment, known as paired-associate learning, each subject is required to learn to associate a response word with a stimulus word. For example, he may have to learn a list of 12 pairs, such as the following:

Stimulus Word	*Response Word*
table	chair
black	white
ruler	queen
:	:
:	:
paper	court

The stimulus words are presented one at a time, and the subject is required to respond with the appropriate response word. The criterion for learning is often set at being able to go through the entire list of 12 pairs on two successive occasions without error.

PAST EXPERIENCE

In laboratory studies, tasks are often selected because they minimise the influence of previous learning. In one such task, called serial learning, the subject is required to learn a list of words or phrases in a serial fashion, somewhat like learning the batting order of a baseball team. Frequently, nonsense syllables like PUY and HEZ are used as the stimulus and response elements. In contrast, much of the learning that takes place in academic settings presupposes certain prerequisite knowledge and experience within a particular area.

SOCIAL EFFECTS

A great deal of the material learned in school is assimilated in the presence of others. With few exceptions, learning theorists conduct their experiments using only one subject at a time. It seems probable that the presence of other students will have some effect upon performance. There is, in fact, evidence that the presence of other people (parents, teachers, peers) does have effects on performance in simple tasks and that such effects depend on the anxiety level of the child. (Cox,[1,2] Stevenson[3]).

The basic research of Spence,[4,5] to be explicated in Chapter 2, contains a well worked-out prediction for the role of anxiety in the performance of simple learning tasks. This research provides the take-off point for some of the educational studies discussed later, as does Sarason's[6] theory of test anxiety. The point of view taken in this book, then, is that basic research on learning, despite all the problems of relevance and the difficulties associated with generalising to more complex tasks and settings, does provide carefully established principles which have been used to good effect in research in Educational Psychology.

Applied Research

Applied research in education builds on basic psychological research and is generally conducted under field conditions. Many educators see psychology as one of the main foundation disciplines on which education is based. The basic principles or laws enunciated in basic research may be used to formulate hypotheses about performance in classroom settings.

In some cases, the results of a field study may suggest that additional variables need to be built into the principles derived from basic research to make them viable in a more complex setting. (See Gaudry and Fitzgerald, Part II, Chapter 20.) While the contribution of applied research to basic research has been relatively limited, it seems that this type of research should be capable of feeding back important information that could well change the course of the basic research enterprise. (For a full discussion of the status of educational psychology as a discipline, and of this point in particular, see McLaughlin and Precians.[7])

Classroom research represents one important type of applied research on learning. Typically, in classroom research one form of teaching or one method of instruction is compared with another, or the performance of one group of children as they progress through a particular curriculum is compared with that of another group which has followed a different course of study. For example, the question might be asked as to whether children learn to read better using a phonetic alphabet than they do using the conventional alphabet, or whether learning via the Physical Sciences Study Committee course (PSSC) leads to greater understanding of physics than progressing through some other course.

There are many difficulties associated with classroom research, and the results of numerous investigations suggest that the research in this area has not led to any systematised body of knowledge about the learning process. In general, the outcome of such studies has been that one investigator reports Method I as superior and then a second one reports Method II as better than Method I. The outcome is often stacked in favour of one method or the other by the nature of the tests used to assess the criterion performance. Even where strict precautions are taken against bias, favourable results tend to shift from one method to another, depending on such factors as the personality of the teacher, the ability level of the children and a host of other variables. As the vast majority of these studies is not directed by any underlying theory, explanations of discrepant findings are, at best, *ad hoc*.

Ausubel[8] maintains that the best way of arriving at an understanding of how people cope with complex verbal material is to conduct experiments using difficult prose material as the learning task. In a series of studies using passages about unfamiliar topics like Buddhism or the metallurgical properties of carbon steel (e.g., Ausubel,[9] Ausubel and Fitzgerald,[10,11] Ausubel and Youssef[12]) Ausubel and his colleagues have built up a convincing case that meaningful learning, as opposed to learning by rote, occurs only where the learner has a structure of relevant ideas to which new materials can be linked or anchored. Where these prerequisite structures do not exist, learning can only be rote in nature. To overcome this problem, Ausubel suggests that appropriate introductions to difficult materials will facilitate both learning and retention.

Ausubel's approach has a great deal of promise and appears likely to provide teachers with sound practical advice on the optimal structure of learning situations so that difficult materials can be learned in a meaningful way. It is unfortunate that his work has touched only tangentially on anxiety and learning, the central topics in this text.

The Construct of Anxiety

Terms like anxiety, intelligence and motivation are abstract constructs which have been advanced to make various facets of performance comprehensible. For example, we may attribute a student's excellent performance in classroom examinations to his superior intelligence as estimated from a high score on a test of ability. Or we may interpret poor performance in terms of a motivational concept, such as anxiety, which interferes with academic achievement. Anxiety level can be inferred in a variety of ways.

VERBAL REPORTS

A student may refuse to make a speech of thanks to a distinguished visitor who has addressed the school assembly. The reluctant speaker may state that he refused to take on the task because he gets so nervous in such situations that he has great difficulty in marshalling his thoughts. Or he may state that he shakes and trembles so much that he becomes incapable of commencing or completing his speech.

PHYSIOLOGICAL INDICATIONS

In everyday life, many of us judge others to be more or less anxious on the basis of overt bodily reactions in stressful situations. The presence of signs such as tremor in the limbs, sweating of the hands and forehead and flushing of the neck and face, is deemed to be an indication of anxiety. In more controlled laboratory situations, physiological measures of heart rate, blood pressure and sweating have been used to assess the extent of emotional response to stressful situations.

GENERAL BEHAVIOUR

The stereotype of the expectant father illustrates the method of evaluating a person as more or less anxious on the basis of his general behaviour. Such signs as pacing around the room, inability to sit in a chair for any length of time, chain smoking and inability to relax are often indicators of high anxiety. Anxiety can also be inferred from behavioural signs, such as restlessness, tenseness of posture, increased rate of speech and general distractibility.

These three examples of ways to assess anxiety level are sufficient to illustrate the complex nature of a scientific construct. They also show that there is no qualitative way to define a psychological construct such as anxiety. Just as we cannot dissect an animal and point to its intelligence, we cannot point to a specific behaviour and unambiguously state that it is "anxiety". However, concepts such as intelligence and anxiety can be "operationally" defined in terms of things people do though not in terms of what they are. For example, intelligence level may be defined by reference to performance on certain tests, and anxiety may be defined in terms of self-reports, physiological signs or general behaviour (Krause[13] lists six different types of evidence for inferring the presence of transitory anxiety).

To put the argument in a different form, a construct such as anxiety becomes useful when it can be related to antecedent or stimulus conditions and consequent or response conditions. For example, a stimulus condition that typically evokes anxiety is that of entering an examination room to take an important test. A student may respond by sweating and trembling, or by verbally reporting feelings of apprehension. From the relationship between stimulus and response, anxiety is inferred and we may then evaluate the performance of students who are rated as either high or low in anxiety.

In the majority of the studies that are referred to in later chapters, anxiety level has been assessed by the use of questionnaires, which require the subject to give introspective reports about how he feels, or about his feelings with respect to a certain delineated class of events or situations, such as taking a test or giving a speech. The validity of these measures assumes, of course, that the respondent is motivated to answer accurately and honestly, and that he is capable of assessing his own reactions. Thus, if an individual reports that he feels anxious, frightened, or apprehensive, or that he is trembling or his heart is beating rapidly, these verbal reports define an anxiety state.

In the following chapter, some of the questionnaires and tests that have been used to assess anxiety level will be described and the theoretical foundation on the basis of which each test was constructed will be made explicit.

References

[1] F. N. Cox, "Some Effects of Test Anxiety and Presence or Absence of other Persons on Boys' Performance on a Repetitive Motor Task". *J. exp. Child Psychol.*, 1966, **3**, pp. 100-12.

[2] F. N. Cox, "Some Relationships between Test Anxiety, Presence or Absence of Male Persons and Boys' Performance on a Repetitive Motor Task". *J. exp. Child Psychol.*, 1968, **6**, pp. 1-12.

[3] H. W. Stevenson, "Social Reinforcement of Children's Behaviour", in L. P. Lipsitt and C. C. Spiker (Eds), *Advances in Child Development and Behaviour,* Vol. 2, Academic Press, New York, 1965.

[4] K. W. Spence, *Behaviour Theory and Conditioning,* Yale University Press, New Haven, 1956.

[5] K. W. Spence, "A Theory of Emotionally Based Drive (D) and its Relation to Performance in Simple Learning Situations". *Am. Psychol.*, 1958, **13**, pp. 131-41.

[6] S. B. Sarason, K. S. Davidson, F. F. Lighthall, R. R. Waite and B. K. Ruebush, *Anxiety in Elementary School Children*, John Wiley & Sons, New York, 1960.

[7] R. McLaughlin and R. Precians, "Educational Psychology: Some Questions of Status", in R. J. W. Selleck (Ed.) *Melbourne Studies in Education*, Melbourne University Press, Melbourne, 1967.

[8] D. P. Ausubel, *Educational Psychology: A Cognitive View,* Holt Rinehart & Winston, New York, 1968.

[9] D. P. Ausubel, "The Use of Advance Organizers in the Learning and Retention of Meaningful Verbal Material". *J. educ. Psychol.*, 1960, **51**, pp. 267-72.

[10] D. P. Ausubel and D. Fitzgerald, "The Role of Discriminability in Meaningful Verbal Learning and Retention". *J. educ. Psychol.*, 1961, **52**, pp. 266-71.

[11] D. P. Ausubel and D. Fitzgerald, "Organizer, General Background and Antecedent Learning Variables in Sequential Verbal Learning". *J. educ. Psychol.*, 1962, **53**, pp. 243-49.

[12] D. P. Ausubel and M. Youssef, "The Role of Discriminability in Meaningful Verbal Learning". *J. educ. Psychol.*, 1963, **54**, pp. 331-36.

[13] M. S. Krause, "The Measurement of Transitory Anxiety". *Psychol. Rev.*, 1961, **68**, pp. 178-89.

Chapter 2

Measures of Anxiety and Their Theoretical Bases

In this chapter, four measures of anxiety are described along with the theoretical foundation on the basis of which each of these measures was constructed. No attempt has been made to cover the total range of anxiety scales. The decision to include a particular scale was determined largely by the extent to which it has been used by the investigators whose research is reported in later chapters.

The Manifest Anxiety Scale (MAS)

Much of the early experimental work on anxiety followed the development of the MAS by Taylor[1] and the subsequent publication of this scale (Taylor[2]). The MAS consists of fifty questions like: "I blush easily"; "I worry more than other people"; "I frequently find myself worrying about something"; "I always have enough energy when faced with difficulty". The subject is asked to indicate whether each statement is true or false about him, and his score is based on the total number of items marked in such a way as to indicate the presence of anxiety as a personality trait.

The development of the MAS was stimulated by the work of the learning theorist K. W. Spence at the University of Iowa. Spence belongs firmly in the "basic research" group. His research into the learning processes was conducted in the laboratory with simple tasks, and, often, with infra-human subjects. As a result of his investigations, and the earlier theoretical and experimental work of Hull,[3] Spence[4] developed two constructs which he believed to play important roles in learning and performance.

The first, called *habit-strength* (H), is the existing tendency to make a response. For example, if a student is asked to respond to the word "table", various associations would be available to him. Responses such as "chair", "cloth", and "brown" might be forthcoming in that order. In Spence's terminology, "chair" has a high habit strength and is high in the response hierarchy, while "brown" has a lower habit strength and is low in the response hierarchy. If "brown" is arbitrarily designated as the correct response, the subject who responds to "table" with "chair" approaches the task with a tendency to make an incorrect response.

Spence's second construct is a motivational one, called *drive* (D). Drive has the capacity to energise or activate the behaviour of the learner. In his studies with animals, Spence defined drive in terms of hours of food or water deprivation, or by the strength of a noxious stimulus, such as a painful electric shock, to which the animal was exposed. The relationship between habit strength and drive is expressed by a mathematical equation which, in simplified form, reads:

$$\text{Performance} = \text{Function of H} \times \text{D}$$

Now in the simple situations with which Spence was dealing—that is, the situations in which the correct response was high in the response hierarchy from the outset—it follows that the higher the drive level, the better the performance. Consider the arbitrary case where H for the correct response has a value of 10 and D can have two values of 6 or 9 units.

Case 1.

$$\text{Performance} = 10 \times 6 = 60 \text{ units}$$

Case 2.

$$\text{Performance} = 10 \times 9 = 90 \text{ units}$$

If these two cases represent two animals who have to perform a task, in which both have the tendency to make the correct response from the outset, then the animal with the higher drive level (that is Case 2) would perform at a higher level than the animal with the lower drive level (Case 1).

Now take two situations where the effects of changing the level of D can be calculated:

Situation 1.

	H for correct response	= 10
	H for incorrect response	= 2
Where D = 4,	performance correct	= 10 × 4 = 40;
	performance incorrect	= 2 × 4 = 8; and the
	absolute difference	= 32 units of strength for the correct response.
Where D = 8,	performance correct	= 10 × 8 = 80;
	performance incorrect	= 2 × 8 = 16; and the
	absolute difference	= 64 units of strength for the correct response.

Situation 2.

	H for correct response	= 2
	H for incorrect response	= 10
Where D = 4,	performance correct	= 2 × 4 = 8;
	performance incorrect	= 10 × 4 = 40; and the
	absolute difference	= 32 units of strength for the incorrect response.

Where D = 8, performance correct = 2 × 8 = 16;
performance incorrect = 10 × 8 = 80; and the
absolute difference = 64 units of strength for the incorrect response.

In Situation 1, an easy task where the correct response is high in the response hierarchy, the effect of doubling the drive level is to *increase* the absolute difference from 32 to 64 units. This is because D energises all existing habits, and the higher the drive the better the performance because there is less interference arising from competing response tendencies. In Situation 2, however, where the correct response is low in the response hierarchy, the effect of doubling the drive level increases the absolute difference in response strength from 32 to 64 units in favour of the incorrect response. Hence, the higher the drive, the worse the performance because competing responses provide greater competition with the correct response.

Thus, the effects of drive on performance will depend on the characteristics of the task. In a simple task where the correct response is dominant, high drive will facilitate performance; in a more complex task, in which incorrect responses are stronger than the correct response, high drive will impair performance.

The MAS was developed and regarded by Spence as a measure of drive for human subjects. Most studies employing the MAS as a measure of D have found that high-anxious *S*s perform better on simple tasks than low-anxious *S*s (e.g., Montague,[5] Taylor and Chapman[6]), but that they perform worse than low-anxious *S*s on complex tasks (e.g., Farber and Spence,[7] Montague,[5] Ramond[8]).

The MAS is a measure of a general "trait" or predisposition to experience anxiety, as can be seen from the use of words such as "often", "frequently", "usually", and "hardly ever" in the scale questions. Subjects are not required to report their emotional state as it exists at a particular moment in time. The Children's Manifest Anxiety Scale (CMAS), developed by Castaneda, McCandless and Palermo,[9] is also a measure of trait anxiety.

Test Anxiety Scales

The Test Anxiety Questionnaire (TAQ) was constructed by Mandler and Sarason (1952) to measure the anxiety reactions of adults taking course examinations or intelligence tests. The Test Anxiety Scale (Mandler and Cowen[10]), known as TAS, is a high school version. The Test Anxiety Scale for Children (TASC) was developed by Sarason and his colleagues (Sarason *et al.*[11]) as a measure of the anxiety that is aroused in children by tests or test-like situations. Their focus on test anxiety was determined, in part, by the fact that test situations are frequently encountered by almost all members of our society. Most persons perceive the testing situation to have an evaluative or assessment purpose, and feel that it is important to do well because " . . . in our culture the lives of people are very frequently affected by their test performance." (Sarason *et al.*,[11] p. 8).

Sarason's conception of anxiety is influenced by psychoanalytic theory which holds that the development of anxiety takes place in the family setting from the earliest years of life. According to this view, the child's behaviour in a wide variety of settings is constantly being evaluated by his parents. Adverse parental evaluations often evoke feelings of hostility in the child which cannot be expressed because of the child's dependence on his parents for approval, direction and support. Instead, feelings of guilt and anxiety are aroused in the child who appears as "dependent, unaggressive, and self-derogatory in test-like situations" (Sarason *et al.*,[11] p. 15).

The test-anxious child often pays more attention to his own anxiety responses in test situations than to the task. Consequently, his performance may be impaired if situations contain cues which tell the child he is being evaluated and therefore in a danger situation. The resulting anxiety interferes with adequate perception of external events and with task performance. School situations arouse test anxiety primarily because of the stimulus similarities between the parent and the teacher. Both are adult authority figures with powers to perform evaluative functions and to dispense rewards and punishments.

The following hypotheses flow from Sarason's theory:

(1) in general, high test anxiety will interfere with performance on school tests or in situations which are "test-like" (e.g., giving a speech);
(2) the greater the test-like characteristics of the task, the more the child's anxiety will be manifested and the more it will interfere with his performance;
(3) conversely, reduction in the test-like characteristics of a task should reduce the impairing effects of anxiety. This might be brought about by eliminating time limits, or by giving cues to the correct answers;
(4) high test-anxious children will be more dependent and unaggressive than low test-anxious children.

The TASC contains 30 questions about test situations to which the child answers "yes" or "no". Some sample questions are: "Do you think you worry more about school than other children?"; "Do you worry a lot *before* you take a test?"; "Do you worry a lot *while* you are taking a test?"; "When you are taking a test, does the hand you write with shake a little?"

The Achievement Anxiety Test (AAT)

Sarason and his colleagues tend to focus on the debilitating effects of anxiety. In contrast, Alpert and Haber[12] constructed the AAT to identify individuals whose academic performance is *facilitated* by the stress of the test situation, as well as those whose performance is *impaired*. The AAT consists of two scales, a nine-item "facilitating anxiety scale" (AAT +), and a ten-item "debilitating anxiety scale" (AAT −). These items were chosen from a larger pool of items on the basis of their ability to predict the grade-point average of college students. Each item is scored on a five-point scale.

The facilitating anxiety scale contains items like: "Nervousness while taking a test helps me to do better"; "I look forward to exams"; "The more important the exam or test, the better I seem to do". Examples of the items in the debilitating anxiety scale are: "In a course where I have been doing poorly, my fear of a bad grade cuts down my efficiency"; "I find myself reading exam questions without understanding them, and I must go back over them so that they will make sense".

Alpert and Haber point out that, in the construction of the TASC and the TAQ, it was implicitly assumed that if a subject has a great deal of debilitating anxiety, he will have little or no facilitating anxiety. In essence, this view assumes that there is a high negative correlation between debilitating and facilitating anxiety. In contrast, Alpert and Haber[12] maintain that, "an individual may possess a large amount of both anxieties, or of one but not the other, or none of either" (p. 32). In other words, facilitating and debilitating anxiety may be uncorrelated. Much of the work with the AAT has been concerned with the clarification of this issue. This research has attempted to demonstrate that facilitating anxiety is not just a mirror image of debilitating anxiety but does, in fact, add a new element.

The State-Trait Anxiety Inventory (STAI)

The questionnaires and tests described in the preceding pages are trait measures which tap individual differences in anxiety proneness. The STAI (Spielberger and Gorsuch,[13] Spielberger, Gorsuch and Lushene[14]) measures two distinct anxiety concepts: state anxiety (A-State) and trait anxiety (A-Trait). These concepts are defined by Spielberger *et al.*[14] (p. 2) as follows:

> State anxiety (A-State) is conceptualised as a transitory emotional state or condition of the human organism that is characterised by subjective, consciously perceived feelings of tension and apprehension and heightened autonomic nervous system activity. A-States may vary in intensity and fluctuate over time.
>
> Trait anxiety (A-Trait) refers to relatively stable individual differences in anxiety proneness, that is, to differences between people in the tendency to respond to situations perceived as threatening with elevations in A-State intensity.
>
> In general, it would be expected that those who are high in A-Trait will exhibit A-State elevations more frequently than low A-Trait individuals because they tend to perceive a wider range of situations as dangerous or threatening. High A-Trait persons are also more likely to respond to stressful situations with increased A-State intensity, especially in situations that involve interpersonal relationships which pose some threat to self-esteem.

Spielberger *et al.*[14] (p. 3) draw the following analogy with the concepts of kinetic and potential energy in physics:

> State anxiety, like kinetic energy, refers to an empirical process or reaction taking place at a particular moment in time and at a given level of intensity. Trait anxiety, like potential energy, indicates differences in the strength of a latent disposition to manifest a certain type of reaction. And where potential energy denotes differences between physical objects in the amount of kinetic energy which may be released if triggered by an appropriate force, trait anxiety implies differences between people in the disposition to respond to stressful situations with varying amounts of A-State.

The concepts of state and trait anxiety have a great deal of significance for the academic learning situation. It seems eminently reasonable to assume that some children may be anxious in many different situations and circumstances while others will rarely experience anxiety states. Furthermore, a child who is high in trait anxiety may show high levels of A-State in some school subjects but not in others.

Take the case of a student who has a particular flair for mathematics (and a history of outstanding success in this area), but a mediocre record in subjects requiring verbal skills. This student would probably have very little anxiety when faced with a mathematics test, but might be very tense in an English test, or if he is required to give a speech. Conversely, a student who is low in A-Trait may be quite calm in most testing situations, but he may react with intense anxiety when faced with an examination in mathematics because of a past history of failure in this area. Thus, classifying individual students as high or low in trait anxiety may have very little validity for predicting state anxiety in a particular situation.

The STAI consists of separate self-report scales for measuring A-State and A-Trait. The A-State scale is comprised of 20 items which require the subject to indicate how he feels at a particular moment in time. The A-State scale contains questions such as: "I feel upset", "I feel calm", "I am tense", "I feel over-excited and rattled". The subject is required to respond to each item by rating the intensity of his feelings on a 4-point scale with the following categories: not at all; somewhat; moderately so; very much so.

The STAI A-Trait scale consists of 20 statements that ask people to describe how they generally feel. The A-Trait scale contains questions such as: "I take disappointments so keenly that I can't put them out of my mind", "I feel pleasant", "I become tense and upset when I think about my present concerns", and "I am a steady person". The subject responds to each item by rating himself on the following 4-point scale: almost never; sometimes; often; almost always.

In his book, *The Psychology of Anxiety*, Levitt[15] reviews and evaluates a number of different anxiety inventories. He concludes that: "The STAI is the most carefully developed instrument, from both theoretical and methodological standpoints of those presented in this chapter. The test construction procedures described by Spielberger and Gorsuch[13] are highly sophisticated and rigorous." (Levitt,[15] p. 71-2.)

References

[1] J. A. TAYLOR, "The Relation of Anxiety to the Conditioned Eyelid Response". *J. exp. Psychol.*, 1951, **41**, pp. 81-92.

[2] J. A. TAYLOR, "A Personality Scale of Manifest Anxiety". *J. abnorm. soc. Psychol.*, 1953, **48**, pp. 285-90.

[3] C. L. HULL, *Principles of Behaviour*, Appleton-Century-Crofts, New York, 1943.

[4] K. W. SPENCE, "A Theory of Emotionally Based Drive (D) and its Relation to Performance in Simple Learning Situations". *Am. Psychol.*, 1958, **13**, pp. 131-41.

[5] E. K. MONTAGUE, "The Role of Anxiety in Serial Rote Learning". *J. exp. Psychol.*, 1953, **45**, pp. 91-98.

[6] J. H. TAYLOR and J. P. CHAPMAN, "Paired-associate Learning as Related to Anxiety". *Am. J. Psychol.*, 1955, **68**, p. 671.

[7] I. E. FARBER and K. W. SPENCE, "Effects of Anxiety, Stress and Task Variables on Reaction Time". *J. Personality*, 1953, **25**, pp. 1-18.

[8] G. RAMOND, "Anxiety and Tasks as Determiners of Verbal Performance". *J. exp. Psychol.*, 1953, **46**, pp. 120-24.

[9] A. CASTANEDA, B. R. MCCANDLESS and D. S. PALERMO, "The Children's Form of the Manifest Anxiety Scale". *Child Dev.*, 1956, **27**, pp. 317-26.

[10] G. MANDLER and J. COWEN, "Test Anxiety Questionnaires". *J. consult. Psychol.*, 1958, **22**, pp. 228-29.

[11] S. B. SARASON, K. S. DAVIDSON, F. F. LIGHTHALL, R. R. WAITE and B. K. RUEBUSH, *Anxiety in Elementary School Children*, John Wiley & Sons, New York, 1960.

[12] R. ALPERT and R. N. HABER, "Anxiety in Academic Achievement Situations". *J. abnorm. soc. Psychol.*, 1960, **61**, pp. 207-15.

[13] C. D. SPIELBERGER and R. L. GORSUCH, "The Development of the State-Trait Anxiety Inventory", in C. D. Spielberger and R. L. Gorsuch (Eds), *Mediating Processes in Verbal Conditioning*. Final report to the National Institutes of Health, U.S. Public Health Service on Grants MH7229 and HD947, 1966.

[14] C. D. SPIELBERGER, R. L. GORSUCH and R. E. LUSHENE, *The State-Trait Anxiety (S.T.A.I.) Test Manual for Form X*, Consulting Psychologists Press, Palo Alto, 1970.

[15] E. E. LEVITT, *The Psychology of Anxiety*, Bobbs Merrill, New York, 1967.

Chapter 3

Behavioural Correlates of the Anxious Student

Research on the personality and behavioural characteristics of the anxious child will be reviewed in this chapter. This research is relevant to academic attainment in a number of ways. For example, if a child has a poor self-image, and is rejected by his teachers and discriminated against by his peers, then the child is not likely to do well in school. Furthermore, his problems are likely to become worse with the passing of time unless he is given special help.

Much of the research in this chapter and those that follow is based on correlational studies in which the emphasis is on discovering whether a relationship exists between anxiety, various measures of adjustment, and academic attainment. Correlations can range between $+1 \cdot 00$ and $-1 \cdot 00$, where $0 \cdot 00$ represents no relationship at all. Correlations of $+0 \cdot 80$ or $-0 \cdot 80$ represent a strong relationship between two variables. However, even quite small correlations of the order of $+0 \cdot 20$ or $-0 \cdot 20$ may be significant, especially where the direction of the relationship is consistent across many studies.

One difficulty with correlational studies is that they do not establish a causal relationship, but merely indicate that two factors are associated. In the tropics, for example, it would be possible to show a positive correlation between sleeping with the windows open and the incidence of malaria. That is, people who sleep with open windows are more likely to contract the disease than those who sleep with closed windows. Although the inference could be drawn that night air causes malaria, a third associated factor, the anopheles mosquito, is the actual causal agent. The problem of causality will be taken up again in Chapter 10 in which we will review the total research evidence on the relationship between anxiety and learning in academic settings.

The research evidence on the behavioural correlates of anxious children has been organised into four major categories. These categories are defined in terms of whether the personality and behavioural characteristics were evaluated by: (1) the child himself (self-image); (2) other children, particularly classmates; (3) teachers and other observers; and (4) parents. This chapter is relevant to academic attainment in many ways. For example, if a child has a poor self-image, is discriminated against by his peers and not recognised by his teachers, then the chances are that the child's problems will become worse with the passage of time.

Self Image

The kinds of verbalisations that people make about themselves have long been of interest to psychologists, particularly personality theorists. These verbalisations have played a major role in the formation of constructs such as ego, superego and self-concept. The following studies, in one form or another, were designed to elicit responses from subjects varying in anxiety level, in order to gain insight into the self-perceptions of the anxious student.

Lipsitt[1] gave the CMAS to children in Grades 4, 5 and 6 together with a self-concept scale. The self-concept scale consisted of 22 adjectives, some of which were positive (e.g., friendly, happy, kind, loyal) and some negative (lazy, jealous, bashful). There was a highly significant negative correlation between CMAS scores and scores on the self-concept scale both for boys and for girls at all three grade levels. Thus, there was a strong tendency for the high-anxious children to be self-disparaging.

Rosenberg[2] in a large scale study involving over 5,000 junior and senior high school students also found a strong negative relationship between self-esteem and anxiety, once again pointing to the low esteem in which anxious students hold themselves. Similarly, at the college level, Suinn and Hill[3] found a substantial negative correlation between self-acceptance and two measures of trait anxiety, the MAS and the TAQ.

Sarason *et al.*[4] present data indicating that anxious children develop self-derogatory attitudes which in turn lead to over-concern with bodily adequacy. These investigators also observed that high-anxious children tended to blame themselves for their failures, to be dependent on others and to have difficulty expressing hostility in a manner appropriate to the situation. In their longitudinal study, Hill and Sarason[5] repeatedly tested two groups of children through the elementary grades. They confirmed earlier findings by Lighthall,[6, 7] that children who obtained high scores on the TASC also admitted to "what may be called universal worry as well as to hostility, feelings of inadequacy and negative effect in general".

A study to be discussed subsequently in greater detail suggests that high-anxious children appear to rely on "safe" ways of expressing anger and hostility. Penney[8] reasoned that the anxious child would, therefore, be less prone to explore unknown and unfamiliar situations. On a "reactive curiosity scale", containing items such as "I like to learn about people who live in other countries," and "It's fun to see inside the big buildings downtown," Penney found that children with high anxiety scores tended to get low "curiosity" scores. The results of this investigation suggest that the anxious child sees himself as unadventurous and preferring the well-known. Extrapolating further, it also suggests that he would prefer a stable, well-articulated school routine, not one in which constant change was taking place, or in which children were largely thrown on their own resources.

Four studies (Singer and Schonbar,[9] Singer and Rowe,[10] Reiter,[11] and Singer[12]) have investigated the relationship between anxiety and frequency of daydreaming. In each of these studies, in which different measures of anxiety and different age groups were used, it was found that high anxiety children reported a higher incidence of daydreaming. Since high anxiety is generally associated with low achievement, it appears that HA children may attempt to compensate for their lack of success by indulging in flights of fancy. In their daydreams, they can accomplish miraculous feats, obtain rich material possessions and reach positions of high status in which they have tremendous power. Summing up his findings, Singer[12] states:

> The evidence . . . indicates that daydreaming frequency does correlate positively at moderately high levels with questionnaire measures of anxiety. . . . This would suggest that persons reporting more frequent daydreams also describe themselves as more anxious, sensitive and fearful.

Classmates' Perceptions of the High-anxious

The three studies discussed in this section all used sociometric ratings to determine how anxious children are perceived by their peers. In the first (Cowen *et al.*,[13] Part II, Chapter 11), the sociometric technique was one called "Class Play". This "test" centres around a hypothetical play to be acted by the class. Half of the roles are positive and half are negative. In the first part of the test, each child nominates as many of his classmates as he wishes for each role. In the second part, each child marks which parts he would like to act and which ones he thinks he would be chosen for by peers and by teachers. Significant positive correlations were found between anxiety scores and both the number and the percentage of negative roles for which a child was nominated by his peers. In part two there was a significant positive relation between anxiety and the percentage of negative choices.

The results of Cowen *et al.* indicate that the high-anxious children are discriminated by peers and reacted against in a negative manner. At the same time, the high-anxious child sees himself as unfit for positive roles and unlikely to be chosen by his peers or teachers for such roles. The authors conclude that "regardless of whether the sociometric ratings are done by peers or the child himself, elevations of nominations for negative roles and reduction of nominations for positive roles are found to be related to high anxiety".

McCandless, Castaneda and Palermo[14] asked the children in six classes at Grades 4, 5 and 6 to rank all children in the class of the same sex as themselves as friends, that is, to put the number 1 after the name of his best friend, 2 after his second-best friend, and so on. The overall result supported the hypothesis of a negative relationship between anxiety and popularity. Although there were variations from grade to grade, the predominant pattern was for high ratings to go to the low-anxious children, as measured by CMAS score. A similar study by Iscoe and Carden[15] showed CMAS scores to be significantly related to sociometric status for girls but not for boys.

Teachers' Perceptions of the High-anxious

Cowen *et al.*[13] (Part II, Chapter 11) correlated teachers' ratings of children with CMAS scores. On one measure, the teachers of 394 third-graders were asked to select from a list of 17 negative nouns (for example, moodiness, immaturity, destructiveness) those which seemed applicable to a given child, and to give an intensity rating of mild, moderate or strong for each selected characteristic. The final score was termed a "Total Adjustment Score". In addition, each teacher rated the child on a single five-point scale ranging from very well-adjusted to very poorly-adjusted. All correlations were significantly positive ranging from 0·21 to 0·29, indicating that teachers see the high-anxious as being more poorly-adjusted, and as possessing more negative personality characteristics. In two previous investigations (Wirt and Broen,[16] Grams, Hafner and Quast[17]), no relationship was found between measures of anxiety and teacher-ratings of adjustment. However, both these studies used a teacher-rating scheme that was not very comprehensive. Further, Wirt and Broen did not ask the children to complete an anxiety questionnaire, using teacher-ratings of anxiety instead.

Sarason *et al.*[18] observed HA (high-anxious) and LA (low-anxious) children for one hour in a classroom situation. They concluded that the HA children, especially the boys, were less secure, less task-oriented and less academically oriented than the LA subjects. In a follow-up study by Davidson and Sarason,[19] three Grade 2 classrooms were observed by trained observers for four months. Once again, the relationship between TASC scores and ratings of observers and teachers was strong for boys but not for girls. High TASC scores for boys were associated with hiding emotions, difficulty in communication, submissiveness, caution, lack of ambition, underactivity, underachievement, lack of attention and lack of responsibility.

Barnard, Zimbardo and Sarason[20] gave the TASC and an intelligence test to children in Grades 2 and 3. Those falling in the top and bottom 15 per cent on TASC were then selected as subjects to be rated by their classroom teachers on 24 personality traits "that have been found in past research to be related to the variable of test anxiety". These characteristics were presented to each teacher in pairs of bipolar trait names, including "dependent-independent", "aggressive-submissive", "impulsive-cautious", and "withdrawn-sociable". The overall result was that teachers did not differentiate between the HA and LA children on any of the 24 characteristics while they did differentiate between high and low IQ children on 14 of the 24 traits. High IQ students were seen to have characteristics such as independence, sensitiveness and ambition whereas those with low IQ were seen to possess the opposite characteristics. No differentiation was made for students who were very different in terms of their own self-report on test anxiousness.

When both anxiety and intelligence were taken into account, bright anxious children were seen to have the "desirable" characteristics of independence, adaptability and aggression while being more sensitive, mature, sociable, popular and active. Barnard *et al.* claim, however, that these ratings probably reflect a halo effect deriving from their high intelligence. They further surmise that since teachers are unable to recognise and identify the high-anxious child, they will not be able to help him to improve his self-image.

Stevenson and Odom[21] asked teachers to rate Grade 4 and 6 children on general learning ability, and then correlated these ratings with the TASC scores obtained from the children. At the Grade 4 level, the correlations were −0·38 and −0·28 for boys and girls respectively. At grade 6 they were −0·40 and −0·27. In contrast to the results of Barnard *et al.*[20] in the previous study, the teachers were differentiating between high- and low-anxious children at least to some extent. The authors state that the teachers were using the children's participation in class discussions and performance in written assignments as the major criteria for their ratings. While there were many differences in the two studies, perhaps the most important was the children's age. It is also possible that the inability of the teachers in the study of Barnard *et al.* to discriminate the high-anxious child may have been due to the fact that fewer verbal productions, oral and written, were available to them in the earlier grades.

Parents' Perceptions of the High-Anxious

The evidence in this area has been gathered primarily by the Yale group headed by Sarason. These researchers interviewed the parents of HA and LA children, and asked both mothers and fathers to rate their own children on 25 personality characteristics. They predicted that the LA children would be described more favourably and with fewer tensions, conflicts and anxieties than the HA boys and girls. This prediction was upheld for the fathers who described their HA children as less mature, less relaxed, more dependent and so on. The mothers, however, evaluated the HA and LA children equally favourably. Failure to find any difference between the mothers of HA and LA children prompted the investigators to examine the proposition that the mothers of the high-anxious were more defensive in evaluating their children and in responding to the interview questions. After extensive sifting of the data, the authors concluded that the mothers of high-anxious children consciously withheld or distorted evidence and were also unconsciously defensive in their replies.

Davidson[22] concluded that the parents of LA children saw them as relatively well-adjusted and as having a variety of ways of expressing anger. In contrast the parents of HA children saw them as less well-adjusted and as tending to express their feelings of anger and aggressive impulses in only one "safe" way, irrespective of the situation. There were also trends in the data which suggested that the parents of HA children saw them as worrying more about missing school because of illness, as having less positive feelings about starting school at the beginning of the year, and as having had more trouble in learning to read.

Other Behavioural Correlates of High Anxiety

Cowen *et al.*[13] (Part II, Chapter 11) obtained from the school records of Grade 3 children the total number of referrals to the school nurse and the total number of days absent in Grade 3. For the total group, all correlations were significant for referrals but not for absences. That is, there was a tendency for the high-anxious children to report to the infirmary more often than the low-anxious, but there was no relationship between anxiety and staying away from school. The interpretation of these findings can only be speculative. Possibly the HA children actually experienced more physical or somatic pain or discomfort than the LA, or perhaps, when faced with anxiety-provoking situations, they tried to escape to a situation where dependency needs can be expressed in safety.

Sutton-Smith and Rosenberg[23] gave the CMAS to children in Grades 4, 5 and 6 and asked the children to state their preferences for games of various sorts. The most important result was that the game choices of the HA boys were not only more feminine in nature than those of LA boys, but also that they tended to choose games typically chosen by younger girls. On the other hand, HA girls tended to choose masculine games typically chosen by older boys.

In summary, the evidence suggests that high-anxious children: (1) are self-disparaging, (2) are unadventurous, (3) possess more negative personality characteristics, and (4) have a strong tendency to indulge in daydreams. Classmates appear to react unfavourably against the high-anxious, while teachers, after the first few years at least, see them as possessing characteristics currently regarded in western culture as negative and unfavourable. Fathers of high-anxious children, perhaps because they are less defensive than their spouses, tend to view their offspring in the same way as the children judge themselves. The mothers, however, seem unable or unwilling to differentiate between HA and LA children on various personality and behavioural characteristics.

Some educational psychologists see one of the primary roles of the skilful teacher, especially in the elementary and secondary school years, as being to promote and sustain a positive self-concept in the child. This notion, as expressed in the work of developmental psychologists such as Havighurst and Erikson, is epigenetic in character. Expressed in another way, failure of the child to achieve the tasks characteristic of a particular developmental stage through which he is passing is thought to be inimical to his progress towards adulthood. If high anxiety interferes with academic achievement (an important developmental task), and if teachers are unable to identify the high-anxious child and take steps to promote a more positive self-concept, then it seems unlikely that the anxious child will achieve a positive sense of identity, a goal which many psychologists see as being necessary for successful personality development in childhood and adolescence.

References

[1] L. P. Lipsitt, "A Self-concept Scale for Children and its Relationship to the Children's Form of the MAS". *Child Dev.*, 1958, **29**, pp. 463-72.

[2] M. Rosenberg, "The Association between Self-esteem and Anxiety". *J. Psychol.*, 1953, **48**, pp. 285-90.

[3] R. M. Suinn and H. Hill, "Influence of Anxiety on the Relationship between Self-acceptances of Others". *J. consult. Psychol.*, 1964, **28**, pp. 116-119.

[4] S. B. Sarason, K. S. Davidson, F. F. Lighthall, R. R. Waite and B. K. Ruebush, *Anxiety in Elementary School Children*, John Wiley & Sons, New York, 1960.

[5] K. T. Hill and S. B. Sarason, "The Relation of Test Anxiety and Defensiveness to Test and School Performance over the Elementary School Years: a Further Longitudinal Study". *Monogr. Soc. Res. Child Dev.*, 1966, **31** (2, serial No. 104).

[6] F. F. Lighthall, "Some Theoretical and Measurement Problems Associated with Changes in Anxiety: Comments on 'Anxiety in Connection with School Performance: III' ". *Pedagogisk Forskning*, 1961, No. 4, pp. 263-76.

[7] F. F. Lighthall, "Defensive and Non-defensive Change in Children's Responses to Personality Questionnaires". *Child Dev.*, 1963, **34**, pp. 455-70.

[8] R. K. Penney, "Reactive Curiosity and Manifest Anxiety in Children". *Child Dev.*, 1965, **36**, pp. 697-702.

[9] J. L. Singer and R. A. Schonbar, "Correlates of Daydreaming: A Dimension of Self-awareness". *J. consult. Psychol.*, 1961, **25**, pp. 1-6.

[10] J. L. Singer and R. Rowe, "An Experimental Study of Some Relationships between Daydreaming and Anxiety". *J. consult. Psychol.*, 1962, **26**, pp. 446-54.

[11] H. H. Reiter, "Some Personality Correlates of the Page Fantasy Scale". *Percept. Mot. Skills*, 1963, **16**, pp. 747-48.

[12] J. L. Singer, *Daydreaming: An Introduction to the Experimental Study of Inner Experience*, Random House, New York, 1966.

[13] E. L. Cowen, M. Zax, R. Klein, L. D. Izzo and M. A. Trost, "The Relation of Anxiety in School Children to School Record, Achievement and Behavioural Measures". *Child Dev.*, 1965, **36**, pp. 685-95.

[14] B. R. McCandless, A. Castaneda and D. S. Palermo, "Anxiety in Children and School Status". *Child Dev.*, 1956, **27**, pp. 385-91.

[15] I. Iscoe and J. A. Carden, "Field Dependence, Manifest Anxiety and Sociometric Status in Children". *J. consult Psychol.*, 1961, **25**, p. 184.

[16] R. D. Wirt and W. E. Broen, "The Relation of the Children's MAS to the Concept of Anxiety as Used in the Clinic". *J. consult. Psychol.*, 1956, **20**, p. 482.

[17] A. Grams, A. J. Hafner and W. Quast, "Children's Anxiety Compared with Parents' Reports and Teachers' Ratings of Adjustment". Paper read at A.P.A. Meetings, St Louis, Mo., 1962.

[18] S. B. Sarason, K. S. Davidson, F. F. Lighthall and R. R. Waite, "Classroom Observations of High and Low Anxious Children". *Child Dev.*, 1958, **29**, pp. 287-95.

[19] K. S. Davidson and S. B. Sarason, "Text Anxiety and Classroom Observations". *Child Dev.*, 1961, **32**, pp. 199-210.

[20] J. W. Barnard, P. G. Zimbardo and S. B. Sarason, "Teachers' Ratings of Student Personality Traits as they relate to IQ and Social Desirability". *J. educ. Psychol.*, 1968, **59**, pp. 128-32.

[21] H. W. STEVENSON and R. D. ODOM, "The Relation of Anxiety to Children's Performance on Learning and Problem-solving Tasks". *Child Dev.*, 1965, **36**, pp. 1003-12.

[22] K. S. DAVIDSON, "Interviews of Parents of High Anxious and Low Anxious Children". *Child Dev.*, 1959, **30**, pp. 341-51.

[23] B. SUTTON-SMITH and B. G. ROSENBERG, "Manifest Anxiety and Game Preferences in Children". *Child Dev.*, 1960, **31**, pp. 307-11.

Chapter 4

Anxiety and Examining Procedures

In many parts of the world, and particularly in the urbanised, industrial countries, there appears to be a developing movement both among teachers and in the community at large to question the current practices of examining students. One aspect of the criticisms of the assessment process in education is the claim that the stress of formal examinations results in such high degrees of anxiety in many students that they are unable to perform at a level which matches the potential they have shown in less stressful situations. It is with research in this field that this chapter is concerned.

Relieving Anxiety During Examinations

McKeachie, Pollie and Speisman[1] have reported a series of studies in which they attempted to improve the performance of students at the University of Michigan by encouraging them to write comments about test items during course examinations. The rationale for this procedure was that if a student taking a multiple-choice test comes across an item that is difficult or ambiguous, this leads to an immediate increase in anxiety and to the manifestation of responses which are not task-relevant. The student's performance may be disrupted because he pays too much attention to his emotional responses and self-centred feelings of inadequacy, and this misdirection of attention interferes with his responses to the test items.

In one of their experiments, McKeachie and his colleagues gave half of the students answer sheets with spaces for comments and instructed them to "feel free to make any comments about the items in the space provided". The other students were given standard answer sheets. The results of this experiment indicated that students in the "comment" group made significantly higher scores on the test than those who used conventional answer sheets. The experiment was repeated three times and comparable results were obtained on each occasion. In a further experiment, the authors found evidence that writing of comments did not affect the scores on the items about which the comments were written, but had an effect on the items that came later in the test.

Smith and Rockett[2] replicated the McKeachie *et al.*[1] study with 217 college students enrolled in the introductory psychology course at Michigan State University who had taken the Sarason Test Anxiety Scale one month before they were given an 80-item multiple choice test. Each subject received one of three answer sheets which were identical in appearance, except for the instructions. The instructions on two sets of answer sheets were the same as those used by McKeachie. The third read, "Please comment on anything unusual about each question."

As can be seen in Table 4.1 the instructions had somewhat different effects on the high and low anxiety groups. Performance of the high-anxious students increased steadily as the instruction to comment increased, while the reverse was true for the low-anxious. These results are in line with McKeachie's and with a study by Sarason, Mandler and Craighill[3] who also found that high-anxious subjects performed better than low-anxious subjects with non-anxiety provoking instructions. It should be noted, however, that the low-anxiety subjects performed worse when they were asked to comment on the test items.

TABLE 4.1

Performance as a Function of Anxiety and Instructions *

	Instructions		
Anxiety	No comment	Feel free	Please comment
Low	54·9	52·8	50·8
High	53·1	54·2	55·0

*Estimated from Fig. 1[3]. By permission of the *Journal of Abnormal and Social Psychology*.

Each of the studies discussed above points to the fact that high-anxious students improve their scores as the opportunity to comment on test items increases. While interpretation of these results can be only of a speculative nature, it is possible that the opportunity to discharge tension built up after encountering a difficult or ambiguous item helps the student feel that he has, even in this indirect way, some personal contact with his instructor. The student's performance may be facilitated by seeing his instructor as a friendly person who wishes to encourage communication, rather than as a powerful authority figure who arbitrarily and punitively assigns grades on which the student's future may depend. Whatever the explanation, the facts are clear: the opportunity to comment helps the highly anxious student and hinders the less anxious.

Another method for reducing the interfering effects of anxiety during examinations is suggested by the test-construction experts, who advise teachers to arrange their test questions so that items are presented in increasing order of difficulty, with the easiest item first and the most difficult last. Lund[4] checked this advice by giving two parallel forms of an untimed test. The first form was arranged so that the items were presented in increasing order of difficulty; the second form included some difficult items in the early part of the test. The *S*s performed worse on the second form of the test.

Lund's results may be explained in terms of the same general principles that probably account for the findings in the studies of McKeachie *et al.*, and Smith and Rockett. We may speculate that the effects of the anxiety aroused by encountering a difficult item early in a test persist over time and cause students to miss easy items that would have been answered correctly if anxiety had not interfered.

Anxiety and Memory Support

In the two studies that are discussed in this section, a method is suggested for reducing the interfering effects of anxiety during examinations. This method involves providing the student with some kind of memory support.

Sinclair[5] (Part II, Chapter 12) used as his subjects 173 male twelfth grade students from three boys' high schools in Sydney, Australia. His main hypothesis was that the debilitating effects of individual differences in anxiety would be most evident under conditions of high ego-involvement. To test this hypothesis, students were given a six-page study passage describing life among the Trobriand Islanders of the South Pacific. This topic was selected because it was "closely related to content typically taught at the high school level and yet there was little chance of the subjects having had any prior experience with it" (Sinclair,[5] p. 301).

Three weeks prior to the time that the students were tested on the study passage, they were given the Test Anxiety Scale and divided into high, medium, and low anxiety groups on the basis of their scores on the TAS. Within each anxiety group, *S*s were allocated at random to either the high or low ego-involvement condition. In the high-ego involvement condition, the *S*s were informed that the test was one of scholastic aptitude and that their results would be made available to their headmaster. In the low-ego involvement condition, the *S*s were told that the purpose of the test was to establish whether the study passage was a good one, or whether the questions were too easy or too difficult.

Two performance measures of learning were taken. The first consisted of 20 multiple-choice factual questions for which the correct answers were explicitly stated in the study passage. Prior to answering the factual learning questions, *S*s were allowed 25 minutes to study the passage. The second performance measure was a reasoning test that required the *S*s to make deductions from the information given in the study passage and to draw inferences and conclusions. The correct answers for the reasoning test were not explicitly stated in the passage. Therefore, in order to ensure that each student had equal access to the factual material on which the answers depended, the *S*s were allowed to consult the passage as they worked on the test.

For the test of factual learning, there were no significant differences between the anxiety groups in the conditions of low ego-involvement, but the LA *S*s were superior to both the MA and HA *S*s in the high ego-involvement condition. In commenting on the implications of these findings, Sinclair[5] states, "in important examinations, the HA student will be at a considerable disadvantage. When competing with other students for scholarships, university entrance, school prizes, employment opportunities, or simply place in class, anxiety will act to interfere with and reduce the level of his performance" (p. 305).

Another important principle is suggested in the results obtained by Sinclair with his reasoning test. Despite the fact that this test appeared to be more difficult than the factual learning test, no significant differences in performance were found in the comparisons of the scores of the three anxiety groups. In fact, in the high ego-involvement conditions, all three anxiety groups did slightly better on the reasoning test than their counterparts in the low ego-involvement condition. Apparently the opportunity to consult the study passage both reassured the high-anxious students and facilitated their performance by reducing task-irrelevant responses.

Within the framework of Spence's Drive Theory, it is reasonable to assume that memory support sufficiently elevates a correct answer in a subject's response hierarchy so that high anxiety (drive) no longer interferes with performance. The following study adds further support to the notion that the interfering effects of anxiety can be ameliorated by the provision of aids to memory.

Sieber and Kameya[6] were interested in discovering ways of lowering the interfering effects of anxiety in classroom learning situations. They hypothesised that the poor performance of high-anxious students in stressful situations is caused, at least in part, by anxiety-produced deficits in memory. Therefore, if some form of memory support were provided, this should help individuals with high anxiety. To test this hypothesis, high- and low-anxious children (matched on IQ) were presented with a form board containing nine holes. The task was to interchange four white marbles that were originally placed to the left of the centre hole with four black marbles originally placed to the right of the centre hole. The rules of the game were such that the task was quite difficult, "since only one sequence of 24 moves results in the solution".

An important characteristic of Sieber and Kameya's task was that previous failures leading to an impasse had to be remembered if success was to be achieved. In order to provide memory support, a variant of the task was constructed in which the subject was given three boards and three sets of marbles. After a mistake was made, the subject was instructed to try again with the second board while the first board was kept in view for reference to help avoid a similar mistake. Rotation of the boards continued until success was achieved.

The total number of errors, and the number of errors recognised by the subject before he removed his hand from an incorrectly moved marble, were used as measures of performance. As predicted, with no memory support the high-anxious children made more errors and failed to recognise more mistakes than the low-anxious children. In contrast, when memory support was provided, the high-anxious children did a shade better than the low-anxious. In commenting on these results, Sieber[7] concludes, "Quite possibly their [the high-anxious] high level of performance under the experimental condition is due, in part, to their cautiousness or motivation to avoid failure, since memory support avails to high-anxious persons a body of information upon which they may operate with their characteristic penchant for accuracy or correctness" (p. 59).

While going a bit beyond the data, the results of these two studies seem to indicate that high-anxious persons should benefit from the use of any technique that helps them to remember and recall previously learned materials. Sieber[7] has suggested that mnemonic devices, diagrams and outlines, and detailed systems for organising general ideas could all be quite useful in helping the high-anxious student perform up to his full potential.

Anxiety and Test Performance under Stress

In this section, two studies are discussed in which attempts were made to discover the effects of using instructions to reduce the stress associated with test situations. The results of these investigations support the conclusion that statements by authority figures which emphasise the importance of good performance tend to work to the disadvantage of high-anxious students, especially on difficult tests.

Wrightsman[8] gave the Manifest Anxiety Scale and a timed measure of intelligence to 234 freshmen at George Peabody College for Teachers in Nashville, Tennessee. Approximately half of the students were given instructions which led them to believe that the results of the test were very important and might affect their entire college career. The remaining students were told that data on the test were being collected for normative purposes. The correlation between the MAS and intelligence test scores was $-0 \cdot 37$ in the "important test" condition and only $-0 \cdot 06$ in the "unimportant test" condition.

Analysed in another way, Wrightsman's results showed that there was little difference in the performance of the LA *S*s in the two conditions, whereas the performance of HA *S*s who were given the stressful instruction ("important test" condition) was almost one standard deviation lower than that of the HA *S*s in the non-stressful condition. These results can be interpreted as indicating that anxiety is unrelated to performance if a test is seen to be of little importance, but when the test is personally important, as is the case with most school examinations, anxiety impairs performance.

In a similar study, Caron[9] gave two groups of high school students a 1,700-word passage about psychological theory to read. One group studied the passage and was tested under examination conditions. The second group ("curiosity" condition) was led to believe that they were studying the passage so they could interpret data on their own personality profiles. Following the study, measures of rote-learning and comprehension were obtained on both groups. The rote-learning measure was a "simple" test that involved only the reproduction of formulae and definitions contained in the passage. The comprehension test was quite complex in that it called for applications of the psychological principles that were presented in the passage.

On the rote-learning test, there were no differences between the HA and LA subjects in either condition. On the comprehension test, there were no differences between the HA and LA *S*s in the "curiosity" condition, but the LA *S*s did significantly better than the HA *S*s in the "examination" condition. These results are quite consistent with those obtained by Wrightsman. The findings in both studies suggest that where the test is difficult, explicit statements about the importance of the results work against the high-anxious student.

Stress, Anxiety, and Performance on Classroom Examinations

Paul and Eriksen[10] used a "real-life" examination to investigate the effects of stress on test performance. The subjects were 118 female students in an introductory psychology course. They were required to participate in an experiment held in the evening following their first hourly examination in the course. When the students reported for the experiment, the examiner informed them that "the purpose of the study was to determine people's feelings, attitudes and reactions to different examining situations since many people felt that feelings of uneasiness and tension kept them from really demonstrating their knowledge" (p. 482). The test anxiety questionnaire was then administered, and after it was completed the students were reassured that the test they were about to take would not count towards their course grade. They were then given a parallel form of the course examination they had taken in class that morning. Throughout the experimental session, the examiners were "as warm, permissive, and understanding as possible".

The hypothesis of interest in this study was that the high-anxious subjects, as compared with the low-anxious, would do relatively better on the non-stressful examination than on the regular course examination. The analysis of the total data showed a trend in the expected direction, but the differences were not significant. It was discovered, however, that the results were obscured by the intelligence variable (see Chapter 8 for development of this point). When subjects with very high and very low intelligence were excluded and the data reanalysed using only the middle 70 per cent of the cases, the results were highly significant. The high-anxious students did better on the examination given under the less stressful condition, and the low-anxious students did better on the more stressful course examination.

Gaudry and Bradshaw[11] (Part II, Chapter 13) also investigated the effects of anxiety on performance in a "real-life" examination situation. They noted that a common practice in Australian schools is to assess students' progress by combining marks obtained from progressive testing with those obtained from terminal examinations. Typically the nature of these two testing situations varies in the amount of stress that is associated with the assessment procedures. Progressive assessment is typically based on class assignments, and on short tests conducted in regular class periods, often in a rather informal manner without stringent time limits. Terminal examinations, on the other hand, usually have strict time limits and are often given in the school auditorium or some other unfamiliar location. Furthermore, written reports of the results of terminal examinations are generally sent to parents. Given the characteristics of these testing situations, it would be predicted from Sarason's theory that high-anxious children would do relatively better under progressive assessment than under the more stressful situation of terminal assessment.

The subjects in the Gaudry-Bradshaw study were Grade 7 and 8 pupils from 14 government schools in Melbourne, Australia. In each of these schools, a single class was selected which contained at least 24 pupils of the same sex. The TASC and an intelligence test were administered to these classes early in the school year, and progressive and terminal marks were obtained from school records as follows:

(1) the progressive mark was the mean for each pupil on at least three progressive assessments;

(2) the terminal mark was the result on a formal examination held either at the end of the first term or at mid-year.

For each class, the mean normalised progressive and terminal marks of high- and low-anxious pupils with high and low intelligence were determined in such a way that each of the 14 schools contributed a pair of scores for each of the four groups. (A more detailed description of the determination of these scores is given in Chapter 13.) The chief results of the study are reported in Table 4.2 which presents the mean scores obtained by the high and low anxiety *S*s on the progressive and terminal examinations.*

TABLE 4.2

Mean Scores for Anxiety Groups on Two Methods of Assessment †

Method of assessment	Anxiety Low	High
Progressive	66·56	63·56
Terminal	67·76	62·64

† The scores in Table 4.2 are based on a mean of 65 and a standard deviation of 14. The means and standard deviations in the original table have been multiplied by 4 and a constant of 33 added to the scores. By permission of the authors and the *Australian Journal of Psychology*.

It may be noted in Table 4.2 that the HA *S*s obtained lower marks on both methods of assessment than did their LA counterparts, and that high anxiety had less interfering effects in the progressive examinations than in the terminal examination. The finding that the HA *S*s did more poorly on the terminal examination supports Sarason's claim that the effects of anxiety on performance will be greater in situations in which "test-like" characteristics are emphasised.

It should be remembered that Gaudry and Bradshaw's findings are based on a comparison of the performance of high- and low-anxious children *in the same classes*, and not on children with high and low anxiety scores in an absolute sense. While a good case could be made for using absolute scores—indeed most experiments have used them—

* The table corresponds to Table 13.2 in Chapter 13 by E. Gaudry and G. D. Bradshaw.

the organisational nature of school systems makes it likely that intra-classroom factors, such as the intelligence and the educational aspirations of classmates, profoundly influence both anxiety level and performance.

Implications of Research on Anxiety and Test Performance for School Examining Procedures

In this chapter, evidence has been reviewed which demonstrates that high-anxious students do better on examinations when they are allowed to comment on the test items. The findings in Lund's study strongly suggest that placing items in increasing order of difficulty reduces anxiety and yields more valid test scores, that is scores that reflect the student's knowledge rather than his anxiety level.

With respect to the effects on anxiety and stress on test performance, the evidence is less clear. Wrightsman, Caron, Paul and Eriksen, and Gaudry and Bradshaw all found significant interactions between anxiety and examination procedures. However, others have failed to find any differences in performance as a function of the amount of stress associated with examination practices (McKeachie, *et al.*,[1] French[12]). Nevertheless, the bulk of the available evidence supports the tentative conclusion that reduction of the test-like characteristics of examination situations will facilitate the performance of high-anxious students.

The studies of Sinclair and of Sieber and Kameya strongly suggest that examining procedures which provide memory support will aid the high-anxious students. Thus, open book examinations, in which students are allowed to consult textbooks and other references, may provide better measures of what a student has actually learned because the results of testing procedures which place a strong emphasis on memory are more likely to be distorted by anxiety.

The comments in the preceding paragraphs are concerned with factors that reduce the stress associated with examining procedures and thereby facilitate the performance of high-anxious students. It must be remembered, however, that stress also appears to facilitate the test performance of low-anxious students. Given the effects on performance of stress and anxiety, examining policies should be determined by the general goals which the assessments are designed to meet. For example, if one were training doctors who would be expected to perform emergency operations under the threat of enemy attack, examinations might be more valid from the standpoint of predicting subsequent performance if they were held under highly stressful conditions. In short, the long-term aims of the assessment procedures should determine the conditions under which the examinations are carried out.

References

[1] W. J. McKeachie, D. Pollie and J. Speisman, "Relieving Anxiety in Classroom Examinations". *J. abnorm, soc. Psychol.*, 1955, **50**, pp. 93-98.

[2] W. F. Smith and F. C. Rockett, "Test Performance as a Function of Anxiety, Instructor and Instructions". *J. educ. Res.*, 1958, **52**, pp. 138-41.

[3] S. B. Sarason, G. Mandler and P. G. Craighill, "The Effect of Differential Instructions on Anxiety and Learning". *J. abnorm. soc. Psychol.*, 1952, **47**, pp. 561-65.

[4] K. W. Lund, "Test Performance as Related to the Order of Item Difficulty, Anxiety and Intelligence". Unpublished Ph.D. thesis, Northwestern University, 1953.

[5] K. E. Sinclair, "The Influence of Anxiety on Several Measures of Classroom Performance". *Aust. J. Educ.*, 1969, **13**, pp. 296-307.

[6] J. E. Sieber and L. Kameya, "The Relationship between Anxiety and Children's Need for Memory Support in Problem-solving". Revised Research Memorandum No. 11, Stanford Center for Research and Development in Teaching, Stanford, 1967.

[7] J. E. Sieber, "A Paradigm for Experimental Modification of the Effects of Test Anxiety on Cognitive Processes". *Am. educ. Res. J.*, 1969, **6**, pp. 46-61.

[8] L. S. Wrightsman, "The Effects of Anxiety, Achievement-Motivation and Task Importance upon Performance on an Intelligence Test". *J. educ. Psychol.*, 1962, **53**, pp. 150-56.

[9] A. J. Caron, "Curiosity, Achievement and Avoidant Motivation as Determinants of Epistemic Behaviour". *J. abnorm. soc. Psychol.*, 1963, **67**, pp. 535-49.

[10] G. L. Paul and C. W. Eriksen, "Effects of Test Anxiety on 'Real-Life' Examinations". *J. Personality*, 1964, **32**, pp. 480-94.

[11] E. Gaudry and G. D. Bradshaw, "The Differential Effect of Anxiety on Performance in Progressive and Terminal School Examinations". *Aust. J. Psychol.*, 1970, **22**, pp. 1-4.

[12] J. W. French, "Effect of Anxiety on Verbal and Mathematical Examination Scores". *Educ. psychol. Measur.*, 1962, **22**, pp. 553-64.

Chapter 5

The Anxious Student and Academic Achievement

Research on the complex relationship between anxiety and academic achievement is reviewed in this chapter. For convenience, this is broken down into two sections, one on school achievement and the other on college achievement. Much of the research is based on correlational studies in which the emphasis is on discovering whether a relationship exists between anxiety and various measures of academic performance.

Academic performance can be assessed in a variety of ways. In the review of the research literature which follows, measures such as grade-point-average, performance on standardised tests such as the Stanford Achievement Test, the Science Research Associates (SRA) tests and standardised tests of reading have been used. In other studies, performance in mathematics, reading and other subject areas has been the variable which has been linked with yet another aspect of performance in the classroom, the verbal behaviour of HA and LA children.

The point at issue is whether these various measures of classroom performance correlate with anxiety level and if such a correlation is indeed found, whether the size of the effects is such as to cause concern. The question of causal relationship is left to the final chapter of the book.

Lunneborg[1] gave three anxiety scales—the TASC, the CMAS and the GASC—to 213 boys and girls in Grades 4, 5 and 6. The scores on these scales were then correlated with reading and arithmetic achievement scores obtained from the Metropolitan Achievement Test battery. For the total group, the correlations between the anxiety and achievement measures for each grade were all negative (range $-0 \cdot 18$ to $-0 \cdot 32$) and statistically significant, indicating that high anxiety was associated with poorer achievement in reading and arithmetic. A breakdown of the results for boys and girls at each grade level is given in Table 5.1 in which it can be seen that:

(1) the negative correlations tended to be larger for girls than for boys,

(2) the negative correlations tended to become stronger with increasing grade level, and

(3) the negative correlation between TASC scores and both achievement measures tended to be larger than was the case for the other two anxiety scales.

TABLE 5.1

Correlations for Males and Females at Each Grade Level*

Anxiety measure	Males						Females					
	Reading			Arithmetic			Reading			Arithmetic		
	Grade			Grade			Grade			Grade		
	4	5	6	4	5	6	4	5	6	4	5	6
CMAS	14	−12	−03	05	−17	−21	−12	−47	−51	−25	−50	−50
TASC	−08	−28	−16	08	−34	−31	−24	−46	−65	−19	−56	−60
GASC	17	−09	−21	12	−16	−41	−32	−50	−47	−29	−48	−52

*Adapted from Tables 4 and 5.[1] Decimal points omitted. By permission of the author and *Child Development*.

Sarason *et al.*[2] present similar data which support Lunneborg's finding that correlations between anxiety level and achievement are negative and tend to become higher with increasing grade level in elementary school. They report correlations of −0·23, −0·26, −0·25 and −0·41 between the TASC and the Stanford Achievement Test for Grades 3, 4, 5 and 6, respectively.

Frost[3] reports a study in which the relation between anxiety and educational achievement was investigated for 310 eleven-year-old London pupils. Frost's anxiety measures consisted of items from the MAS, the CMAS, the GASC and the TASC which were arbitrarily assigned to two different anxiety scales, a "School Anxiety" scale and a "General Anxiety" scale. For both boys and girls, these two anxiety measures were negatively correlated with four performance measures: Vocabulary, Reading Comprehension, Mechanical Arithmetic, and Problem Arithmetic.

Stevenson and Odom[4] tested 318 children attending Grades 4 and 6 in Minneapolis. Correlations were obtained for boys and girls at both grade levels between the TASC and scores on the five subtests of the Iowa Tests of Basic Skills. All twenty correlations were negative, ranging from −0·11 to −0·40, and fifteen of the twenty correlations were significant. There was no tendency, however, for the negative relationship to be any stronger for Grade 6 pupils than for Grade 4 pupils, nor was this relationship any stronger for girls than for boys.

Further evidence on the relationship between anxiety and academic achievement is provided in a study by Cowen *et al.*[5] for 394 Grade 3 pupils in Rochester, New York (Part II, Chapter 11). For two separate groups of Grade 3 pupils, they calculated the correlations between CMAS scores and various achievement measures, including grade-point average at the end of the school year and five SRA tests: Reading Comprehension, Vocabulary, Arithmetic Reasoning, Computation, and Concepts. Of the ten correlations involving SRA scores, all were negative, ranging from −0·06 to −0·30. The correlations between CMAS scores and GPA for the two groups were −0·29 and −0·30, respectively. These results indicate a consistent tendency, even at this early stage of schooling, for high anxiety to be associated with poorer performance.

The Relationship Between Anxiety and Measures of Arithmetic and Reading

In his study of Grade 4 and Grade 5 pupils in Australia, Cox[6] (Part II, Chapter 14) found that arithmetic scores were negatively correlated with TASC scores, and that reading scores were uncorrelated. While similar data were reported by Lynn[7] in a study of the performance of school children in England, no consistent differences in the relationship between anxiety, reading and arithmetic were found in the studies of Feldhausen and Klausmeier,[8] nor in Lunneborg's[1] study which was previously discussed (see Table 5.1). In contrast, some studies, such as those of Sarason *et al.*[2] and Stevenson and Odom,[4] reported reading achievement to be more negatively correlated with anxiety than arithmetic.

In a longitudinal approach in which the same children were followed up over a period of several years, Hill and Sarason[9] administered the TASC just prior to obtaining measures of achievement or intelligence. They confirmed the finding that the relation between anxiety and test performance continued to increase in the negative direction over the entire elementary school period. In this study, there was also suggestive evidence that reading and anxiety were more strongly correlated in the early grades than arithmetic and anxiety, and that the arithmetic-anxiety and reading-anxiety correlations tended to become more similar in the later grades. Hill and Sarason cite studies of high school and college students (e.g., S. B. Sarason,[10] I. G. Sarason,[11, 12] Walter, Denzler and Sarason[13]) in which correlations between anxiety and measures of arithmetic and reading performance were negative and about equal in magnitude, to support their conclusion that ". . . anxiety is more strongly related to reading than to arithmetic in the early elementary-school years, but that the difference weakens during the course of the elementary-school years and disappears in the late elementary or junior-high school years" (Hill and Sarason,[9] p. 63).

Given the tremendous importance that is attached to learning to read in the first years of school, Hill and Sarason's conclusion appears quite tenable. Learning to read is a tangible accomplishment in which a child can readily assess his progress relative to that of his classmates. On the other hand, progress in arithmetic in the lower grades, particularly in the "New Mathematics", is probably less obvious to the child. Consequently, arithmetic may be less anxiety-provoking until later in school when increasing attention is paid to solving problems and to computations. Failure to grasp the mathematical concepts and relationships which were taught earlier results in poorer performance in advanced work which is more obvious to the child.

While this tentative conclusion does not explain the findings of Cox or Lynn, it may be that cross-cultural differences were at work. Possibly the teaching of mathematics in England and Australia at the time these two studies were conducted was more formal and heavily emphasised than in the United States.

The Relation Between Anxiety and Achievement for Boys and Girls

The differential relationship between anxiety scores and school achievement for boys and girls was mentioned in the discussion of Lunneborg's study in which the negative relationship between these variables was found to be stronger for girls than for boys. Davidson,[14] using LA and HA children in Grades 2 through 5 who were matched on intelligence, found that LA children performed significantly better than HA children on total school performance. In contrast to Lunneborg's results, Davidson noted that the interfering effects of anxiety were more marked for boys than for girls, and he concluded that a high anxiety score for males would more likely lead to interference with performance whereas high scores for females may produce either facilitating or interfering effects. This interpretation was not supported by Stevenson and Odom,[4] however, who found no differences for the two sexes in the relationship between anxiety and school achievement. Similarly, the twelve correlations between TASC scores and reading and arithmetic obtained by Hill and Sarason revealed no consistent pattern of differences for boys and girls.

The most likely conclusion appears to be that the relationship between anxiety and achievement is equally strong for the two sexes overall but this relationship may vary as a function of complex situational factors, such as the sex of the teacher or a teacher's value system. For example, in a classroom where there is a female teacher who allows girls to be dependent, and who sees high achievement as more important for boys than for girls, the negative relationship between anxiety and achievement may be stronger for boys than for girls. Much more research is needed, however, to clarify this issue.

Long-term Effects of Anxiety on Academic Achievement

In the studies reported so far, a clear case has been made for the existence of a consistent negative relationship between anxiety and various measures of performance. A crucial issue in the interpretation of this relationship is whether or not these effects have long-term consequences which are reflected in school performance. One way to study this is to evaluate gains in scores on standardised achievement tests over a period of time.

Gaudry and Bradshaw,[15] whose experiment is described in full in Chapter 13, gave the TASC to fourteen classes of children in Grades 7 and 8, and then collected marks from progressive and terminal school tests. The children in each class were divided into HA and LA groups on the basis of the median TASC scores. It was found that the LA children averaged 67·2 marks on the total test compared with an average score of 63·1 for the HA groups. This difference of 4·1 score points is considerable when it is remembered that the groups were split at the median. While the question of magnitude of the difference that might have been found for more extreme anxiety groups, especially for children with very high anxiety scores, has not been answered, it is likely that this difference would have been even greater.

A more dramatic example of the size of the effect is reported by Hill and Sarason[9] who found a clear relationship between change in anxiety level and various measures of achievement during the elementary school years. Perhaps the most striking result in this study was that children who showed a drop from initially high levels of anxiety to a lower level (HA-LA) did significantly better than children who showed an increase in anxiety level from a low level to a high level (LA-HA). For example, the reading scores for the HA-LA group increased by an average of 39·5 months from Grade 2 to Grade 5 compared with 29·9 months for the LA-HA group. In another sample of children, measured at Grades 3 and 6, the HA-LA group improved 37·8 months as compared with 25·2 months for the LA-HA group.

The verbal behaviour of children is an aspect of school performance which is increasingly stressed in the design of new courses, especially in the humanities. Barnard, Zimbardo and Sarason,[16] in tape-recorded interviews lasting about 30 minutes, asked children a number of questions about a variety of topics. These questions varied from emotionally loaded ones like, "Tell me about a time when you had a fight with one of your good friends", to more neutral, general questions like, "Tell me about the different things you did last summer". Half the children were interviewed in a permissive atmosphere, while the other half was told there was to be a test following the interview. For the children in the evaluative interview situation, the HA children (as measured by the TASC) used a greater proportion of negative expressions than did the LA children. This difference between HA and LA children was not found in the more permissive situation. Furthermore, in describing people who were important to them, the HA children tended to be more concrete than the LA children. Their responses were also generally less well-organised and less comprehensible than the responses of the LA children.

In the Barnard *et al.* study, the behaviour of third grade children in a face-to-face interview situation was studied, and it would be interesting to know whether the same behaviour pattern would hold for the verbal exchanges which occur in the classroom. If so, awarding marks or grades for participation in class discussions would discriminate against the high-anxious pupil in the same way as do more formal tests. Some teachers contend that it is fairer to the student to grade him on the basis of classroom performance rather than formal tests because he is under less stress. One could argue, however, that as soon as the basis for grading became known, as it inevitably would, the classroom performance of HA children would be impaired by their anxiety responses and they would not be able to do themselves justice.

Grade Repetition and Optimal Level of Motivation

Two important issues remain to be presented in this section—grade repetition and optimal level of anxiety or motivation. Hill and Sarason[9] provide evidence on the former topic. In their longitudinal study, they compared the TASC scores of children repeating a grade with those of non-repeaters, and found a distinct tendency, especially among girls, for repeaters to be more anxious than children making normal progress through the grades. While this result is suggestive, more comprehensive and systematic studies of this relationship need to be conducted.

The second issue arises from the psychological theory of Hebb[17] in which it is strongly argued that the optimal level of motivation for effective performance lies in the middle ranges, rather than at the high or low end. This hypothesis is formalised in what is known as the Yerkes-Dodson Law, which states that the relationship between motivation (anxiety) and learning takes the form of an inverted U-shaped curve. A further and related hypothesis is that, as the task becomes more difficult, the optimal drive level becomes lower and lower.

A study by Cox[18] supports the Yerkes-Dodson Law. In this study, school examination marks of ten- and eleven-year-old boys were evaluated as a function of anxiety level as measured by the TAS. The relationship of scores on the TAS to school examination marks is indicated in Table 5.2 for low anxiety (LA), medium anxiety (MA), and high anxiety (HA) students. It may be noted that about three-quarters of the MA group were in the top half of the class, as compared with approximately half of the LA group and less than one-third of the HA group.

TABLE 5.2

Relationship of Scores on TAS to School Examination Marks *

School Marks	TAS Scores LA	MA	HA
Above median	16	22	10
Below median	15	7	26

* Adapted from Table 2[18]. By permission of the *Australian Journal of Psychology*.

The application of the Yerkes-Dodson principle to classroom learning seems entirely reasonable, but even with well-controlled laboratory studies there is sufficient contrary evidence to make for caution in accepting this law too readily. For example, Trapp and Kausler,[19] using a rather difficult task involving nonsense syllables, found that HA subjects performed best and MA subjects performed worst. Similarly, Maltzman *et al.*[20] found that a MA group made significantly more errors than either HA or LA groups. Gaudry[21] using a paired-associate learning task with elementary school children, also found that a MA group took more trials to reach the criterion of two successive, errorless trials than did LA and HA groups.

Anxiety and College Achievement

In commenting on the trend toward increasing reliance on objective tests of aptitude and intelligence in the selection of candidates for college, I. G. Sarason[22] has suggested that certain personality variables which correlate negatively with aptitude and intelligence should also be taken into account in evaluating applicants. Sarason obtained scores on thirteen intellectual measures for 738 men and women enrolled in introductory psychology and sociology courses at the University of Washington, and correlated each of these measures with scores on six different personality scales. The intellectual measures included high-school averages in English, mathematics, foreign languages and natural science, together with the test scores on Co-operative English Usage, Social Studies, and Mathematics. The personality variables were test anxiety, general anxiety, lack of protection, hostility, need for achievement and defensiveness.

The results showed that test anxiety was the only personality variable which related consistently to the measures of academic aptitude and achievement. All of the correlations involving test anxiety were negative, and eleven of thirteen were statistically significant. The correlations between test anxiety and entrance scores were more negative than those obtained with high-school grade-point averages. In discussing this point, Sarason reasons that the anxious student has an opportunity in high school to overlearn material, and to get to know and impress his instructors in the classroom, possibilities largely absent in group aptitude testing.

Spielberger[23] examined the relationship between anxiety and dropout rate resulting from academic failure for male students at Duke University (Part II, Chapter 15). Academic failure was defined as: (1) having been dismissed by the University because of poor academic performance; and/or (2) having left the University with a grade-point average below 1·75 (a GPA of 1·90 was required for graduation). Only eight of 138 LA students dropped out of college because of academic failure as compared with 26 of 129 HA students who dropped out. Thus, more than 20 per cent of the HA students failed as compared with less than 6 per cent of the LA students. On the basis of aptitude test scores, Spielberger classified these students into five levels of ability and found that a much larger percentage of HA students were academic failures at all levels, except the highest for which there was no difference.

Alpert and Haber[24] gave a battery of six anxiety scales to male students taking introductory psychology at Stanford University and evaluated the ability of these scales to predict college success. Their main interest was in comparing general anxiety scales, as represented by the MAS, the Welsh Anxiety Index (AI),[25] and the Freeman Anxiety Scale (AS),[26] with more specific test or achievement anxiety scales, as represented by the TAS, and the AAT + and AAT – scales. Table 5.3 summarises the results.

These data indicate that the specific anxiety scales tended to have higher negative correlations with measures of academic achievement than did the general anxiety scales. Only one of the eleven correlations for the general anxiety scales was large enough to be considered statistically significant, compared with nine of the twelve correlations involving the specific scales. It appears that specific and general anxiety scales measure something different, and that the former are better predictors of academic performance at the college level than the latter.

A study which appears to cast some doubt on the usefulness of the

TABLE 5.3

Correlations between Six Anxiety Scales and Four Measures of Academic Performance *

Test	GPA	Course grade	Final exam grade	Mid-term exam grade
General anxiety scales				
MAS	01	−08	−02	−19
AI	−04	−05	−03	−22
AS	−06	14	15	—
Specific anxiety scales				
TAS	−24	−21	−16	−32
AAT−	−35	−26	−28	−25
AAT+	37	23	26	21

* Adapted from Table 2[24]. By permission of the *Journal of Abnormal and Social Psychology*. Decimal points omitted.

TAQ as a predictor of academic success was reported by Grooms and Endler[27] for college students at Pennsylvania State University. They found that HA students did not differ significantly from LA students on any of the aptitude or achievement measures used in their study. In discussing these results in the context of other positive findings, the authors pointed out the fact that they used sophomores and juniors may have influenced the anxiety-achievement relationship because "students with poor averages would have been dropped or withdrawn from the University prior to entering the sophomore year" (p. 303).

General Conclusions

The most consistent general finding noted in this chapter is that high anxiety is associated with relatively low performance at both the school and university level. This conclusion is based on the negative correlations that were obtained in a number of different studies between different measures of anxiety and a variety of measures of academic aptitude and achievement.

For elementary school children, the evidence suggests that negative correlations between anxiety and achievement tend to increase in size for the higher grade levels, provided that the anxiety scales are given in reasonably close proximity to the achievement test. In addition, the following three tentative conclusions appear to be supported by research findings: (1) reading is more strongly associated with anxiety in the earlier grades than is arithmetic; (2) arithmetic (mathematics) becomes increasingly associated with anxiety towards the end of the elementary grades; and (3) differential relationships between anxiety and performance for boys and girls may depend upon situational factors.

Two studies were cited in which evidence was found that anxiety interferes with other aspects of academic achievement, but more data are required to clarify this relationship. One study suggested that the verbal behaviour of HA children was inferior to that of LA children in an interview situation, while another reported that children who are required to repeat grades tend to be more anxious than their peers who are making normal progress through school.

At the college level, there is evidence that anxiety tends to be associated with lower grades and higher dropout rates. In addition, it has been found that specific anxiety scales, such as the TASC and the AAT, are better predictors of academic success than are the general anxiety scales.

References

[1] P. W. LUNNEBORG, "Relations among Social Desirability, Achievement and Anxiety Measures in Children". *Child Dev.*, 1964, **35**, pp. 169-82.

[2] S. B. SARASON, K. S. DAVIDSON, F. F. LIGHTHALL, R. R. WAITE and B. K. RUEBUSH, *Anxiety in Elementary School Children*, John Wiley & Sons, New York, 1960.

[3] B. P. FROST, "Anxiety and Educational Achievement". *Br. J. educ. Psychol.*, 1968, **38**, pp. 293-301.

[4] H. W. STEVENSON and R. D. ODOM, "The Relation of Anxiety to Children's Performance on Learning and Problem-solving Tasks". *Child Dev.*, 1965, **36**, pp. 1003-12.

[5] E. L. COWEN, M. ZAX, R. KLEIN, L. D. IZZO, and M. A. TROST, "The Relation of Anxiety in School Children to School Record, Achievement and Behavioural Measures". *Child Dev.*, 1965, **36**, pp. 685-95.

[6] F. N. COX, "Test Anxiety and Achievement Behaviour Systems Related to Examination Performance in Children". *Child Dev.*, 1964, **35**, pp. 909-15.

[7] R. LYNN, "Temperamental Characteristics Related to Disparity of Attainment in Reading and Arithmetic". *Br. J. educ. Psychol.*, 1957, **27**, pp. 62-67.

[8] J. F. FELDHAUSEN and H. J. KLAUSMEIER, "Anxiety, Intelligence and Achievement in Children of Low, Average and High Intelligence". *Child Dev.*, 1962, **33**, pp. 403-09.

[9] K. T. HILL and S. B. SARASON, "The Relation of Test Anxiety and Defensiveness to Test and School Performance over the Elementary School Years: A Further Longitudinal Study. *Monogr. Soc. Res. Child Dev.*, 1966, **31** (2, serial No. 104).

[10] S. B. SARASON, "Text Anxiety, General Anxiety and Intellectual Performance". *J. consult. Psychol.*, 1957, **21**, 485-90.

[11] I. G. SARASON, "Intellectual and Personality Correlates of Test Anxiety". *J. abnorm. soc. Psychol.*, 1959, **59**, pp. 272-78.

[12] I. G. SARASON, "Test Anxiety and Intellectual Performance". *J. abnorm. soc. Psychol.*, 1963, **66**, pp. 73-75.

[13] D. WALTER, L. S. DENZLER, and I. G. SARASON, "Anxiety and Intellectual Performance of High School Students". *Child Dev.*, 1964, **35**, pp. 917-26.

[14] K. S. DAVIDSON, "Interviews of Parents of High Anxious and Low Anxious Children". *Child Dev.*, 1959, **30**, pp. 341-51.

[15] E. GAUDRY and G. D. BRADSHAW, "The Differential Effect of Anxiety on Performance in Progressive and Terminal School Examinations". *Aust. J. Psychol.*, 1970, **22**, pp. 1-4.

[16] J. W. BARNARD, P. G. ZIMBARDO and S. B. SARASON, "Anxiety and Verbal Behaviour in Children". *Child Dev.*, 1961, **32**, pp. 379-92.

[17] D. O. HEBB, *A Textbook of Psychology*, Saunders, London, 1958.

[18] F. N. COX, "Correlates of General and Text Anxiety in Children". *Aust. J. Psychol.*, 1960, **12**, pp. 169-77.

[19] E. P. TRAPP and D. H. KAUSLER, "Motivation and Cue Utilization in Intentional and Incidental Learning". *Psychol Rev.*, 1960, **67**, pp. 373-79.

[20] I. MALTZMAN, E. EISMAN and L. J. MORRISETT, "Rational Learning under Manifest and Induced Anxiety". *Psychol Rep.*, 1961, **8**, pp. 357-66.

[21] E. GAUDRY, "Parameters of Learning Curves". Unpublished doctoral dissertation, University of Melbourne, 1967.

[22] I. G. SARASON, "Test Anxiety and the Intellectual Performance of College Students". *J. educ. Psychol.*, 1961, **52**, pp. 201-06.

[23] C. D. SPIELBERGER, "The Effects of Manifest Anxiety on the Academic Achievement of College Students". *Ment. Hyg., N.Y.*, 1962, **46**, pp. 420-26.

[24] R. ALPERT and R. N. HABER, "Anxiety in Academic Achievement Situations". *J. abnorm. soc. Psychol.*, 1960, **61**, pp. 207-15.

[25] G. S. WELSH, "An Anxiety Index and an Internalization Ratio for the MMPI". *J. consult. Psychol.*, 1952, **16**, pp. 65-72.

[26] M. J. FREEMAN, "The Development of a Test for the Measurement of Anxiety: A Study of Its Reliability and Validity". *Psychol. Monogr.*, 1953, **67** (3, whole No. 353).

[27] R. R. GROOMS and N. S. ENDLER, "The Effect of Anxiety on Academic Achievement". *J. educ. Psychol.*, 1960, **51**, pp. 299-304.

Chapter 6

*Anxiety and Ability Grouping**

Classroom teachers have always been faced with the difficulty that pupils begin each new lesson with differing amounts of relevant knowledge and interest in the subject-matter. Different children also process new information at varying rates. With this heterogeneity at the outset, the rather curious educational goal has been, in many cases, to bring each pupil to the same point by the end of the lesson.

Given wide individual differences in ability and a fixed curriculum through which children must work to reach predetermined standards, the conscientious teacher is faced with a difficult dilemma. If he ignores individual differences in entering behaviour and pitches his teaching at the broad middle range of the class, the bright students are likely to become bored and restless while the slower-learning students flounder helplessly. If he attempts to cope with differences in ability and maturation by individualised teaching, the workload increases enormously.

One partial answer has been to stream children by ability, placing the high-flyers in one class and those having trouble in learning in another. A great deal of research has centred around this streaming process. While issues such as whether pupils streamed into subgroups achieve better than those randomly grouped have been the chief concern, claims that ability-grouping leads to better study methods have also been advanced and possible effects on social adjustment and status among peers have been investigated. Some educators have condemned ability-grouping on the grounds that it leads to changes in self-concept, with the bright children becoming arrogant and the less bright ones tending to develop feelings of inferiority and anxiety about school. This chapter is concerned with a facet of this last claim.

In recent years, some interesting research on the relationship between educational streaming and anxiety level has been reported. For example, Sarnoff *et al.*[1] conducted a cross-cultural study of English and American children which has stimulated other investigators to examine the streaming issue in more detail. A striking similarity in results has been found, with children in lower streams generally showing higher levels of anxiety. The difficulty comes in establishing a causal connection between ability grouping and anxiety. It is with this area of research that this chapter is concerned.

* Based on E. Gaudry, "Anxiety and Ability Grouping: A Review of Some Non-experimental and Experimental Studies". *Aust. J. Educ.*, 1971, **15** (in press).

In deciding to conduct a cross-cultural study, Sarnoff and his colleagues pointed to the differences between the educational policies and practices that were then current in England and America. They characterised the English system as heavily influenced by the "Eleven-plus" examinations. All children at or near the completion of Grade 5 must take a series of examinations which, in effect, determine the type of secondary education each pupil will receive. Consequently, the results of the examination greatly influence later vocational choice. While successful candidates may proceed to pursue academic courses at grammar schools with the option of subsequent university entrance, unsuccessful children are placed in secondary modern schools which are not concerned with academic preparation for university entrance.

An associated practice of British primary schools is that of streaming children into upper and lower ability groups at the end of the second or third grade, a process that is highly visible to both parents and children. In contrast, in the American system there is less formality and presumably less stress; the pupil may progress from grade to grade, often even without final examinations. Where ability-grouping is used, it tends to be within classes where the accelerated group in reading might contain different students than the high ability group in mathematics.

Overall, Sarnoff *et al.* saw the English system as more likely to foster anxiety about tests than the American system. They proceeded to examine this hypothesis by selecting over 500 English children in Grades 1 through 4 who were compared with nearly 600 American children, matched as closely as possible for grade, sex and social class background. They predicted that English children would be more *test-anxious* than their American counterparts, and that there would be no great differences in the mean level of *general anxiety*. Using the TASC and the GASC as anxiety measures, the authors report results in accordance with their predictions. The mean text-anxiety score for English children was 10·0 as compared to only 7·15 for American children, and there were no significant differences in the general anxiety scores of these children. Thus, the observed differences in test-anxiety appeared to be associated with educational practices rather than with more general differences in national temperament.

Cox[2] predicted that children in an "inferior" or lower stream would have higher test-anxiety scores than children in the "superior" or upper stream and that there would be no great differences in the level of general anxiety of these children. A total of 266 Grade 4 and 5 children living in Canberra, Australia, who had been placed in superior or inferior streams at the end of Grade 3 were given the same scales used

TABLE 6.1
Comparison of Children from Two Educational Streams on Test Anxiety Scores *

	Grade 4		Grade 5	
Sex	Superior	Inferior	Superior	Inferior
Male	9·0	15·1	11·5	19·7
Female	12·0	17·8	14·2	20·8

* Estimated from Fig. 1 in Cox[2]. By permission of the author and of *Child Development*.

by Sarnoff after they had been streamed 11 months and 23 months respectively. At both grade levels and for both sexes, children in the inferior streams had much higher test-anxiety scores than those in the upper streams, as shown in Table 6.1. In contrast, when boys and girls were considered separately, mean scores on general anxiety were very similar in Grades 4 and 5.

To test the consistency of this finding, Cox and Hammond[3] (Part II, Chapter 16) investigated levels of test-anxiety in a wide range of schools in Melbourne, Australia. Grade 9 and 10 classes in government, private and technical schools were used. In six out of seven comparisons, the mean test-anxiety scores were higher in the lower stream than in the upper stream and, once again, there were no significant differences in general anxiety.

While it is tempting to conclude that streaming *causes* an increase in test-anxiety, not one of the three studies discussed above demonstrates a causal relationship. In each of these studies some other factor related to streaming may actually be the causal agent. One such factor is suggested in the results of a longitudinal study by Levy, Gooch and Kellmer-Pringle[4] who gave the TASC on three separate occasions. In one of the two schools used in this investigation, the children were assigned to classes according to date of birth, and stayed together until the group was streamed at the beginning of the fourth year. The TASC was administered towards the end of the third year, at the beginning of the fourth year after streaming had been completed, and again six months later after the "Eleven-plus". On the first testing (prior to streaming) the mean scores for the boys who were later placed in streams A, B, and C were 7·3, 11·0 and 11·9 respectively: the corresponding scores for girls were 12·6, 13·0 and 14·3. The authors conclude: "Thus, there is no necessary conclusion that streaming raises the anxiety of C stream children relative to those of A stream children; the usual negative relationship between test anxiety and ability may well be a sufficient reason for Cox's 'effect of streaming'."

Bradshaw and Gaudry[5] (Part II, Chapter 17) put forward the hypothesis that continued experiences of failure cause the level of test-anxiety to rise. If the school policy is to stream on the basis of past performance, then it follows that those placed in the lower stream would tend to have a higher level of test-anxiety, not because of the act of being streamed, but because they have more frequently experienced anxiety about past failures.

To investigate this possibility, Bradshaw and Gaudry conducted an experiment using pupils from ten Grade 9 classes drawn from the Melbourne metropolitan area. Within each class, the pupils were randomly assigned to two groups: the first group was given an experience of success, the second was given an experience of failure. The TASC was subsequently administered to both groups, and the pupils' scores were analysed to determine whether just one single experience of failure caused a rise in test-anxiety. Two vocabulary tests were prepared—an easy form for the success group and a difficult one for the failure group. The seating was so arranged that the pupils in one group were unaware that those in the other group were doing a different task.

Each pupil marked his own test and compared his scores with norms that were prominently displayed. All pupils in the success group, in fact, obtained a score rated as "very good", while almost all in the failure group fell below a score rated as "poor". The analysis of the TASC scores obtained after the success and failure experiences showed the failure group scoring significantly higher than the success group. Thus, the conclusion may be drawn that a single experience of failure does in fact *cause* an immediate rise in test-anxiety. Therefore it seems reasonable to assume that the cumulative effects of failure will lead to higher levels of test-anxiety. Furthermore, since children who fail are placed in lower streams, it would be expected that they would have a higher mean level of test-anxiety than those in the upper stream, as was observed in the previous studies.

It seems reasonable to suppose that if, following placement in a lower stream, children are given a programme of work appropriate to their level of attainment with correspondingly easier examinations, then one would expect to find a drop in test-anxiety. That is, any change in educational practice which decreases the relative frequency of failure in the lower stream, such as differential teaching and examining, should lead to a decline in test-anxiety. Unfortunately, the prevailing practice is to stream, but then to continue to expect that students in the lower streams will master the same material and pass the same examinations as those in the upper streams. This practice is justified on the grounds that it enables a student who has been relegated to a lower stream to fight his way back into the upper stream.

Let us now return to the study of Levy *et al.*[4] which highlights the complexity of the relationship between ability-grouping and anxiety. In this study, two junior schools in the Midlands were used to examine the effects of repeated administration of the TASC and GASC in relation to differences in school regime, streaming, sex, and the "Eleven-plus" examination. In the "traditional" school (School T), which had an "adult-directed, traditional form of education, in which academic competition, streaming by achievement, class teaching and progress testing are among the educational factors emphasised", the results of the investigation were different from those obtained from the second school (School P), in which there was a child-centred approach. In School P, "children were allocated to classes within an age group according to

TABLE 6.2

Mean TASC Scores by School, Sex, Stream and Testing Occasion *

		School T			School P		
	Stream	A	B	C	A	B	C
	Occasion:						
Boys	1st	10·1	10·5	12·8	7·3	11·0	11·9
	2nd	8·6	8·1	11·0	7·1	11·5	9·7
	3rd	5·7	4·1	10·1	8·3	6·8	8·5
Girls	1st	14·1	14·3	11·9	12·6	13·0	14·3
	2nd	12·0	11·8	7·8	10·3	16·8	16·7
	3rd	11·0	9·2	13·0	10·0	13·8	16·7

* From Levy *et al.*[4]. By permission of the *British Journal of Educational Psychology.*

date of birth and stay together throughout the first three years of junior school. Academic achievement and progress testing are said not to be emphasised in the classroom."

While the findings were complex and difficult to summarise in any meaningful way, an inspection of Table 6.2 should indicate the difficulties of making simple generalisations about anxiety and streaming. In interpreting these results it should be borne in mind that: (1) A is the highest stream and C the lowest; (2) in School T the streaming had taken place before the first testing occasion whereas School P was streamed between the first and second testing occasion; and (3) the "Eleven-plus" examination occurred for both groups between the second and third occasion. While the mean TASC scores rose steadily across streams A, B and C, this varied with the occasion, school and sex. The authors correctly note the dangers inherent in interpreting overall results which combine data from different schools, from both sexes, and from several testing occasions.

References

[1] I. Sarnoff, F. F. Lighthall, R. R. Waite, K. S. Davidson and S. B. Sarason, "A Cross-cultural Study of Anxiety amongst American and English School Children". *J. educ. Psychol.*, 1958, **49**, pp. 129-37.

[2] F. N. Cox, "Educational Streaming and General and Test Anxiety". *Child Dev.*, 1962, **33**, pp. 381-90.

[3] F. N. Cox and S. B. Hammond, "Educational Streaming and Anxiety in Children". *Aust. J. educ.*, 1964, **8**, pp. 85-90.

[4] P. Levy, S. Gooch and M. L. Kellmer-Pringle, "A Longitudinal Study of the Relationship between Anxiety and Streaming in a Progressive and a Traditional Junior School". *Br. J. educ. Psychol.*, 1969, **39**, pp. 166-73.

[5] G. D. Bradshaw and E. Gaudry, "The Effect of a Single Experience of Success or Failure on Test Anxiety". *Aust. J. Psychol.*, 1968, **20**, pp. 219-23.

Chapter 7

Programmed Learning and Computer-Based Instruction

Ability grouping is, at best, only a limited attempt to cope with the problem of individual differences in intellectual ability and the relevant background knowledge and experience which students bring to new learning tasks. If we have, for example, 120 students at Grade 6 streamed into four classes of thirty pupils, each class will certainly be more homogeneous in ability or knowledge than the total group. But there will still be a considerable spread of talent within each class and even students with the same level of ability may differ in knowledge and motivational factors.

Many plans have been put forward as alternatives to the inflexible system that characterises the traditional self-contained classroom in which children work through a fixed curriculum and move from grade to grade by annual examination. Some of these plans are listed below.

THE NON-GRADED SCHOOL

This approach depends upon the construction of a curriculum through which pupils can progress at their own pace. Probably the first comprehensive attempt to implement a non-graded school programme was at Western Springs, Illinois, in 1934, and numerous difficulties were encountered. There are, for example, a great many practical problems in administering such programmes, particularly if the number of students involved is large; there are also problems in reporting progress to parents. Furthermore, teachers whose experience is in more traditional systems often find it difficult to adapt to the non-graded approach. Probably for a combination of these reasons, Western Springs abandoned the plan and very few school systems have subsequently adopted this method.

PARTIAL GRADING

This method is perhaps best exemplified by the Dalton Plan, evolved about 1915. The curriculum was divided into two parts. In the first part—the skills component—pupils proceeded through the basic subjects of mathematics and English at their own pace. For the second part of the curriculum, students stayed with their own classes, and were taught as a group in subject-areas, such as history and geography. Similarly, the Winnetka Plan preserved the normal grade structure while providing for differential progress in the curriculum through an emphasis on individual assignments.

DUAL PROGRESS

In dual progress programmes, each day is divided into two parts. Specialist teachers attempt to promote individual progress during half of the day, while group activity is coordinated and supervised by the class teacher in the other half.

Programmed Learning

These brief references highlight the fact that in educational circles throughout the world, at least since John Dewey set up his laboratory school at the University of Chicago in the 1890s, there has been a great deal of interest in individualising instruction according to the needs and abilities of the individual student. As with the non-graded school, most of these procedures have been tried and abandoned, not because they lacked intrinsic value but because practical methods for implementing the basic ideas were not available.

Midway through the twentieth century, Professor B. F. Skinner, a prominent psychologist whose main interest is in the learning process, published an article entitled "The Science of Learning and the Art of Teaching".[1] In this article, Skinner proposed using reinforcement, in the form of immediate knowledge of results, to shape human behaviour towards the mastery of complex subject-matter. Since 1954, there has been a great deal of interest and research devoted to the application of Skinner's ideas in the field of education. Among the products of these efforts are the development of programmed textbooks and the allied field of computer-based instruction.

In programmed learning, the material which is to be taught is broken down into major concepts, and then further subdivided into smaller units, called "frames", which are then assembled in hierarchical order to constitute self-instructional units. The student works through the programmed materials at his own pace, responding to each frame by composing or selecting an appropriate answer. After each response, immediate reinforcement is provided in the form of information about the correctness or incorrectness of the response.

A set of frames on a single topic, such as mathematics or spelling, is called a programme. Great care goes into the development of each programme which may consist of several thousand frames. A programme is usually revised a number of times in the light of the responses made by students in the preparation phase. In brief, the general principles which guide the preparation of a programme for learning include:

(1) progress must be made in small steps, so that the student may gradually proceed from relatively simple to more complex tasks;

(2) by means of this gradual progression and the careful use of prompts and hints, the student should make relatively few errors; and

(3) care must be taken not to reward or reinforce any behaviour that is not compatible with the desired responses.

The presentation of programmed materials can be carried out in a number of ways. The use of programmed textbooks, teaching machines and computers in the presentation of such materials is described below.

PROGRAMMED TEXTBOOKS

In most programmed texts, *linear programmes* are used. The frames in linear programmes are arranged so that the student: (a) reads the first frame; (b) makes a response; (c) uncovers the correct answer by sliding a masking device down the page; (d) checks his answer; and then (e) moves to the next frame which is immediately below the first frame. There may be as many as 15 to 20 frames on a single page of a programmed text.

A slight variation of the format for the linear programme is to organise the layout of the text so that Frame 1 is at the top of page 1, Frame 2 is at the top of page 2, and so on for 12 pages. Frame 13 is found on the second level of page 1; Frame 14 is found on the second level of page 2, and so on.

When the text contains a great deal of material to be absorbed, *branching programmes* are often used. Typically, a question about the material is presented and the student responds by selecting an answer, as in a multiple-choice test. Depending on the answer selected, he is directed to another page of the book. If his choice was correct, he will be told that he was correct and then presented with more material. If he chose an incorrect answer, he will be told that he was wrong and then given some remedial help before being sent back to try the question again.

TEACHING MACHINES AND COMPUTERS

These vary in size and sophistication, from simple machines costing a few dollars which offer little advantage over the programmed text to highly versatile computers costing many thousands of dollars. The more sophisticated teaching machine can be used to regulate the sequence in which the pupil completes the programme and the rate of presentation of the frames. Such devices can also present branching sequences, with audio as well as visual materials, and keep a complete record of performance.

The use of high-speed computers in education has been hailed as a development that may finally solve the problem of individualising instruction. The implementation of computer-based learning systems in the United States, England and the U.S.S.R. is already under way with such success that the future of this approach seems assured. A brief description of the work being done at Stanford University should suffice to show the tremendous flexibility flowing from the use of computers as instructional devices.

With the computer-assisted instruction system at Stanford, it is possible to handle (a) university students taking a course in elementary Russian, (b) eleven-year-old pupils who are learning spelling, and (c) younger children taking a course in elementary mathematics, *all at the same time.* Furthermore, at any given time, an individual student in one of these groups may be at a different point in the course from any of his classmates.

Because of its tremendous speed of operation, a computer can keep track of the progress of each individual student and, if required, it can print out reports on each lesson which the student may use as a study guide. A further advantage of computer-based instruction is that the students can work at centres that are located many miles away from the computer facility. Since a computer terminal can be linked to the central processor of the computer by conventional telephone wires, only access to the terminal at which the programmes are presented is required.

From the brief description of programmed and computer-based instruction, it can be seen that this approach is solitary and highly structured. Each student proceeds independently at his own pace, with little or no reference to the work of other students. Great emphasis is placed on individual progress through a series of small steps that are carefully designed to keep the error rate to a minimum. A central feature of this approach is that the student is provided with immediate knowledge of results. The student is also constantly reassured that he is making good progress, and there is no competition brought about by individual differences in speed, or by either overt or covert comparisons between students of unequal ability.

Anxiety and Programmed Learning

The preceding section of this chapter was devoted to showing a connection between early attempts to cope with the problem of individual differences in education and more recent efforts which integrate learning theory with new developments in educational technology. The remainder of the chapter deals with research on the relationship between anxiety and learning in studies using some form of programmed instruction.

In general, programmed instruction is about as far removed from the stresses of the test situation as one can get. From Sarason's point of view (see Chapter 2, pp. 12-13), this approach provides a learning environment in which the anxious student should not be at a disadvantage. Unlike the traditional classroom, there are no time pressures and the student can practise task-relevant responses without fear of negative evaluation by his teacher. From Spence's theoretical frame of reference (see Chapter 2, pp. 10-12), programmed learning with its gradual progression in small, easy steps, resembles an easy task on which few errors are made. It might even be expected that high anxiety would facilitate performance if the programme writer has been successful in reducing competing error-tendencies to a minimum.

More than a decade of research on programmed learning has centred mainly on the characteristics of programmes and the various qualities of students' responses to them. In the last several years, however, some evidence has been reported on the personality characteristics of students and how individual differences in personality affect performance in programmed-learning tasks. Five recent investigations of anxiety and programmed learning are described below.

Campeau[2] attempted to demonstrate experimentally that feedback (knowledge of results) is a critical factor in the performance of anxious students in programmed learning. Two versions of a programmed lesson on earth-sun relationships were prepared, one with feedback and one without. The subjects in the experiment were boys and girls with high and low scores (upper and lower 27 per cent) on Sarason's TASC, who were selected from two Grade 5 classes in San Francisco. Campeau found that the high-test-anxious girls in the feedback condition did better on the criterion test than the low-anxious girls (25·85 *v.* 19·42), but they did worse in the no-feedback condition (16·47 *v.* 23·53). Although no significant differences were found for boys, the author interpreted her results as supporting the hypothesis that feedback minimised erroneous responses and was less threatening than no feedback. While these results suggest that programmed instruction assists the high-anxious student, replication with a larger sample is needed.

Kight and Sassenrath[3] (Part II, Chapter 18) gave a series of linear-type programmed booklets, dealing with the construction and analysis of classroom achievement tests, to 139 undergraduate students in Educational Psychology at Indiana University. Prior to the learning session, the Mandler-Sarason[4] Text Anxiety Questionnaire and a measure of achievement motivation were given to these students. The results showed that the high test-anxious students made significantly fewer errors than the low-anxious (16·8 *v.* 23·3), and completed the programme in less time (112·3 min *v.* 116·4 min). While these findings support the hypothesis that programmed instruction facilitates the performance of anxious students, two further results of this study need to be borne in mind. First, no significant differences were found in the scores of the high and low anxiety groups on an achievement test given at the conclusion of the programmed instruction (HA = 23·8, LA = 22·1). Secondly, in the time data there was a significant interaction between test-anxiety and achievement motivation. The authors interpreted this latter finding as indicating that high test-anxiety is associated with faster performance only for students with high achievement motivation.

Ryan[5] gave fourth grade students five linear programmes centred on the geography of Japan, and required the students to complete one programme on each of five consecutive school days. A test was conducted to assess knowledge of specific facts, along with generalisations and applications of these facts. As in the Kight and Sassenrath study, Ryan found no significant difference in the test scores of the high and low test-anxious subjects. But in contrast to Kight and Sassenrath, Ryan's high-anxious students took longer to complete the programme. One possible explanation for the inconsistency in these results lies in the different populations that were used in the two studies. Using fourth grade students, Gifford and Marston[6] showed that high-anxious subjects took significantly longer to complete a reading rate test than did low-anxious students. Although comparative data on reading rate are not available for college students, since the negative correlation typically found between intelligence and test-anxiety in children seems to disappear at the college level, it seems reasonable to suggest that reading rate and test-anxiety are negatively related in school children, but not in college students.

O'Neil, Spielberger and Hansen[7] (Part II, Chapter 19) investigated the relationship between state anxiety (A-State) and performance on a computer-assisted learning task. The subjects were 29 undergraduate students at Florida State University who were given difficult and easy mathematical concepts to learn by computer-assisted instruction. A unique feature of this study was that measures of A-State were obtained while the subjects performed the learning task. It was found that scores on Spielberger's *et al.*[8] STAI A-State scale and measures of systolic blood pressure increased while students worked on the difficult learning materials, and decreased when they responded to the easy materials. Furthermore, students with high A-State scores made more errors on the more difficult materials and fewer errors on the easier materials than low A-State subjects. Assuming that A-State reflected drive level, the authors interpreted these findings as indicating that high A-State activated error-tendencies on the more difficult CAI materials for which error rate was relatively high, and enhanced the probability of giving correct responses on the easier CAI materials on which error rate was relatively low. This complex interactive relationship between A-State and errors would be predicted by Spence's[9] theory of emotionally-based drive.

The findings of one study appear to run against the general trend of results discussed in the previous paragraphs. Flynn and Morgan[10] worked with 96 students ("primarily sophomores") in six geometry classes from a New Jersey public high school. Three of the six intact classes were randomly assigned to receive instruction from a branched programme text on vector geometry, while the other three were teacher-directed. The results included two findings of interest:

(1) achievement did not differ significantly for students with high and low test-anxiety; and

(2) there was no significant interaction between method of instruction and level of test-anxiety. That is, the achievement for the high-anxious students in programmed instruction and under teacher instruction was not different from that of the low-anxious.

The line of argument advanced in this chapter would lead to the prediction that the high-anxious student would do relatively better than the low-anxious student under the programmed-instruction method, and not as well under the teacher-directed method. Since Flynn and Morgan did not present mean scores on their anxiety scales or their performance measures, it is not possible to say how well their groups were matched or whether there were any trends in their results supporting the interactive hypothesis.

A serious methodological criticism of Flynn and Morgan's study is that the *classes* were allocated at random to methods of instruction, but the data were analysed as if *students* had been randomly assigned. One can sympathise with the authors because this very dilemma causes constant trouble in educational research. The problem is whether to make a study much larger and to use, say, twenty classes which are evaluated as classes, or to assume, as Flynn and Morgan did, that individual students had been randomly assigned to classes. If the latter course is adopted, a minimum precaution would be to give some form of pre-test in order to show that the groups were reasonably similar before the differential treatments were given. No such precaution was taken by Flynn and Morgan.

Some Concluding Considerations

In summary, evidence is accumulating that programmed learning and computer-based instruction may help to nullify the interfering effects of high anxiety on academic achievement. Since programmed textbooks and computer systems also offer practical methods for coping with individual differences in the ability to handle new material, these technological advances have great promise for the future. If this promise is to be realised, however, the educational programmes written for textbooks or computers will require considerable improvement. Educational programmes could be improved by:

(1) introducing greater variety in the presentation format;

(2) making provisions for the use of ancillary media, such as tapes, slides, films and textbooks;

(3) providing an opportunity for cumulative note-taking and the discussion of programmed materials in small groups;

(4) making access to sections of the programme easier to permit reviews of specific topics with which the student is having difficulty.

Many valid criticisms have been levelled at the programmed movement in education, but most of the faults lie with the programme writers rather than being inherent in the approach. Given insightful programmers who can produce stimulating programmes, modern educational technology shows great promise. We now have practical ways of implementing the basic notions which led to streaming and to the Dalton and Winnetka Plans. And, at the same time, we can help anxious students to realise their full potential by providing less stressful, less threatening learning environments.

References

[1] B. F. Skinner, "The Science of Learning and the Art of Teaching". *Harv. educ. Rev.*, 1954, **24**, pp. 86-97.

[2] P. L. Campeau, "Test Anxiety and Feedback in Programmed Instruction". *J. educ. Psychol.*, 1968, **59**, pp. 159-163.

[3] H. R. Kight and J. M. Sassenrath, "Relation of Achievement Motivation and Test Anxiety to Performance in Programmed Instruction". *J. educ. Psychol.*, 1966, **57**, pp. 14-17.

[4] G. Mandler and S. B. Sarason, "A Study of Anxiety and Learning". *J. abnorm. soc. Psychol.*, 1952, **47**, pp. 155-73.

[5] F. L. Ryan, "Advance Organizers and Test Anxiety in Programmed Social Studies Instruction". *Calif. J. educ. Res.*, 1968, **19**, pp. 67-76.

[6] E. M. Gifford and A. R. Marston, "Test Anxiety, Reading Rate and Task Experience". *J. educ. Res.*, 1966, **59**, pp. 303-06.

[7] H. F. O'Neil, C. D. Spielberger and D. N. Hansen, "The Effects of State-anxiety and Task Difficulty on Computer-assisted Learning". *J. educ. Psychol.*, 1969, **60**, pp. 343-50.

[8] C. D. Spielberger, R. L. Gorsuch and R. E. Lushene, *The State-Trait Anxiety Inventory. (S.T.A.I.) Test Manual for Form X*, Consulting Psychologists Press, Palo Alto, 1970.

[9] K. W. Spence, "A Theory of Emotionally Based Drive (D) and its Relation to Performance in Simple Learning Situations". *Am. Psychol.*, 1958, **13**, pp. 131-41.

[10] J. T. Flynn and J. H. Morgan, "A Methodological Study of the Effectiveness of Programmed Instruction through Analyses of Learner Characteristics". *Proc. 74th Ann. Conven. A.P.A.*, 1966, pp. 259-60.

Chapter 8

The Interactive Effects of Intelligence and Anxiety

In his presidential address to the American Psychological Association on "The Two Disciplines of Scientific Psychology", Cronbach[1] pointed to the division of psychology into two domains represented, on the one hand, by the psychometricians and, on the other, by the experimentalists. Progress toward a unification of these disparate fields, with their different objectives and methods, was assessed in a symposium on "Learning and Individual Differences" held in 1965 at the University of Pittsburg. The compelling conclusion which follows from reading the papers presented at the Pittsburg Conference (Gagné[2]) is that very little integration has occurred. There was, however, considerable agreement on the general strategy needed to effect such integration. In his summary comments on the conference, Melton[3] (p. 239) succinctly expressed this strategy as follows: "What is necessary is that we frame our hypotheses about individual difference variables in terms of the process constructs of contemporary theories of learning and performance." For many teachers, intelligence is regarded as the individual difference variable which is most closely related to academic achievement. In the following paragraphs, we attempt to extend Spence's Drive Theory to incorporate the intelligence variable. Research evidence from both the laboratory and the classroom will then be presented in an endeavour to assess the viability of our theoretical development.

Anxiety, Intelligence and Learning

Spence's theory of emotionally based drive begins with the assumption that the effect of anxiety or drive level (D) on performance depends upon the relative strength of the correct and competing response tendencies that are evoked by a learning task (see Chapter 2). On simple tasks, in which correct response tendencies are stronger than competing responses, high D facilitates performance; on complex or difficult tasks, in which competing response tendencies are stronger than correct responses, high D interferes with performance, at least in the initial stages of learning. Drive Theory has been strongly supported by research findings in which the Manifest Anxiety Scale (MAS) was used as an operational measure of individual differences in D (e.g., Lucas,[4] Montague,[5] Ramond,[6] Rosenbaum,[7] Spence,[8] Spence and Spence,[9] Spielberger and Smith,[10] Taylor and Chapman[11]).

The present extension of Spence's Drive Theory to encompass individual differences in intelligence takes into account the following variables: difficulty of the learning task, stage of learning and type of performance measure. The primary hypothesis from which this extension proceeds, first explicated by Spielberger,[12] is that the difficulty of a learning task will depend on the intelligence level of the subject. More specifically, it is assumed that the subject's IQ will determine, in part, the relative strengths of the correct and competing response tendencies elicited by a learning task. The implications of this assumption for Drive Theory are discussed below for tasks which vary in difficulty.

In simple learning tasks, few error tendencies are evoked. High anxiety (HA) would therefore be expected to facilitate the performance of all *S*s irrespective of their intellectual ability if number of errors or number of trials to criterion is used as the performance measure. However, where speed of response is used, covert error tendencies may be detected by this very sensitive measure. Therefore, it might be expected that high anxiety would impair performance early in learning, especially for low IQ *S*s. On the other hand, high anxiety might be expected to enhance learning on very easy tasks from the outset. If this were the case, more rapid performance as well as fewer errors would be observed, especially for high IQ *S*s.

A learning task of intermediate difficulty would be relatively easier for high IQ *S*s than for low IQ *S*s. In other words, fewer competing error tendencies would be evoked in high IQ *S*s and the strength of correct response tendencies would be stronger. In contrast, the same task might be quite difficult for low IQ *S*s in whom numerous competing error tendencies were generated and the strength of correct response tendencies was relatively low. On such tasks, high anxiety would facilitate the performance of high IQ *S*s, while leading to performance decrements in *S*s with low intelligence. However, if repeated practice is given, it would be expected that the habit strength of correct responses would increase relative to that of error tendencies so that, at a later stage in learning, high anxiety might begin to facilitate performance for low ability *S*s.

For very difficult learning tasks, it would be predicted that the performance of LA *S*s would initially be superior to that of HA *S*s of comparable ability. As the task becomes easier with repeated practice, performance should come to resemble that on the early trials of a task of intermediate difficulty, with high anxiety eventually facilitating the performance of high IQ *S*s. Whether or not high anxiety would ever facilitate the performance of low IQ *S*s on difficult tasks would depend on whether these *S*s could gain sufficient mastery of the task so that it could assume the characteristics of an easy task after repeated practice trials.

It seems unlikely that the inherently difficult materials typically encountered by students in the classroom can be mastered sufficiently so that they will become relatively easy. Therefore, it would be expected that such materials would be poorly handled by the high-anxious, especially those with low ability. In the following sections, the research evidence on the interactive effects of intelligence and anxiety on performance is examined for learning tasks that vary in difficulty.

Effects of Intelligence and Anxiety on Simple Tasks

Gaudry and Spielberger[13] investigated the effects of anxiety and intelligence on paired-associate learning using two levels of anxiety and two levels of intelligence. The subjects were students enrolled in a course in Educational Psychology at the Balmain Teachers College, Sydney, Australia. They were required to learn the following list of easy paired-associates: butterfly-insect; sheep-animal; sickness-health; table-chair; needle-thread. The words were selected so that, for each pair, the response word was the most frequent association to the stimulus word and none of the stimulus words was given as a response to any other stimulus word.

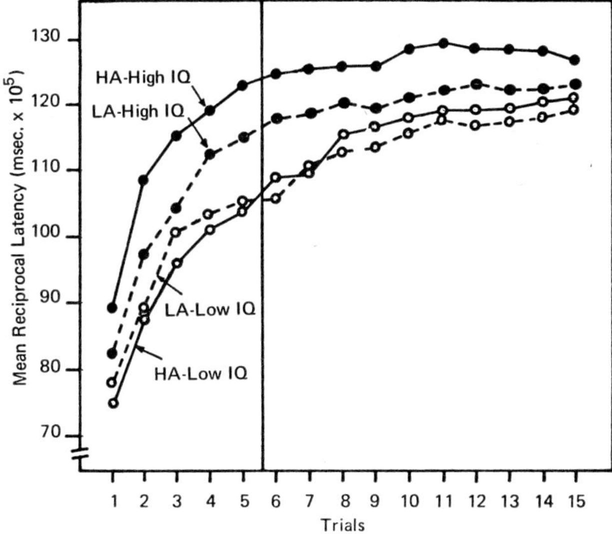

Fig. 8.1 Mean reciprocal latency scores over trials for the four experimental groups. From Gaudry and Spielberger.[13] By permission of the *Journal of Educational Psychology.*

Errors and latency measures were obtained over 15 anticipation trials, and separate factorial statistical analyses were made for the early and later stages of learning (trials 1-5 and 6-15). The results of the study are shown in Fig. 8.1 in which mean reciprocal latency scores (speed of response) are presented. The results of the statistical analyses showed that:

(1) early in learning, high anxiety facilitated performance for high IQ *S*s and impaired performance for low IQ *S*s relative to their low anxiety counterparts;

(2) later in learning, high anxiety tended to facilitate performance for both high and low IQ *S*s;

(3) at both stages of learning the performance of high IQ *S*s was superior to that of low IQ *S*s.

In general, these results are consistent with the prediction that the learning task generated fewer competing response tendencies for high IQ *S*s than for low IQ *S*s. It must be emphasised, however, that virtually no errors were made in this task, and that the performance measure was the latency (speed) for the correct response.

The results of a study reported by Harleston[14] are consistent with those obtained by Gaudry and Spielberger. Harleston used four paired-associate word lists which differed in terms of the association value of the stimulus and response items. His easiest list, for which both the stimulus and response items had high association values, can be properly classified as a relatively simple task. Harleston's subjects were HA and LA students who were divided into groups of fast and slow learners. For his easiest list, Harleston found a "significant trial-blocks by ability level by anxiety interaction". This finding indicated that the HA *S*s who were slow learners (presumably lower in IQ) performed more poorly than LA *S*s of comparable ability on the first 15 trials, but they performed better than the LA *S*s on the last 15 trials. Thus, high anxiety impaired performance on this easy task for the slow learners on early trials, but subsequently facilitated performance for these same *S*s relative to the performance of low anxiety *Ss* of comparable ability.

Conflicting evidence is found in the results of a discrimination reaction-time experiment reported by Stabler and Dyal[15] who used a speed of response measure with subjects who differed in anxiety and intelligence. They found reliable IQ effects but no evidence of an anxiety by intelligence interaction. Their high intelligence *S*s were superior over trials, irrespective of their level of anxiety. Since the findings in this study are inconsistent with those of Harleston, and of Gaudry and Spielberger, several important methodological problems need to be considered in interpreting them. First, the task was quite simple in that each *S* had only to learn to press one of three buttons as a response to one of three lights. Thus, the large number of errors that were made over trials seems rather odd. Secondly, the 60 *S*s in this study were selected from a prison population of 265 after it had been found necessary to eliminate 33 *S*s because they either misunderstood directions or refused to participate. Furthermore, 36 additional *S*s were excluded because of high lie scores. The large number of errors and the nature of the selection procedures suggests that perhaps a prison population is not the ideal group to use in testing hypotheses concerning motivational variables!

Effects of Intelligence and Anxiety on Tasks of Moderate Difficulty Level

A study by Denny[16] provides the best evidence in this area. He used an ingenious concept formation task with male college students at Duke

University. In this task, the *S*s were required to deduce the attributes which constituted a conjunctive concept from information that was given to them in separate "instances". It had been previously determined in pilot work that there were minimal floor and ceiling effects for this population. That is, low intelligence *S*s rarely achieved the worst possible score and high intelligence *S*s rarely made the best possible score. Denny found that high anxiety facilitated the performance of high IQ *S*s, but impaired the performance of LA *S*s of comparable ability. These results are presented graphically in Fig. 8.2.

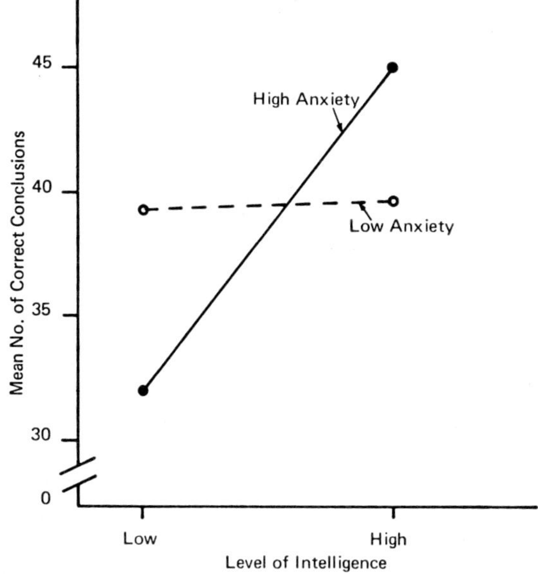

Fig. 8.2 Mean number of correct conclusions formed by each of the four experimental groups. After Denny[16]. By permission of the author and the *Journal of Experimental Psychology.*

Katahn[17] also found that anxiety and ability had an interactive effect on performance for a task of moderate difficulty. Although no differences were found for HA and LA *S*s with relatively low mathematical aptitude scores, the performance of the HA *S*s with high aptitude was superior to that of LA *S*s with comparable ability. This latter finding is similar to the results reported by Denny, and to the findings for high ability *S*s in the Gaudry-Spielberger and Harleston studies.

It was previously noted that, for Harleston's easiest paired-associate word list, anxiety and intelligence influenced performance in an interactive manner that was consistent with the extension of drive theory proposed in this chapter. However, for Harleston's other three word-lists, which can probably be regarded as learning tasks of intermediate difficulty, no such interactions were found. The most likely explanation is that the anxiety groups may not have been comparable in intelligence to begin with. It may be recalled that Harleston used performance on a practice list as his measure of ability. Since performance on the practice list may have been influenced by anxiety, this leaves the ability level of the various groups somewhat in doubt.

The findings in two verbal learning studies reported by Deese, Lazarus and Keenan[18] also bear on the question of the effects of anxiety and intelligence on performance. In one study, conducted at the Johns Hopkins University, an institution noted for the quality of its students, the performance of HA *S*s was superior to that of LA *S*s. These same authors also refer to an unpublished study "with the identical design and task used in the present experiment, but with a population of lower intelligence [in which] high anxious *S*s performed more poorly than low anxious *Ss*" (Footnote 2, p. 59). Thus, high anxiety apparently facilitated the performance of *S*s with high intelligence in the first study, while leading to performance decrements on the same task for the less able *S*s in the second.

Effects of Intelligence and Anxiety on Difficult Tasks

No laboratory studies of anxiety and intelligence could be found in which the experimental task could be classified as difficult for the most able students. Accordingly, evidence on the relationship between anxiety and college grades will be examined on the assumption that the academic task is relatively difficult for most students.

Spielberger and Weitz[19] present data on two groups of male college students at Duke University which appear to fit the requirements. These results are shown in Fig. 8.3. For the upperclassmen, high anxiety facilitated the performance of *S*s at the highest level of ability, but had detrimental effects on students with low or average ability. This finding, which suggests that the academic task was apparently not too difficult for the brightest upperclassmen, contrasts with the results for the freshmen in Section B of Fig. 8.3, in which high anxiety is associated with somewhat poorer performance, especially for the high ability group.

In a *post-hoc* explanation of their findings, Spielberger and Weitz note that the level of academic aptitude of students entering the university rose consistently each successive year during the time the data were collected. Consequently, by 1959, the academic task for entering freshmen was apparently no longer easy, even for the very high ability students. The exclusion of less able students led to a more homogeneous population of high ability, and this produced a much keener competition for grades. It also probably resulted in more difficult examinations on which anxiety interfered with performance, even for the most able students.

The failure to find any differences due to anxiety in the academic performance of low-ability freshmen was also attributed by Spielberger and Weitz to the changing characteristics of the student body. As the academic requirements for entrance to the university were raised, only those low-aptitude students with excellent high school grades were admitted, and it was found that the low-aptitude students with high anxiety had better study habits, as measured by the Brown-Holtzman[20] scale, than the low-aptitude students with low anxiety. Thus, the superior study habits of the low-aptitude students with high anxiety appeared to counteract the adverse effects of their higher anxiety level.

The evidence of an interactive effect of anxiety and intelligence on academic achievement outlined in the previous paragraphs is included only because of the absence of research from more controlled studies. While the *post-hoc* explanations of the findings are plausible, and serve to show the complexity of the phenomena in question, a more direct test of the hypothesis of an interaction between anxiety and intelligence in a school setting is contained in a recent study by Gaudry and Fitzgerald (Part II, Chapter 20). In this investigation, the performance of junior high school pupils in six different subject-matter areas was evaluated.

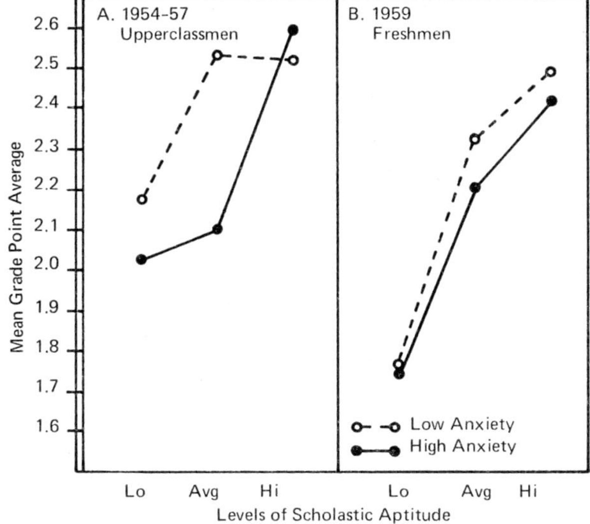

Fig. 8.3 The relationship between anxiety and grades as a function of scholastic aptitude for: (A) upperclassmen (1954-57); (B) freshmen who entered the university in the fall term of 1959; from Spielberger and Weitz[19]. By permission of the authors and the American Psychological Association.

Gaudry and Fitzgerald gave the Test Anxiety Scale for Children (TASC) and the Australian Council for Educational Research Intermediate Test D, a measure of intelligence, to the pupils in twelve Grade 7 classes in Melbourne. The marks obtained by these pupils on the half-yearly school examination in English, Mathematics, History, Geography, French, and Science were collected and standardised to yield distributions with a mean score of 50 and a standard deviation of 10. Since the investigation was concerned with performance within class settings, the data for the *S*s in each class were separated by sex, then divided into high and low anxiety groups by splitting at the median, and further subdivided into five levels of intelligence.

It was predicted that only the most able students would find school examinations easy. Therefore, the performance of the students at the highest level of ability (level 5) was compared with that of students in the four lower ability groups (levels 1, 2, 3, 4). The results for this comparison are shown in Table 8.1 in which it may be noted that the HA *S*s with low ability did more poorly than the LA *S*s with comparable ability in all six subject-matter areas. For students at the highest level of ability, the HA *S*s were superior in two areas, Geography and History, and the difference in favour of the LA *S*s in the other areas was considerably smaller than was the case for the low ability students.

TABLE 8.1

Mean Scores for Intelligence by Anxiety Interaction *

	English		Maths		History		Geography		French		Science	
Anxiety	IQ level		IQ level		IQ level		IQ level		IQ level		IQ level	
	1234	5	1234	5	1234	5	1234	5	1234	5	1234	5
High	46·4	56·4	45·1	56·4	47·0	56·0	46·3	58·1	46·8	56·2	46·4	57·7
Low	49·1	57·3	49·3	57·6	49·4	54·3	49·7	55·3	49·3	56·8	48·6	58·0

* E. Gaudry and D. Fitzgerald. See Chapter 20.

In the statistical analyses of the data, the anxiety by intelligence interaction was significant only for Geography, and approached significance for Mathematics and History. While the findings in all six subject-matter areas were in the direction of the predicted interaction, the variability of the performance scores was such that the statistical analyses did not yield significant results. However, when the students in levels 4 and 5 were compared, the anxiety by intelligence interactions were significant for Geography, History, Mathematics, and French, and of borderline significance in the other two school subjects (see Chapter 20 for a fuller description of these findings). Thus, the anxiety by intelligence interaction was most marked in the comparison of the two highest levels of ability.

The results of the two studies reported in this section certainly indicate that academic performance is an extremely complex matter as Pervin[21] has pointed out, and that grades may be influenced by a multiplicity of variables. In the studies that were reviewed in Chapter 5, it may be recalled that the effects of anxiety on school achievement were different for boys and girls in various subject-matter areas, and that the results of any given study often depended upon the particular measure of anxiety that was used. Perhaps the only conclusion that may be safely drawn in this area is that research on anxiety and attainment must take intellectual ability into account.

References

[1] L. J. CRONBACH, "The Two Disciplines of Scientific Psychology". *Am. Psychol.*, 1957, **12**, pp. 671-84.

[2] R. M. GAGNÉ, *Learning and Individual Differences*, Charles E. Merrill Books, Columbus, 1967.

[3] A. W. MELTON, "Individual Differences and Theoretical Process Variables: General Comments on the Conference", in R. M. Gagné (Ed.), *Learning and Individual Differences*, Charles E. Merrill Books, Columbus, 1967.

[4] J. D. LUCAS, "The Interactive Effects of Anxiety, Failure and Intra-serial Duplication". *Am. J. Psychol.*, 1952, **65**, pp. 59-66.

[5] E. K. MONTAGUE, "The Role of Anxiety in Serial Rote Learning". *J. exp. Psychol.*, 1953, **45**, pp. 91-98.

[6] G. RAMOND, "Anxiety and Task as Determiners of Verbal Performance". *J. exp. Psychol.*, 1953, **46**, pp. 120-24.

[7] G. ROSENBAUM, "Stimulus Generalization as a Function of Experimentally Induced Anxiety". *J. exp. Psychol.*, 1953, **45**, pp. 35-43.

[8] K. W. SPENCE, "Anxiety (drive) Level and Performance in Eyelid Conditioning". *Psychol. Bull.*, 1964, **61**, pp. 129-39.

[9] K. W. SPENCE and J. T. SPENCE, "Sex and Anxiety Differences in Eyelid Conditioning". *Psychol. Bull.*, 1966, **65**, pp. 137-42.

[10] C. D. SPIELBERGER and L. H. SMITH, "Anxiety (drive) Stress and Serial Position Effects in Serial-verbal Learning". *J. exp. Psychol.*, 1966, **72**, pp. 589-95.

[11] J. H. TAYLOR and J. P. CHAPMAN, "Paired-associate Learning as Related to Anxiety". *Am. J. Psychol.*, 1955, **68**, pp. 671.

[12] C. D. SPIELBERGER, "The Effects of Anxiety on Complex Learning and Academic Achievement", in C. D. Spielberger (Ed.), *Anxiety and Behaviour*, Academic Press, New York, 1966.

[13] E. GAUDRY and C. D. SPIELBERGER, "Anxiety and Intelligence in Paired-associate Learning". *J. educ. Psychol.*, 1970, **61**, pp. 386-91.

[14] B. W. HARLESTON, "Task Difficulty, Anxiety Level, and Ability Level and Factors affecting Performance in a Verbal Learning Situation". *J. Psychol.*, 1963, **55**, pp. 165-68.

[15] J. R. STABLER and J. A. DYAL, "Discrimination Reaction Time as a Joint Function of Manifest Anxiety and Intelligence". *Am. J. Psychol.*, 1963, **76**, pp. 484-87.

[16] J. P. DENNY, "Effects of Anxiety and Intelligence on Concept Formation". *J. exp. Psychol.*, 1966, **72**, pp. 596-602.

[17] M. KATAHN, "Interaction of Anxiety and Ability in Complex Learning Situations". *J. Personal. soc. Psychol.*, 1966, **3**, pp. 475-79.

[18] J. DEESE, R. S. LAZARUS and J. KEENAN, "Anxiety, Anxiety Reduction and Stress in Learning". *J. exp. Psychol.*, 1953, **46**, pp. 55-60.

[19] C. D. SPIELBERGER and H. WEITZ, "Improving the Academic Performance of Anxious College Freshmen: A Group-counselling Approach to the Prevention of Underachievement". *Psychol. Monogr.*, 1964, **78** (No. 13, whole 590).

[20] W. F. BROWN and W. H. HOLTZMAN, "A Study-attitudes Questionnaire for Predicting Academic Success". *J. educ. Psychol.*, 1955, **46**, pp. 75-84.

[21] L. A. PERVIN, "Aptitude, Anxiety and Academic Performance: A Moderator Variable Analysis". *Psychol. Rep.*, 1967, **20**, pp. 215-21.

Chapter 9

Stress, Anxiety and Performance

To explain the complex effects of anxiety on performance, a theory of learning is required that takes into account both the drive characteristics and the interfering response properties of anxiety states. We have seen that Spence's theory of emotionally-based drive, which was described in Chapter 2, pays a great deal of attention to the anxiety or drive (D) level of the learner, and that this theory is concerned with the strength of the correct responses and the interfering error-tendencies that are aroused in learning tasks.

Research on anxiety and performance in academic settings also demands specification of the conditions under which anxiety states are aroused and which takes into account the various kinds of stress that are encountered in school environments. The effects of different kinds of stress on state anxiety is a central feature in the Spielberger,[1] Spielberger *et al.*,[2] Trait-State Anxiety Theory which is discussed in the following section.

Trait-State Anxiety Theory

An adequate theory of anxiety must distinguish between anxiety as a transitory state (A-State) and as a relatively stable personality trait (A-Trait). It must also differentiate between anxiety states, the stressful environmental conditions or circumstances which evoke these states, and the psychological defence mechanisms that serve to avoid or ameliorate them. Another major task for Trait-State Anxiety Theory is to identify the characteristics of stressful situations that evoke differential levels of A-State in persons who differ in A-Trait.

The words "stress" and "threat" are often used interchangeably by those who research anxiety phenomena. In Trait-State Anxiety Theory, however, these terms denote different aspects of a sequence of events that culminate in the arousal of an anxiety state. *Stress* refers to variations in environmental conditions or circumstances that are characterised by some degree of objective danger. *Threat* refers to the subjective appraisal or interpretation of a particular situation as ominous, frightening or dangerous. The term *state anxiety* (A-State) refers to the complex emotional reaction that is evoked in an individual who interprets a stressful situation as personally threatening to him.

According to this usage, then, *stress* refers to the objective stimulus properties of a situation, whereas *threat* refers to an individual's idiosyncratic perception of a situation as physically or psychologically dangerous or frightening for him. It is conceivable that objectively stressful situations will not be interpreted by some individuals as threatening because they do not appraise these situations as dangerous. Conversely, situations that most people regard as benign may be perceived as highly threatening by some people for whom they have special traumatic significance.

Trait-State Anxiety Theory assumes that an individual who perceives a particular situation as threatening will respond to it with an elevation in A-State irrespective of the presence or absence of any real (objective) danger. The intensity and duration of this A-State reaction will be determined by the amount of threat that the individual attributes to the situation, and by the persistence of his appraisal of the situation as threatening. While a given situation may be regarded as objectively dangerous by most people, whether or not it is perceived as threatening by a particular individual will depend upon his own personal appraisal of the situation, and this will be determined largely by his past experience.

With regard to the characteristics of stressful situations that evoke differential A-State reactions in persons who differ in A-Trait, Atkinson[3] suggests that a "fear of failure" motive is reflected in measures of A-Trait, while Sarason *et al.*[4] emphasise the special significance for individuals with high A-Trait of failure situations which arouse self-depreciating tendencies. In general, the research literature is consistent with the hypothesis that situations which impose direct or implied threats to self-esteem produce higher levels of A-State in persons with high A-Trait than in those who are low in A-Trait. For example, individuals with high A-Trait tend to perform more poorly than persons who are low in A-Trait under conditions that involve "ego-involving" instructions, negative evaluation of performance, or failure (Spence and Spence[5]). It might be expected, therefore, that academic situations and intelligence tests would be especially threatening to persons with high A-Trait because they involve the evaluation of personal adequacy and the risk of failure.

A difficult academic task, such as an advanced course in mathematics or physics, might tend to evoke high levels of A-State in most individuals with high A-Trait. However, such tasks are not likely to be regarded as threatening by a student with high A-Trait who has the requisite skills and background to do well in them. On the other hand, a recreational course in physical education that most students find interesting and pleasurable might be very threatening to a particular individual with low A-Trait for whom the course has special traumatic significance. Thus, while measures of A-Trait provide useful information regarding the *probability* that high levels of A-State will be aroused, the impact of any given situation on a particular person can be best ascertained by taking actual measurements of A-State in that situation.

There is some evidence that persons with high A-Trait do not perceive physical dangers as any more threatening than individuals with low A-Trait. For example, the results of two studies (Katkin,[6] Hodges and Spielberger[7]) indicated that the threat of electric shock produced significant increases in physiological measures of A-State, but the magnitude of change in the A-State measures was unrelated to the level of A-Trait. Similarly, Spielberger *et al.*[8] found that viewing a stressful movie depicting accidents in a woodworking shop evoked marked increases in A-State, but these were unrelated to level of A-Trait. It is tempting to generalise from these data that persons with high A-Trait do not perceive physical dangers or physical pain to be any more threatening than individuals with low A-Trait, but there is not yet sufficient evidence to justify this conclusion.

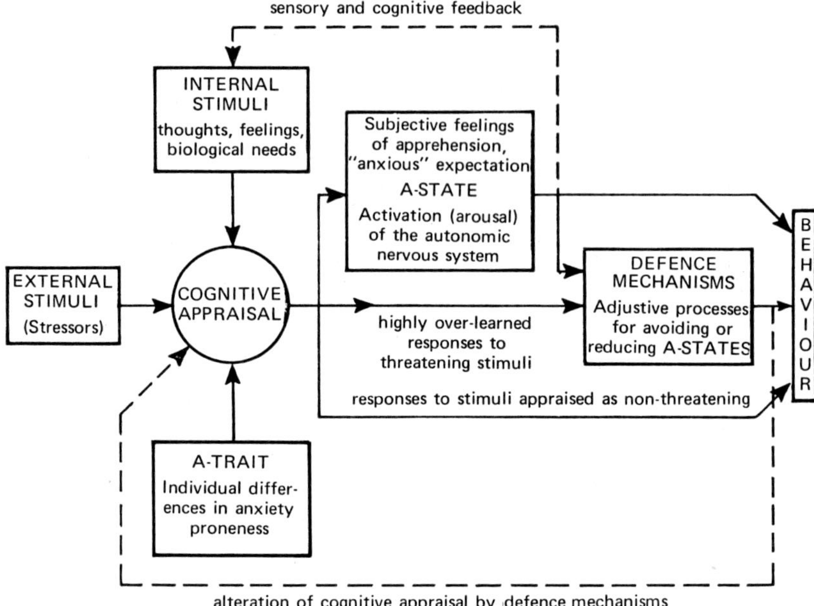

Fig 9.1 A Trait–State conception of anxiety in which two anxiety concepts, A-Trait and A-State, are posited and conceptually distinguished from the stimulus conditions which evoke A-State reactions and the defences against A-States. It is hypothesised that the arousal of A-States involves a sequence of temporally ordered events in which a stimulus that is cognitively appraised as dangerous evokes an A-State reaction. This A-State reaction may then initiate a behaviour sequence designed to avoid the danger situation, or it may evoke defensive manoeuvres which alter the cognitive appraisal of the situation. Individual differences in A-Trait determine the particular stimuli that are cognitively appraised as threatenlng. By permission of Academic Press.

The Trait-State Theory of Anxiety outlined in the preceding paragraphs is presented in the form of a diagram in Fig. 9.1. The theory assumes that the arousal of an anxiety state involves a process or sequence of temporally ordered events that begins with the cognitive appraisal of a situation as dangerous or threatening to the individual. This process may be initiated by an external psychological stress, such as the threat to self-esteem that is encountered when a student is called upon to recite in class, or by internal stimuli which cause an individual to think about or anticipate a frightening situation. For example, an intense A-State reaction might be evoked in a student who suddenly remembers that he has failed to prepare for an examination that is scheduled for the next class period. The main assumptions of Trait-State Anxiety Theory may be summarised as follows:

(1) for all situations that are appraised by an individual as threatening, an A-State reaction will be evoked;
(2) individuals with high A-Trait will perceive situations or circumstances that involve failure or threats to self-esteem as more threatening than will persons who are low in A-Trait;
(3) the intensity of the A-State reaction will be proportional to the amount of threat that the situation poses for the individual;
(4) the duration of the A-State reaction will depend upon the persistence of the individual's interpretation of the situation as threatening;
(5) high levels of A-State will be experienced as unpleasant through sensory and cognitive feedback mechanisms;
(6) elevation in A-State has drive properties which may be expressed directly in behaviour, or which may serve to initiate psychological defences that have been effective in reducing A-States in the past;
(7) stressful situations that are encountered frequently may cause an individual to develop coping responses or psychological defence mechanisms which reduce A-State by minimising the threat.

In summary, the schematic diagram of Trait-State Anxiety Theory presented in Fig. 9.1 provides a cross-sectional analysis of anxiety phenomena. The theory posits two different anxiety constructs, A-State and A-Trait, and notes the importance of the stimulus conditions which evoke A-States and the defences that help individuals to avoid or reduce them. The theory also provides a conceptual frame of reference for classifying the major variables that should be considered in anxiety research, and suggests possible interrelationships among them. Some important implications of Trait-State Anxiety Theory for research on anxiety and learning are discussed in the next section.

Anxiety, Stress and Serial Learning

Spielberger and Smith[9] investigated the effects of anxiety on performance in serial rote-learning in two studies in which the learning task consisted of a moderately difficult list of twelve nonsense syllables (e.g., BEW, HAJ, SOZ . . .). On the basis of Spence's Drive Theory it was expected that the performance of HA *S*s would be inferior to that of LA *S*s early in learning, and superior to the LA *S*s in the later stages of learning. It was further expected that the facilitative effects of high anxiety or drive (D) would occur earlier in learning for words at the extremes of the list (easy words), than for words in the middle of the list (hard words). Learning typically proceeds more rapidly for words at the beginning and at the end of a serial list than for embedded words because there are more competing error-tendencies associated with the latter.

The subjects in the first study were undergraduate males at Duke University who had extreme scores (upper and lower 20 per cent) on the MAS. They were given standard instructions for the serial anticipation method of verbal learning and then repeatedly presented with the list of nonsense syllables until each *S* attained the learning criterion of two successive perfect trials, or received a maximum of 25 trials. The mean number of correct anticipation responses given by the HA and LA *S*s on successive trial blocks is indicated in Fig. 9.2.

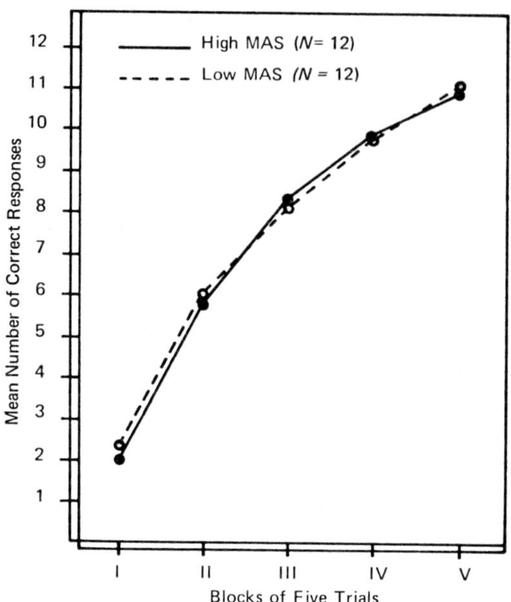

Fig. 9.2 Mean number of correct responses given by high and low anxiety subjects on successive trial-blocks. From Spielberger and Smith.[9] By permission of Academic Press.

Since the curves for the HA and LA groups did not differ in any perceivable respect, the predictions from drive theory were obviously not supported by the results. One explanation for the failure to find the expected differences in the performance of HA and LA *S*s is suggested by Trait-State Anxiety Theory. Since the MAS is a trait-anxiety measure, *S*s with high scores on this scale would be expected to have higher D than LA *S*s only in situations in which they experience failure or some threat to self-esteem. Perhaps there was insufficient stress in the serial learning experiment to cause the *S*s to interpret the situation as threatening.

To test this possibility, a second experiment was carried out in which the *S*s were led to believe that their intelligence was being evaluated. They were told that performance on the serial learning task was highly related to IQ. In all other respects the experimental procedures were exactly the same as in the previous study. The mean number of correct responses given by the HA and LA *S*s over successive trial blocks is shown in Fig. 9.3 in which it may be noted that the performance of HA *S*s was inferior to that of LA *S*s early in learning and superior later in learning.

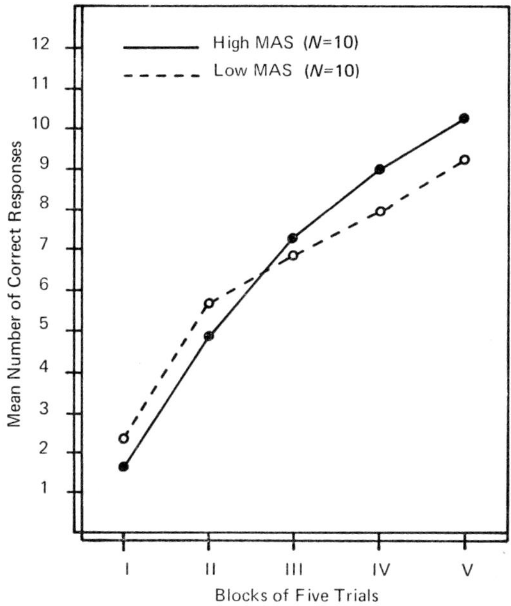

Fig. 9.3 Mean number of correct responses given by high and low anxiety subjects on successive trial blocks under ego-stress conditions. From Spielberger and Smith.[9] By permission of Academic Press.

The consistency of these results with Spence's Drive Theory is further demonstrated in Fig. 9.4 which presents the mean number of correct responses for hard and easy words given by the HA and LA *S*s on successive trial blocks. In the statistical analysis of the data, the significant triple interaction involving anxiety, hard-easy words, and trial blocks indicated that anxiety had different effects on performance at different stages of learning. High anxiety facilitated performance for the easy words at an earlier stage of learning than was the case for the hard words.

The findings in the second study were strikingly different from the results obtained in the first study. Since the two experiments differed only in the instructions given to the *S*s, the following interpretative conclusions are suggested: (a) the "neutral" instructions in the first

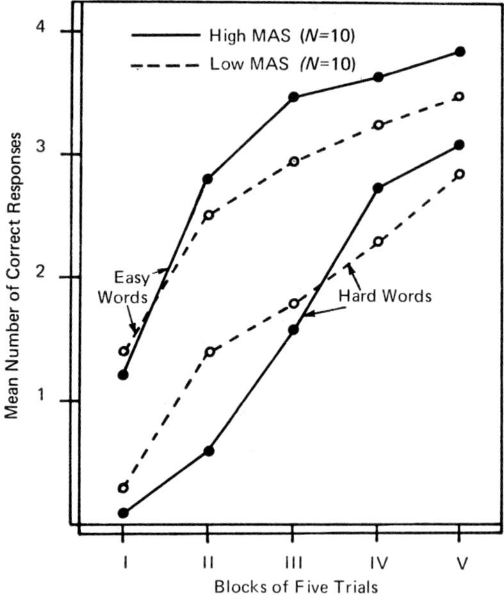

Fig. 9.4 Mean number of correct responses given by high and low anxiety subjects for easy and hard words on successive trial blocks. From Spielberger and Smith.[9] By permission of Academic Press.

study failed to induce differential amounts of state anxiety in the HA and LA *S*s; (b) the ego-stress instructions in the second study induced higher levels of A-State in the HA *S*s than in the LA *S*s and, presumably, higher levels of D; (c) the higher drive level of the HA *S*s impaired their performance relative to LA *S*s where error-tendencies were strong, and facilitated performance at those stages of learning where correct responses were strong or dominant.

As in most studies of anxiety and learning, Spielberger and Smith used a self-report anxiety measure, the MAS, to select *S*s who were assumed to differ in drive level. This procedure now seems questionable. Anxiety scales, such as the MAS, appear to be measures of A-Trait, and whether or not individuals with high scores on these measures will be higher in D than persons with low scores will depend upon the nature and the amount of stress that is associated with the learning situation.

While Spence's Drive Theory does not differentiate between trait and state anxiety, it would seem more logical to infer differences in D from measures of A-State than to select *S*s who are presumed to differ in D on the basis of their A-Trait scores. The extent to which drive theory has been supported in the research literature is probably due to the fact that most studies in the drive theory tradition have exposed *S*s who were selected on the basis of A-Trait measures to ego-involving or failure instructions. According to Trait-State Anxiety Theory, such conditions would be expected to evoke higher levels of A-State in HA *S*s than in LA *S*s, and presumably higher levels of D.

Ideally, research on anxiety and learning should take into account the nature and the amount of stress that is involved in a learning situation and its differential impact on level of A-State for persons who differ in A-Trait. A study of anxiety and memory in which all of these factors were considered is reported in the following section.

State Anxiety and Memory

Hodges and Spielberger[10] (Part II, Chapter 21) investigated the relation between measures of state and trait anxiety and performance on a memory task under stressful and non-stressful experimental conditions. The *S*s were 72 male undergraduate students from an introductory psychology course at Vanderbilt University who had extreme scores (upper and lower 25 per cent) on the MAS. The memory task was an adaptation of the Digits Backwards (DB) subtest of the Wechsler[11] Adult Intelligence Scale (WAIS).

Prior to the experiment each *S* was assigned either to the failure (stress) or the control (non-stress) condition. The DB test from the WAIS was individually administered with standard instructions to determine the *S*'s memory limit for repeating digits backwards. After determining this limit, each *S* was given two practice series of digits just below his limit, and then six more series of digits of the same length. The number of series out of the six in which all the digits were correctly reversed defined the *S*'s performance scores.

After the performance scores were obtained, the *S*s in the stress condition were told that they did not seem to be doing as well as other students, and those in the non-stress condition were told they were doing fine. Following this feedback, each *S* was given six more series of digits of the same length and the number of series correctly reversed defined the *S*'s *test* score. In order to evaluate the effects of the experimental conditions on level of A-State, each *S* was given the Zuckerman[12] Affect Adjective Check List (AACL) and instructed to check those adjectives which indicated how he felt "while repeating the last few series of digits". The AACL is a self-report measure of A-State.

The results of the study indicated that the negative feedback in the stress condition produced significant decrements in performance on the DB task in the test period as compared with the performance period, whereas there were no differences between performance and test scores in the non-stress condition. No relationship was found between A-Trait and performance on the memory task in either the stress or non-stress conditions. That is, the DB scores of the HA and LA *S*s in the two experimental conditions were quite comparable in the performance and text periods.

Next, the relationship between A-State and performance was evaluated. For this analysis, the data for the stress and non-stress conditions were combined. The mean scores on the DB task for the high A-State and low A-State *S*s are shown in Fig. 9.5. It may be noted that the two groups did not differ in the performance period, but that the DB scores of the high A-State group were significantly lower in the

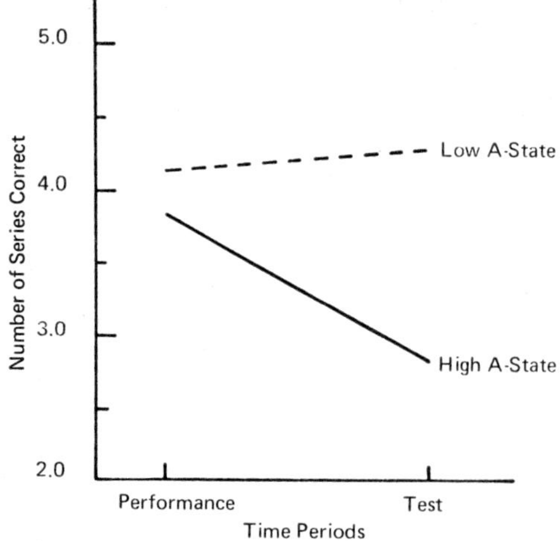

Fig. 9.5 The effects of low A-State and high A-State levels on Digits Backwards during the Performance and Test Periods ($N = 27$ per group). From Hodges and Spielberger.[10] By permission of the *Journal of Consulting and Clinical Psychology.*

test period than those of the low A-State group. The finding that lower DB scores in the test period were associated with higher levels of A-State suggested that the performance decrements on the memory task were produced by the elevations in A-State.

The results in this study demonstrate the importance of obtaining measures of A-State in the experimental situation rather than attempting to infer differences in A-State from A-Trait scores. While *S*s with high A-Trait were more disposed to manifest higher levels of A-State in the stress condition, performance on the memory task was unrelated to A-Trait scores. The reason for this can be seen in the fact that more than half of the *S*s with high A-Trait responded with high levels of A-State in the non-stress condition, even though they were told they were doing well, and almost half of the *S*s with low A-Trait responded with high levels of A-State in the stress condition.

State Anxiety and Performance

In the serial verbal-learning study described in the previous section (Spielberger and Smith[9]), level of state anxiety was inferred from measures of A-Trait taken prior to the experiment, and performance on the learning task was related to A-Trait only in the stress condition, in which *S*s were told they were taking an intelligence test. In the study of anxiety and memory (Hodges and Spielberger[10]), the stress condition produced decrements in performance on the memory task for *S*s with high levels of A-State, but no relationship was found between A-Trait scores and performance. While the *S*s with high A-Trait in the stress condition had higher levels of A-State, as would be predicted by the Trait-State Anxiety Theory for situations which involve a threat to self-esteem, this relationship was far from perfect. In both studies, the findings clearly indicate that stress and task variables must be taken into account in determining the effects of trait anxiety on performance.

The complex relationship between A-State and performance is also illustrated in the study of anxiety and computer-assisted learning described in Chapter 7 (O'Neil *et al.*,[13] Part II, Chapter 19). In this study, A-State increased while students worked on difficult CAI learning materials and decreased when they responded to easy materials. As in the study of anxiety and serial learning, the *S*s with high A-State made more errors on the more difficult materials than *S*s with low A-State and they made fewer errors on the easier materials. This interactive relationship between anxiety and performance on a learning task which varied in difficulty would be predicted from Spence's Drive Theory.

The findings of O'Neil *et al.* were subsequently confirmed in a follow-up study of anxiety and CAI reported by Spielberger, O'Neil and Hansen.[14] In this study, the STAI was used to obtain measures of both A-Trait and A-State. While no relationship between A-Trait and errors was found, *S*s with high levels of A-State made more errors than *S*s with low A-State on the CAI learning materials for which overall error rate was high. However, there was relatively little difference in the performance of the high and low A-State *S*s on learning materials for which overall error rate was relatively low in this study. Thus, whether individual differences in A-State impair, facilitate, or have no effect on performance depends upon the relative strength of the correct responses and the competing error-tendencies that are associated with the learning task.

In the studies reviewed in this chapter, high levels of A-State were induced either by stressful experimental conditions or by the intrinsic complexity of difficult learning tasks. Once aroused, however, the effects of high A-State on performance were determined by the relative strengths of correct responses and competing error-tendencies, irrespective of the conditions which induced the higher levels of A-State. The fact that interactive effects of A-State on performance were observed under circumstances in which A-Trait and performance were unrelated would seem to indicate that high drive level (D) is associated with higher levels of A-State, and not directly related to A-Trait.

With regard to the relationship between A-Trait, A-State and performance, one final point should be noted. Only in situations or circumstances that involve failure or threats to self-esteem will individuals who are high in A-Trait manifest higher levels of A-State than persons with low A-Trait. The fact that high-anxious persons harbour intense self-derogatory attitudes and have poor self-images apparently makes them more vulnerable to failure experiences and to negative evaluations by their parents, their teachers and their peers.

References

[1] C. D. SPIELBERGER, "Theory and Research on Anxiety", in C. D. Spielberger (Ed.), *Anxiety and Behavior*, Academic Press, New York, 1966.

[2] C. D. SPIELBERGER, R. E. LUSHENE and W. G. MCADOO, "Theory and Measurement of Anxiety States", in R. B. Cattell (Ed.), *Handbook of Modern Personality Theory*, Aldine, Chicago (in press), 1971.

[3] J. W. ATKINSON, *An Introduction to Motivation*, Van Nostrand, Princeton, N.J., 1964.

[4] S. B. SARASON, K. S. DAVIDSON, F. F. LIGHTHALL, R. R. WAITE and B. K. RUEBUSH, *Anxiety in Elementary School Children*, John Wiley & Sons, New York, 1960.

[5] K. W. SPENCE and J. T. SPENCE, "Sex and Anxiety Differences in Eyelid Conditioning". *Psychol. Bull.*, 1966, **65**, pp. 137-42.

[6] E. S. KATKIN, "The Relationship between Manifest Anxiety and Two Indices of Autonomic Response to Stress". *J. Personal. soc. Psychol.*, 1965, **2**, pp. 324-33.

[7] W. F. HODGES and C. D. SPIELBERGER, "The Effects of Threat of Shock on Heart Rate for Subjects who Differ in Manifest Anxiety and Fear of Shock". *Psychophysiology*, 1966, **2**, pp. 287-94.

[8] C. D. SPIELBERGER, R. L. GORSUCH, and R. E. LUSHENE, *The State-Trait Anxiety Inventory. (S.T.A.I.) Test Manual for Form X*, Consulting Psychologists Press, Palo Alto, 1970.

[9] C. D. SPIELBERGER and L. H. SMITH, "Anxiety (drive) Stress and Serial Position Effects in Serial-verbal Learning". *J. exp. Psychol.*, 1966, **72**, pp. 589-95.

[10] W. F. HODGES and C. D. SPIELBERGER, "Digit Span: An Indicant of Trait or State Anxiety?" *J. consult. clin. Psychol.*, 1969, **33**, pp. 430-34.

[11] D. WECHSLER, *Manual for the Wechsler Adult Intelligence Scale*, Psychological Corp., New York, 1955.

[12] M. ZUCKERMAN, "The Development of an Affect Adjective Checklist for the Measurement of Anxiety". *J. consult. Psychol.*, 1960, **24**, pp. 457-462.

[13] H. F. O'NEIL, C. D. SPIELBERGER and D. N. HANSEN, "The Effects of State-anxiety and Task Difficulty on Computer-assisted Learning". *J. educ. Psychol.*, 1969, **60**, pp. 343-50.

[14] C. D. SPIELBERGER, H. F. O'NEIL and D. N. HANSEN, "Anxiety, Drive Theory, and Computer-assisted Learning", in B. A. Maher (Ed.), *Progress in Experimental Personality Research*, Academic Press, New York (in press), 1971, Vol. **6**.

Chapter 10

Anxiety and Educational Attainment: An Overview

The principal aim of this book is to examine the relationship between anxiety and learning in educational settings. Although some studies report no relationship, and a few show that anxiety facilitates performance, the overwhelming weight of evidence consistently points to a negative relation between anxiety and various measures of learning and academic achievement. It is also apparent that variations in the learning environment and in examining conditions may have appreciable influence on the relationship between anxiety and school performance.

As a scientific concept, anxiety is useful to the extent that it can be measured objectively and contributes to the prediction of complex behaviour, such as performance on examinations and in school work. In Chapter 1, we discussed the construct of anxiety and noted that anxiety level may be inferred from such diverse indices as questionnaires and rating scales, from physiological measures such as heart rate and blood pressure, and from behavioural signs such as restlessness, distractibility, and chain-smoking. A meaningful theory of anxiety must account for its effects on complex behaviour in the classroom as well as in laboratory studies of the learning process.

Four anxiety inventories that are widely used in studies of anxiety and performance were described in Chapter 2. For each of these self-report scales, the theoretical foundation that stimulated its development and that has governed its use in research was also discussed. For example, investigations using the Manifest Anxiety Scale have been strongly influenced by Spence's Drive Theory, and research with the various test anxiety scales has been notably stimulated by Sarason's conception of anxiety which, in turn, is firmly rooted in Freud's psychoanalytic theory. At a more empirical level, Alpert and Haber observed that anxiety could facilitate as well as impair achievement, and this led them to develop the Achievement Anxiety Test which contains both facilitating and debilitating anxiety scales.

Unfortunately, as was noted in Chapter 9, much of the research with anxiety scales has failed to distinguish between anxiety as a personality trait and as a transitory emotional state. Trait-anxiety (A-Trait) implies relatively stable differences between people in the disposition or tendency to respond to situations perceived as threatening with elevations in state anxiety. State anxiety (A-State) refers to subjective, consciously perceived feelings of tension and apprehension, and heightened autonomic nervous system activity that is associated with these feelings. A-States may vary in intensity and fluctuate over time as a function of the environmental and interpersonal stresses that are encountered by an individual.

The MAS, the AAT and the various test anxiety questionnaires all appear to be measures of individual differences in trait anxiety or anxiety proneness. The State-Trait Anxiety Inventory, also described in Chapter 2, was developed by Spielberger *et al.* to provide self-report measures of both state and trait anxiety.

The pervasive and subtle effects of high levels of anxiety on personality and behaviour were highlighted in Chapter 3. The evidence clearly points to the fact that high-anxious persons tend to be self-disparaging, and lacking in self-confidence, and they have an unfavourable self-image. They also tend to be low in curiosity and adventurousness, and to be characterised by a high incidence of day-dreaming.

Classmates have little difficulty in identifying their high-anxious peers and react to them in a negative manner. Teachers, at least after the first few years of school, also tend to have negative reactions to the high-anxious child, regarding him as less well-adjusted and as possessing many other undesirable personality characteristics. Even the fathers of high-anxious children see them as less mature, less well-adjusted and more dependent. Given the hostile environment in which they live, it is certainly not surprising that the anxious child does worse in school than his less anxious classmates.

An important role of the teacher, especially in the elementary school years, is to promote the development of a positive self-concept in the child. For the high-anxious child, it would be particularly helpful if ways could be found to alleviate the interfering effects of anxiety on his school work, and especially in examinations. The available evidence reviewed in Chapter 4 suggests that providing high-anxious students with an opportunity to comment on test items improves their performance. Arranging test items is an increasing order of difficulty, so that the student does not encounter a very difficult item early in an examination, also appears to facilitate performance by keeping anxiety at a lower level. Providing memory support, such as in "open book examinations", also helps the anxious person to reach closer to his potential. Progressive examining, which is conducted in a more informal and relaxed manner than terminal examinations, has been shown to favour the high-anxious student. But any procedure which emphasises the importance of an examination or its evaluative aspects appears to have an adverse influence on the performance of the high-anxious student.

As previously noted, high anxiety is consistently associated with a lower level of academic achievement at both the school and the university level. The evidence suggests that negative correlations between anxiety and achievement increase in magnitude as school children progress through the elementary grades. In the earlier grades, reading is more adversely influenced by anxiety than arithmetic, but performance in both of these areas is impaired by high anxiety by the end of the elementary grades. While differences in performance level between HA and LA children are most marked on written tests, there is also evidence that the verbal behaviour of HA children in interview situations is inferior to that of LA children.

At the college level, high anxiety is associated with lower grades and higher dropout rates due to academic failure. In investigations of the relationship between anxiety and academic achievement, scales that are more specific to the school situation, such as the Academic Achievement Test and the various test anxiety questionnaires, are generally better predictors of academic success than more general anxiety scales.

Not only is there a negative relationship between anxiety and school performance, but there is also a moderate but consistent negative relationship between anxiety scales and various measures of intelligence. This has led some psychologists to suggest that the lower performance levels of high-anxious students can be explained in terms of their lower intelligence. There are, however, a number of factors which suggest that this hypothesis is not viable, and that high anxiety evoked by stressful situations is the causal factor which interferes with effective performance. The most compelling evidence comes from research in non-stressful situations in which high-anxious persons often do as well, and sometimes even better, than low-anxious persons of comparable ability. Results of this type have been reported for laboratory learning tasks, intelligence tests, and measures of attainment in which students were led to believe that their personal adequacy was not being evaluated.

The evidence from research on anxiety and programmed learning presented in Chapter 7 indicates that HA students perform at least as well as LA students, especially on the non-stressful, highly-structured tasks that are typically associated with computer-based instruction. These findings tend to rule out intelligence as the causal factor in determining negative relationships between anxiety and academic attainment since it seems unlikely that students of lower ability could perform as well as high-ability students in non-stressful situations but not in stressful situations, if anxiety were not a factor. Thus, a more likely explanation of the negative relationship between anxiety and intelligence is that when intelligence tests are given with standard instructions, HA students react to the test situation much as they would to a stressful course examination. Under such circumstances, HA students do not perform as well as they do under less stressful conditions. But when intelligence tests or learning tasks are given under non-test-like conditions, it has been demonstrated by Sarason *et al.*,[1] Wrightsman[2] and others, that HA *S*s perform as well or better than LA *S*s.

The alarmingly high college dropout rate for high-anxious students, which was noted in Chapter 5, surely must be cause for concern. Early identification and differential treatment for anxious students would seem to be a high-priority consideration if this trend is to be arrested. It is clear from the evidence reviewed in Chapter 6, however, that ability grouping is not a likely answer to this problem. Higher levels of test anxiety are typically found for children placed in the lower groups, reflecting the fact that these children have faced failure in the past.

In contrast to the many difficulties associated with ability-grouping, programmed learning or computer-based instruction provides a highly structured learning situation which appears to be especially favourable to the high-anxious student, as was noted in Chapter 7. Programmed instruction also provides a learning environment that can stimulate and evoke the best efforts in students with low anxiety by allowing them to proceed at their own pace.

The use of high-speed computers in education shows great promise for providing a solution to the problem of truly individualised instruction. Tailoring of learning situations to suit the personality and ability of each child is an extremely complex matter, as was illustrated in the longitudinal study by Hill and Sarason[3] described in Chapter 5. In this study, changes in children's anxiety level over time were dramatically linked with performance. Here, we are faced with the problem of causality. Did performance drop because of an increase in anxiety level? Or did anxiety level increase because the child experienced a long series of failures? While there is little evidence on which to decide between these alternatives, the data on ability-grouping suggests that the latter alternative is a more likely explanation.

The problem of causality is a difficult one in educational research, particularly where individual difference variables such as intelligence and anxiety are involved. Experimental studies which permit us to make causal statements are generally not feasible because true experiments require the random assignment of subjects to experimental conditions. A full discussion of this issue in the present context would take us too far afield, but it is worthwhile to note that subjects cannot be randomly assigned to high or low intelligence groups, or to high or low anxiety groups, because these characteristics are not randomly distributed in the population. Thus, only quasi-experiments are possible. The most reasonable approach is to conduct quasi-experiments which are designed to rule out rival hypotheses.

Evidence presented in Chapter 8 supported the proposition that anxiety and intelligence have interactive effects on performance. For persons with high intelligence, high anxiety will facilitate performance on simple tasks, and on most tasks of moderate difficulty. In contrast, high anxiety will generally lead to performance decrements for individuals of low ability, except on very easy tasks or in the later stages of learning in tasks of moderate difficulty. Since earning good grades in school is relatively difficult for most students, it follows that high anxiety will generally interfere with academic achievement, and most studies of this relationship report negative correlations.

It should be noted, however, that academic attainment is an extremely complex matter that involves a multiplicity of skills and habits, as was indicated in the studies conducted by Gaudry and Fitzgerald with junior high school students, and by Spielberger and Weitz at the college level. In addition to the variables considered in laboratory investigation of the learning process, many other variables must be taken into account in research on academic achievement if laws derived from basic learning theory are to play a useful part in the prediction of academic attainment.

With regard to the effects of anxiety on academic attainment, some of the conditions that facilitate the achievement of high-anxious students may have adverse effects upon the low-anxious. Thus, a unitary educational strategy would not be ideal for either HA or LA students. Furthermore, an educational programme based on the consideration of individual differences in personality would be difficult to implement because it would entail personality testing on repeated occasions. Since most classroom teachers have very little training in the discipline of psychology, it would be inappropriate for this testing to be assigned to them. The most viable alternative is that each school district or system use the services of qualified psychologists to consult with and aid teachers in working out procedures that are most suitable for each child. This approach is, of course, already in operation in some educational fields. In remedial education, for example, individual programmes are devised by psychologists and implemented by specially trained teachers, either in special classes or as part of the normal school routine.

Influences outside the school setting play a major role in the failure of some children to make adequate progress but many instances of failure must be attributed to unfortunate learning experiences within the school itself. To the extent that the learning situation can be tailored to suit the personality and ability of each child, this should lower the incidence of failure at all levels of academic work. The preceding paragraph contains recommendations which seem to us to flow logically from the data that we have reviewed. While they may be somewhat visionary in nature, the impetus toward individualisation of instruction and associated developments in educational technology may help this vision to become a reality within a shorter span of years than might appear likely at the moment.

This volume will have served its purpose if it has sensitised the reader to the important role that anxiety plays in the learning process. Learning should not be restricted to the acquisition of knowledge and skills, but should be extended to include development within the child of a spirit of intellectual curiosity that stimulates and motivates him to utilise his full range of personal resources. In helping the anxious child to achieve these goals, however, it must be recognised that he is likely to become upset if suddenly plunged into unstructured situations where he must rely entirely on his own resources. Thus, the merits of the "discovery learning" and the "teaching for creativity" movements may be wasted on anxious children, for whom these approaches may provide poor learning situations. The anxious child requires more gradual transitions that involve frequent experiences of success if he is to overcome his dependence upon safe, well-structured situations and develop a greater ability to cope with more complex and stressful learning environments.

Many of the studies reviewed in this volume stemmed from basic psychological research. It is our hope that sufficient interest will have been aroused to spur future teachers to study areas such as learning theory and personality theory in greater depth. As previously noted, some educators have tended to reject the basic research approach as unfruitful and inappropriate. We hope the contents of this volume will help convince the reader that education has much to gain from the assimilation of basic research findings from psychology and the other social sciences.

References

[1] S. B. SARASON, K. S. DAVIDSON, F. F. LIGHTHALL, W. R. WAITE and B. K. RUEBUSH, *Anxiety in Elementary School Children*, John Wiley & Sons, New York, 1960.

[2] L. S. WRIGHTSMAN, "The Effects of Anxiety, Achievement, Motivation and Task Importance upon Performance on an Intelligence Test". *J. educ. Psychol.*, 1962, **53**, pp. 150-56.

[3] K. T. HILL and S. B. SARASON, "The Relation of Test Anxiety and Defensiveness to Test and School Performance over the Elementary School Years: A Further Longitudinal Study". *Monogr. Soc. Res. Child Dev.*, 1966, **31** (2, serial No. 104).

Part Two

Selected Readings

Chapter 11

The Relation of Anxiety in School Children to School Record, Achievement, and Behavioural Measures

EMORY L. COWEN, MELVIN ZAX, and ROBERT KLEIN
University of Rochester

LOUIS D. IZZO and MARY ANN TROST
Rochester City School District

Responses of two independent samples of 9-year-old children (N = *178 and 216, respectively*) *on the Children's Manifest Anxiety Scale were correlated with performance on a variety of intellectual, achievement, behavioural, and sociometric measures. A very high proportion of significant* r*'s always quite low in magnitude but very consistent across the two samples, emerged from these analyses. High anxiety was thus found to relate negatively to IQ and achievement scores and positively to teachers' ratings of maladjustment, discrepancy between self and desired self, tendency to nominate oneself or to be nominated by peers for negative roles in a sociometric situation, and manifestation of physical complaints in the school setting.*

For some years now, stimulated by the early formulations derived from psychoanalytic theory, there has been mounting interest in the experi-

---

Participation of Robert Klein, currently at Stanford University, was made possible through the NSF Undergraduate Fellowship Program. Emory Cowen's address: Department of Psychology, University of Rochester, River Campus Station, Rochester, N.Y. 14627.

From *Child Development*, 1965, **36**, pp. 685-95.

Reprinted by permission of E. L. Cowen, M. Zax, R. Klein, L. D. Izzo and Mary Ann Trost and *Child Development*.

mental study of anxiety as a concept central to the psychology of personality and adjustment. Varied approaches have been employed, depending largely on one's predilection for viewing anxiety as a hypothetical construct or as a response. For those with the latter preference, the past decade has witnessed a sharp burgeoning in the development of anxiety scales (Sarason and Gordon,[1] Taylor[2]). Such anxiety scales were, and continue to be, widely used, very likely because of their simplicity in administration and scoring. Obviously, a limiting factor to the anxiety scale is the willingness of the respondent to admit to certain symptomatology or to ascribe socially undesirable characteristics to himself. Although such factors tended initially to be overlooked in scale anxiety studies with adults, their increasing recognition in more recent years (Blake and Mouton,[3] Hill,[4] Jessor and Hammond,[5] Sarason[6]) has led to an undermining of our confidence in the construct validity of such scales.

It is conceivable, however, that such apparent limitations upon the validity of anxiety scales with adult *S*s may not exist or may exist to a lesser extent with other groups. For example, the possibility of franker responses to an anxiety scale should, in theory, be present with young children, who may be more inclined to accept questions at face value and who may be less aware of cultural stereotypes about certain types of undesirable self-referent statements. The utility of the instrument as a measure of a given class of content material is increased to the extent that test responses are not distorted by such stylistic determinants.

It is perhaps, in part, with this consideration in mind that the development of a response-based anxiety scale for children (the Children's Manifest Anxiety Scale) was undertaken (Castaneda, McCandless and Palermo[7]). Evidence from a number of independent empirical investigations since then (Castaneda *et al.*,[7] Cowen *et al.*,[8] Holloway,[9, 10] Kitano,[11] Muuss[12]) indicates, indeed, that the correlation between anxiety as measured by the CMAS and the tendency to falsify as measured by an 11-item Lie (*L*) scale does not differ significantly from zero, thus supporting the assumption that *A*-scale responses of young children relate more closely to the content and meaning of the test items than is the case with adults.

The present study uses a generalised scale anxiety measure (the CMAS) and is directed primarily to consideration of certain intellectual, behavioural, achievement, and sociometric correlates of such anxiety. In this context, it may be appropriate to look at the profile of prior data relevant to these areas. Such a review will be brief, since the topics have had recent and quite exhaustive coverage by Ruebush.[13]

There have been quite a number of investigations in which CMAS scores of school children, primarily between ages 10 and 12 (fourth–sixth grade), have been related to measures of intelligence and achievement (Hafner and Kaplan,[14] Hafner, Pollie and Wapner,[15] McCandless and Castaneda,[16] Muuss,[12] Reese[17]). For the most part, these studies, and a number of others like them, report low negative and significant correlations between anxiety scores and measures of intelligence and achievement. Essentially the same relation holds when other anxiety indexes such as the Test Anxiety Scale for Children (TASC) (Sarason *et al.*[18]) is used as the measure of anxiety (Broen,[19] Ruebush,[13] Sarason *et al.*[20]). That there are also several studies which find no relation between anxiety and intelligence or achievement measures (e.g. Kitano,[11] L'Abate,[21] Wirt and Broen[22]) is surprising in view of differences in ages, intelligence, socio-economic status, and geographic location among the samples studied, not to mention actual differences in the criterion tests of intelligence and achievement used.

On several occasions attempts have been made, without success, to relate anxiety-scale scores to teachers' ratings of behaviour (Grams, Hafner and Quast,[23] Wirt and Broen[22]). The argument has been offered (Ruebush[13]) that the weak outcomes of these studies may be attributable to low reliability of the teacher ratings. Also relevant to the present research is the study by Lipsitt[24] relating CMAS scores to scores on a verbal self-concept scale and an investigation by McCandless, Castaneda and Palermo[25] in which high anxiety as measured by the CMAS was found to relate significantly to low sociometric status among peers for children between the ages of 10 and 12.

Although there have been several studies involving anxiety scales with children as young as 7 or 8, the preponderant majority of such studies are based on children between the ages of 10 and 12, or older. A principal purpose of the present research is to explore, with 9-year-old children and in a relatively systematic way, possible relationships between CMAS anxiety and a relatively broad spectrum of intellectual, achievement, behavioural, and sociometric measures. Some of these latter (e.g., IQ) have been examined in relation to anxiety quite extensively among older children. Others (e.g., sociometric status and self-concept) have been studied only relatively infrequently in relation to anxiety even among older groups, and still other actual behavioural measures (e.g., referrals to the school nurse; total days absence) have not yet been tapped in this context.

Method

SUBJECTS

Data for the present investigation are based on two samples of 178 and 216 9-year-olds (third graders) from three public elementary schools in Rochester, New York. Eighty of the first sample and 85 of the second were pupils in a school in which a preventive mental-health programme had been in progress for several years. The remaining 98 and 131 making up the respective samples were selected from two other elementary schools in similar neighbourhoods which had been designated as control schools for the prevention project (Cowen *et al.*[8]). All three schools were considered to draw children primarily from the upper-lower socio-economic bracket, and the average IQ in each school was slightly above 100. The first sample was made up of 87 boys and 91 girls; the comparable figures for the second were 122 and 94, respectively. All subsequent analyses are based on the total groups and the two sex subgroups for both samples.

MEASURES

In all, a total of 22 criterion measures were studied in relation to CMAS scores. One of these, the CMAS *L* score was essentially a control measure designed to provide a check on the validity of the *A*-scale responses. *Behavioural measures* taken from the school records included: total number of referrals to the school nurse (third grade); total number of referrals to the school nurse (cumulative); total days absent (third grade). Three *intelligence* estimates (non-verbal, verbal, and total IQ all taken from the Otis Quick-Scoring Mental-Ability Test) and five *achievement* scores from the SRA tests (Reading Comprehension and Vocabulary and Arithmetic Reasoning, Computation and Concepts) were available for each child based on data from routine city-wide testing of all public-school children in the third grade. Two additional *achievement-type measures* used were the child's grade-point average based on his end-of-year third-grade report card and an Achievement-Aptitude Discrepancy Index (*D* score). This score was computed by converting both grade-point ratio and total IQ scores into standard scores and subtracting the latter from the former. Thus, low *D* scores reflect underachievement, and high *D* scores reflect over-achievement. Two *adjustment* measures were developed using teachers' ratings. A Total Adjustment Score (T) was derived by having the teacher check, for each child, those negative behavioural characteristics (e.g., moodiness, immaturity, destructiveness) that seemed applicable from a list of 17, and to provide an intensity rating on a three-point scale (mild, moderate, strong) for each characteristic checked. Thus the theoretical range of scores on this scale was 0–51. In addition, an Over-all Adjustment Score (O) was based on a single summary rating of the child by the teacher along a five-point scale ranging from very well adjusted to very poorly adjusted. These measures are described more fully elsewhere (Cowen *et al.*[8]).

The remaining seven *self-concept* and *sociometric* scores are based on two tests, "Thinking About Yourself" (TAY) and "Class Play", developed by Bower,[26] and Bower and Lambert.[27] The TAY consists of a series of descriptions of concrete attributes of children. The child respondent is asked to indicate those attributes that actually describe him (self-concept) and those he feels he'd like to have (desired self). The discrepancy between these two scores is taken as an index of self-dissatisfaction; presumably the greater the discrepancy the greater the dissatisfaction.

The Class Play is a two-part test which, throughout, presumes for the child a series of concrete roles in a hypothetical play to be enacted by the class. Half of these roles are positive ones, and half are negative. In Part I, a free-response sociometric estimate, each child nominates as many of his classmates as he wishes for each role. Although a variety of scores can potentially be derived (Zax *et al.*[28]), for purposes of the present investigation only three were used: total positive choices, total negative choices, and percentage of negative choices. It is the last of these three indexes that has been considered the most sensitive (Bower[26]). On Part II of the Class Play, the child indicates, within a fixed multiple-choice framework for 30 sets of four roles (2 positive and 2 negative), which parts *he* would like to play and which ones he thinks he would be chosen for by peers and by teachers. Part II essentially yields a single score reflecting percentage of negative roles selected by the child.*

Results and Discussion

Pearson product-moment correlations relating anxiety-scale scores to scores on each of the other 22 variables were computed for males, females, and total groups for both samples. These correlational analyses are presented in Table 11.1. The number of significant differences in *r*'s between the male and female groups, as tested by *r* to *z* transformations, does not exceed chance expectancy.

It may first be noted, in a "control" sense, that the correlation between the *A* and *L* scales, comparable to what has been noted above for prior investigations, is negative and very low (—·069 for Group II and —·183 for Group I). Although the latter figure reaches significance at $p = \cdot 05$, the absolute magnitude of the intercorrelations would indicate that the *A*-scale scores are not suffering any noticeable distortion from a generalised tendency to falsify or to place oneself in a maximally favourable light.

It may be appropriate, before discussing any specific findings, to comment generally on some of the more salient attributes of the correlational data reported in Table 11.1 First of all, a very substantial proportion of the observed *r*'s (16 of 21 for Total Group I and 16 of 22 for Total Group II) are significant; moreover, the bulk of these significances occur at $p = \cdot 01$ or beyond. Despite the fact that some of the criterion measures are highly interdependent, it nevertheless seems likely, based on the number, breadth, and reliability of the significant *r*'s, that some genuine substantive relations are reflected in the matrix. On the other hand, these significant *r*'s tend, for the most part, to be quite low in the absolute sense; thus, relatively little common variance is reflected in any given significant relationship. Second, there appears to be good consistency across the two sets of data. This is not to say that when an *r* is significant in one group it is *always* significant in the other. There are no evident reversals, however, and among those *r*'s that reach significance in one group but not in the other there is always directional consistency. Somewhat greater discrepancies may be found by comparing *r*'s for the same sex across groups or by comparing the two sexes within groups, but even these differences do not exceed chance expectancy. Finally, the results are quite logical and internally consistent, each significant relation seemingly consistent with the consensus of current clinical thinking and empirical findings with respect to correlates of anxiety and how we might expect an anxious person to perform in a variety of areas.

Turning now to the specific findings, among the behavioural measures

* Percentage of negative roles is slightly preferable to total negative roles because it is more accurate when one or more items have been skipped by the respondent. With a fixed total of 30 items, the two scores correspond perfectly when all items have been answered. Actually, both sets of scores are included in the results table.

TABLE II.I

Intercorrelations Between CMAS Scores and Criterion Measures for Two Samples by Total Group, Males and Females

Variable	Total Group I (N=178)	Total Group II (N=216)	Males I (N=87)	Males II (N=122)	Females I (N=91)	Females II (N=94)
Cumulative nurses' referrals[a]	...	·22**	...	·15	...	·26*
Nurses' referrals, current year	·26**	·22**	·26*	·12	·27**	·30**
Days absent, current year	·03	·09	·07	·11	·02	·03
Grade-point ratio	—·29**	—·30**	—·34**	—·33**	—·27**	—·31**
Otis non-verbal IQ	—·10	—·10	—·18	—·08	—·01	—·14
Otis verbal IQ	—·22**	—·20**	—·36**	—·12	—·08	—·28**
Otis total IQ	—·18*	—·17*	—·29**	—·10	—·05	—·24*
SRA reading comprehension	—·26**	—·23**	—·35**	—·32**	—·16	—·14
SRA reading vocabulary	—·23**	—·20**	—·26*	—·22*	—·20*	—·18
SRA arithmetic reasoning	—·10	—·29**	—·06	—·25**	—·13	—·31**
SRA arithmetic concepts	—·19*	—·27**	—·20	—·27**	—·14	—·27**
SRA arithmetic computation	—·06	—·30**	—·11	—·25**	·02	—·39**
Achievement-Aptitude DISC	—·02	—·13	·05	—·23**	—·12	—·02
Teacher's rating, total	·29**	·21**	·42**	·20*	·16	·23*
Teacher's rating, over-all	·25**	·23**	·35**	·26**	·18	·24*
CMAS *L* Score	—·18*	—·07	—·18	—·13	—·23*	·04
TAY *D* Score	·35**	·46**	·51**	·51**	·16	·38**
Class Play, Ib (total negative)	·21**	·10	·26*	·18*	·20	·02
Class Play, Ic (percentage negative)	·21**	·12	·25*	·24**	·20*	·01
Class Play, I (total positive)	—·19*	—·16*	—·24*	—·19*	—·12	—·08
Class Play, IIc (percentage negative)	·24**	·23**	·27*	·25**	·22*	·29**
Class Play, II (total negative)	·25**	·27**	·28**	·26**	·24*	·30**

[a] Not available for first sample
* Significant at $p =$ ·05 or beyond
** Significant at $p =$·01 or beyond

there is a significant positive relation between anxiety and the number of times the child reports to the school nurse's office for some accident or physical complaint during the school year. This relation holds whether based solely on third-grade data or on the child's cumulative health record since he entered school. Apparently, the highly anxious child either experiences somewhat greater somatic and physical discomfort in the school situation than does the non-anxious child, or else he reacts more strongly in terms of seeking out help in the school nurse's office, given the same amount of discomfort.

Consistent with the weight of prior findings reported in the literature, a low but significant negative relation obtains between CMAS anxiety and both verbal and total IQ. This significant relation is not found when the non-verbal score is used as the IQ measure. Indeed, one might judge from the magnitude of these three sets of correlations that it is due primarily to the CMAS—verbal-IQ relationship that the CMAS–total-IQ correlation reaches significance. By and large, the anxiety measure relates similarly to the SRA achievement indexes. Of the 10 relevant total correlations for the two groups, all are low negative and eight are significant. Reading comprehension and vocabulary and arithmetic concepts reach significance for both groups, while arithmetic reasoning and computation do so only for Group II. Of the two other achievement-type measures, there is a significant *r* between anxiety and grade-point ratio for both groups but not between anxiety and achievement-aptitude *D* score. All these significant anxiety-achievement *r*'s are quite low, ranging between $-\cdot 17$ and $-\cdot 30$. While there has been considerable prior empirical evidence indicating the low negative relation between scale anxiety and measures of intelligence and achievement, the bulk of these data pertain to somewhat older children; moreover, there is additional evidence suggesting that the relation becomes stronger with age (Ruebush[13]). Our findings now indicate that these same relations are, in fact, present among 9-year-old children and, whatever the interfering effects of anxiety may be with respect to such intellective and achievement indexes, they are to be found quite early in the child's career.

Of particular interest are the down-the-line significant correlations between the two sets of teachers' behaviour-ratings and anxiety, with greater anxiety relating to higher-rated maladjustment. It is not that such a finding is illogical. To the contrary, since both classes of measure seemingly touch on some component of maladjustment, an interrelationship might well be expected. The interest stems rather from the fact that two prior investigations (Grams *et al.*,[23] Wirt and Broen[22]) failed to find the relationship. Ruebush[13] has speculated that this failure may be largely attributable to the unreliability of teachers' ratings. In the present instance, modest but significant reliabilities of teachers' ratings have been established (Cowen *et al.*[8]); perhaps these make possible the significant substantive relation. Other differences between this study and preceding ones may also be noted. Our measure of teachers' ratings was a relatively comprehensive one and, unlike the Wirt and Broen[22] measure, did not deal simply and specifically with teacher-rated anxiety. Also, there are undoubtedly differences in sample attributes, not the least of which is the relatively young subject group in our study. It is difficult to know for sure what the active ingredient in the present significant findings may be. We do attach some importance to them, however, since the teachers' rating scale represents an outside measure which is quite independent of the child's own verbal test-taking behaviour.

Turning next to the self-concept and sociometric indexes, we may note first that the highest single correlation, for both groups, occurs between the anxiety score and the TAY *D* score. The latter, reflecting a discrepancy between real self and desired self should, according to Rogerian theory (Rogers[29]) be construed as a maladjustment index (i.e., the greater the discrepancy, the greater the maladjustment). Literal translation of the correlation would then read: high anxiety is related to high self-dissatisfaction and maladjustment. In this sense, the finding accords well with those of Lipsitt.[24] On the other hand, it should be kept in mind that both of these measures, based as they are on the direct, unvarnished, verbal productions of the respondent to a paper and pencil questionnaire, are quite probably subject to common response sets (Jackson and Messick,[30] Ruebush,[13] Sarason[6]). Such sets would operate to spuriously inflate the correlation between the two measures.

Of somewhat greater interest then, even though the *r*'s are of lesser magnitude, are the relationships involving the Class Play measures. Significant positive correlations are found between anxiety score and either the number or the percentage of negative roles for which a child is nominated by his peers in a free-response situation. Similarly, there is a significant negative relation between anxiety and the total number of positive roles for which the child is nominated. In actuality, these three sets of correlations are highly interdependent and represent a single factor. The child with relatively high anxiety as measured by his CMAS responses is more likely to be picked for negative and undesirable roles, in a hypothetical class-play situation, by his peers. Thus he can be discriminated by his 9-year-old classmates and be reacted to in a negative way. The importance of such selections lies in the fact that children presumably are also guided in their actual behaviour by the same perceptions that motivate their sociometric responses. These findings are quite consistent with those reported for older children by McCandless *et al.*[25] In the present study, their particular importance comes from the downward age extension (to a 9-year-old group) and from the fact that in these ratings by peers we once again have a source of data that is independent of the subject's own test-taking behaviour and verbal responses.

We may also note a significant positive relation between anxiety and the percentage (or number) of negative choices on Part II of the Class Play. The latter measure is an indication of (1) the child's perception of himself and (2) how he thinks he is seen by his peers and teachers. Thus, regardless of whether the sociometric ratings are done by peers or by the child himself, elevation of nominations for negative roles and reduction of nominations for positive roles are found to be related to high anxiety. The highly anxious child appears to be sociometrically identifiable and sociometrically disadvantaged. Finally, several summary comments may be in order. The most impressive aspect of the present set of data is the ubiquity of the relation between the anxiety variable and a host of dependent measures, cutting across a broad spectrum of the child's school-functioning variables — intellectual, achievement, behavioural, self-conceptual, and sociometric. These relations are duplicated essentially in two independent samples. The absolute magnitude of the significant relationships is consistently low, suggesting that there is very little predictive potential generated by awareness of any given child's *A*-scale status. Yet, on a group basis, there appear to be stable, logical, internally consistent, and replicable correlates of CMAS performance in diverse areas. It is of some further interest to note that it is the CMAS measure, presumably a generalised anxiety index, rather than the more specific TASC, which has here been shown to relate systematically to indexes derived almost exclusively from the school setting.

A further aspect of the findings of some considerable interest is that the present network of interrelations has now been found to be present with children as young as 9 years old, which, considering the nature of the various measures used, is perhaps as far back as they can be studied. That these relations are based on more than simply the verbal behaviour of the subject is strongly suggested by the fact that at least three types of estimates independent of the *S*s verbal behaviour are included in the matrix: indexes of actual day-to-day behaviour (nurses' referrals), teachers' behaviour-ratings, and sociometric ratings by peers.

We conclude, then, that high anxiety, as measured by the CMAS scale, is inversely related to IQ and educational achievement among 9-year-old children and that it is positively related to teachers' ratings of maladjustment, discrepancy between self and desired self, tendency to nominate oneself or to be nominated by peers for negative roles in a sociometric situation, and a tendency to manifest physical complaints in the school situation.

References

[1] S. B. SARASON and E. M. GORDON, "The Test Anxiety Questionnaire: Scoring and Norms". *J. abnorm. soc. Psychol.*, 1952, **47**, pp. 561-65.

[2] JANET A. TAYLOR, "A Personality Scale of Manifest Anxiety". *J. abnorm. soc. Psychol.*, 1953, **48**, pp. 285-90.

[3] R. R. BLAKE and JANE S. MOUTON, "Personality", in P. R. Farnsworth and Q. McNemar (Eds), *Annual Review of Psychology*, Annual Reviews, Palo Alto, Calif., 1959, **10**, pp. 203-32.

[4] W. F. HILL, "Comments on Taylor's 'Drive Theory and Manifest Anxiety' ". *Psychol. Bull.*, 1957, **54**, pp. 490-93.

[5] R. JESSOR and K. HAMMOND, "Construct Validity and the Taylor Anxiety Scale". *Psychol. Bull.*, 1957, **54**, pp. 161-70.

[6] I. G. SARASON, "Empirical Problems and Theoretical Findings in the Use of Anxiety Scales". *Psychol. Bull.*, 1960, **57**, pp. 403-15.

[7] A. CASTANEDA, B. R. MCCANDLESS and D. S. PALERMO, "The Children's Form of the Manifest Anxiety Scale". *Child Dev.*, 1956, **27**, pp. 317-26.

[8] E. L. COWEN, L. D. IZZO, H. MILES, E. F. TELSCHOW, M. A. TROST and M. ZAX, "A Preventive Mental Health Program in the School Setting: Description and Evaluation". *J. Psychol.*, 1963, **56**, pp. 307-56.

[9] H. D. HOLLOWAY, "Reliability of the Children's Manifest Anxiety Scale at the Rural Third Grade Level". *J. educ. Psychol.*, 1958, **49**, pp. 193-96.

[10] H. D. HOLLOWAY, "Normative Data on the Children's Manifest Anxiety Level at the Rural Third Grade Level". *Child Dev.*, 1961, **32**, pp. 129-34.

[11] H. H. L. KITANO, "Validity of the Children's Manifest Anxiety Scale and the Modified Revised California Inventory". *Child Dev.*, 1960, **31**, pp. 67-72.

[12] R. E. MUUSS, "The Relationship between 'Causal' Orientation, Anxiety, and Insecurity in Elementary-school Children". *J. educ. Psychol.*, 1960, **51**, pp. 122-29.

[13] B. K. RUEBUSH, "Anxiety", in H. W. Stevenson, J. Kagan and C. Spiker (Eds), *Child Psychology*, University of Chicago Press, Chicago, 1963, pp. 460-516.

[14] A. J. HAFNER and A. M. KAPLAN, "Children's Manifest Anxiety and Intelligence". *Child Dev.*, 1959, **30**, pp. 269-71.

[15] A. J. HAFNER, D. M. POLLIE and I. WAPNER, "The Relationship between CMAS and WISC Functioning". *J. clin. Psychol.*, 1960, **16**, pp. 322-23.

[16] B. R. MCCANDLESS and A. CASTANEDA, "Anxiety in Children, School Achievement and Intelligence". *Child Dev.*, 1956, **27**, pp. 378-82.

17 H. W. Reese, "Manifest Anxiety and Achievement Test Performance". *J. educ. Psychol.*, 1961, **52**, pp. 132-35.

18 S. B. Sarason, K. S. Davidson, F. F. Lighthall and R. R. Waite, "A Test Anxiety Scale for Children". *Child Dev.*, 1958, **29**, pp. 105-13.

19 W. E. Broen, "Anxiety, Intelligence and Achievement". *Psych. Rep.*, 1959, **5**, pp. 701-4.

20 S. B. Sarason, K. S. Davidson, F. F. Lighthall, R. R. Waite and B. K. Ruebush, *Anxiety in Elementary School Children*, John Wiley & Sons, New York, 1960.

21 L. L'Abate, "Personality Correlates of Manifest Anxiety in Children". *J. consult. Psychol.*, 1960, **24**, pp. 342-48.

22 R. D. Wirt and W. E. Broen, "The Relation of the Children's MAS to the Concept of Anxiety as used in the Clinic". *J. consult. Psychol.*, 1956, **20**, p. 482.

23 A. Grams, A. J. Hafner and W. Quast, "Children's Anxiety Compared with Parents' Reports and Teachers' Ratings of Adjustment". Paper read at APAP Meetings, St. Louis, Mo., 1962.

24 L. P. Lipsitt, "A Self Concept Scale for Children and Its Relationship to the Children's Form of the Manifest Anxiety Scale". *Child Dev.*, 1958, **29**, pp. 463-72.

25 B. R. McCandless, A. Castaneda and D. S. Palermo, "Anxiety in Children and School Status". *Child Dev.*, 1956, **27**, pp. 385-91.

26 E. M. Bower, *Early Identification of Emotionally Handicapped Children in School*, Charles C. Thomas, Springfield, Ill., 1960.

27 E. M. Bower and Nadine A. Lambert, *A Process for In-school Screening of Children with Emotional Handicaps*, California State Department of Education, Sacramento, Calif., 1961.

28 M. Zax, E. L. Cowen, L. D. Izzo and Mary A. Trost, "Identifying Emotional Disturbance in the School Setting". *Am. J. Orthopsychiat.*, 1964, **34**, pp. 447-54.

29 C. R. Rogers, *Client Centered Therapy*, Houghton-Mifflin, Boston, 1951.

30 D. M. Jackson and S. Messick, "Content and Style in Personality Assessment". *Psychol. Bull.*, 1958, **55**, 243-52.

Chapter 12

The Influence of Anxiety on Several Measures of Classroom Performance

KENNETH E. SINCLAIR
School of Education, University of Sydney

The area of research concerned with the influence of anxiety on human learning and performance has significance for both educational practice and psychological theory. Within an educational context it has particular relevance for procedures used in student evaluation and testing. We live today in a highly test-conscious culture. Decisions of major consequence to the individual are increasingly being made on the basis of his performance in tests. It is important, therefore, that the various factors that influence test performance be identified and the nature of their influence determined. There is growing evidence that anxiety is a factor of considerable importance in influencing test performance.

Beyond its relevance for educational measurement, research in this area is also contributing directly to a more precise understanding of human learning and performance. Investigators from quite varied backgrounds have carried out research in this area. Behaviourists (Spence and Spence[1]), neuropsychologists (Hebb,[2] Malmo[3]) and psychologists adopting a more psychoanalytic position (Sarason *et al.*[4]) have all developed rival theories designed to explain the influence of anxiety on learning and performance. Within an educational context, Sarason's psychoanalytic position has been found to have greatest relevance.

The influence of anxiety on performance in a variety of laboratory tasks is now quite well documented. Laboratory studies have established

This research was supported by a University of Sydney Research Grant. The cooperation of the N.S.W. Department of Education and the principals, staff and students of the Canterbury, Crows Nest and Drummoyne Boys' High Schools is gratefully acknowledged.

From the *Australian Journal of Education*, 1969, **13**, pp. 296-307. Reprinted by permission of K. E. Sinclair and the *Australian Journal of Education*.

that the complexity of the task to be performed and the level of stress (usually defined in terms of level of ego-involvement) inhering in the task are two factors, in particular, which must be considered in explaining the influence of anxiety. Anxiety appears to facilitate performance on simple, straightforward tasks where there is little response competition and to interfere with performance on more complex tasks where response competition is likely (Taylor,[5] Spence and Taylor,[6] Taylor and Spence,[7] Montague,[8] Standish and Champion[9]). In conditions where ego-involvement is low, a number of studies have found anxiety to be unrelated to performance (Lucas,[10] Deese, Lazarus and Keenan,[11] I. G. Sarason,[12] Kalish *et al.*,[13] Nicholson,[14] Feshbach and Loeb[15]), although some studies have found that anxiety facilitated performance (I. G. Sarason,[16, 17] Longnecker[18]). In conditions of high ego-involvement, anxiety has typically been found to interfere with performance (I. G. Sarason,[16, 17] Nicholson,[14] Harleston[19]).

While these relationships have frequently been demonstrated in relation to laboratory tasks, rather fewer studies have dealt with the question of the relationship between anxiety, task complexity, level of stress, and performance in more naturally occurring situations such as the classroom. Wrightsman,[20] however, in one study, varied level of stress in relation to aptitude test performance. He found no relationship ($r = -\cdot 06$) between anxiety and performance in the low ego-involvement condition and a significant negative relationship ($r = -\cdot 37$) in the condition of high ego-involvement. While there had been little change in the performance of low-anxious (LA) subjects in the two conditions, the performance of high-anxious (HA) subjects was reduced by almost one standard deviation by the stress of the instructions.

In a study with college students as subjects, Paul and Eriksen[21] carried out a similar analysis using a classroom achievement test. A regular psychology class examination was administered on the morning of the experiment (the high stress condition) and a parallel form of the test was administered to the same individuals at night under conditions designed to minimise anxiety (the low stress condition). When their data were analysed using only subjects from the middle range of intelligence, a significant interaction was found between level of stress and level of anxiety. In the high stress condition, LA subjects were superior to HA subjects, while, in the relaxed condition, the HA subjects were superior.

The absence of experimental control over the learning materials and process may be a limiting factor in this study. Wide variation would be expected among the subjects as to the notes and texts used in studying for the examination, as well as for the time spent in studying for the examination.

These difficulties were substantially overcome in a study carried out by Caron.[22] He presented high school students with a 1,700 word passage (consisting of an explanation of Atkinson's motive-expectancy-incentive model) to be studied in the experimental situation and, following the study period, obtained measures of rote learning and comprehension. The rote learning questions involved the reproduction of formulae and the definition of symbols contained in the passage, while the comprehension questions required the subjects to apply principles concerning risk preference that were presented in the passage. One half of his subjects studied the passage and were tested under examination conditions while the other half did so under conditions designed to induce curiosity. The curiosity condition was established by informing the subjects that the purpose of studying the passage was to enable them to interpret their own personality profiles which had been obtained in a previous testing session. For the rote learning task, there were no differences between HA and LA subjects in either treatment condition. For the comprehension task, there was no difference between HA and LA subjects in the curiosity condition. In the examination condition, however, LA subjects were superior to HA subjects. Caron[22] (p. 537) interpreted these findings as supporting the conclusion, " . . . that the performance of anxious subjects on 'simple' tasks does not deteriorate under stress . . . whereas on 'complex' tasks their output suffers markedly".

While Caron's study contains many attractive features, a problem in interpreting some of his results arises because of the shortness of his measuring instruments. Only six rote-learning questions and four comprehension questions were used (personal communication) and this may have operated to reduce reliability and, through this, the possibility of obtaining significant differences between the LA and HA subjects. With respect to the rote-learning task, a significant difference in favour of the LA subjects might well have been expected in the examination condition. The subjects were given only fifteen minutes to study the 1,700 word passage so that learning that took place might be expected to be rather unstable and unorganised, resulting in considerable response competition in the performance situation. As has already been noted, in these circumstances anxiety may be expected to disrupt performance.

In the present study, the influence of anxiety on the performance of typical classroom tasks was again studied. As in Caron's investigation, the subjects were required to study a prose passage in the experimental situation and were then tested on several performance measures. In the present investigation, the measures obtained were of factual learning and reasoning and by increasing the number of questions asked, an attempt was made to ensure that a satisfactory level of reliability was reached for each measure. On the basis of scores on the High School Form of the Test Anxiety Scale, groups of LA, MA (moderately anxious) and HA high school students were obtained who completed the performance tasks in conditions of either high or low ego-involvement.

Hypotheses

Anxiety is conceived of as a hypothetical construct mediating between certain situational stimuli and various specifiable responses. The stimulus situation which evokes the anxiety reaction is assumed to be such that the individual anticipates a strong threat to his self-esteem. In classroom test situations, the anticipated threat to self-esteem is, most often, failure on the test.

In learning and performance situations, it is the view of Sarason and his colleagues (Mandler and Sarason,[23] Sarason *et al.*[4]) that anxiety acts as a cue to elicit both responses that are relevant to the learning or performance task, and responses which are irrelevant. Task-relevant responses are observed in an increase in effort, concentration, and in procedural strategies previously found to facilitate learning and reduce anxiety. Task-irrelevant responses may be observed in the intrusion of thoughts concerning the consequences of failure, of self-depreciating ruminations and by ego-defensive avoidant responses designed to protect the individual from loss of self-esteem. These task-irrelevant responses compete with responses relevant to the task and typically have an interfering effect on learning and performance.

The extent to which interference to performance is caused by anxiety will depend upon level of ego-involvement and task complexity. When ego-involvement is low and performance is not perceived as having important ego-related consequences, little anxiety and few associated task-irrelevant responses will be elicited. In such a situation, therefore, performance for all individuals would be expected to be relatively free of the influence of anxiety. As ego-involvement increases, however, so will the tendency to react with anxiety increase and with this the tendency for interfering task-irrelevant responses to be elicited. When ego-involvement is high, individuals reacting with high levels of anxiety will respond with many more task-irrelevant responses than individuals who react to the same conditions with lower levels of anxiety. When the task is complex requiring concentration and careful processing of information, the intrusion of these task-irrelevant responses would be expected greatly to disrupt performance, so that level of anxiety would be inversely related to performance.

In the present study, the complexity of both performance tasks was such that anxiety, when elicited, was expected to have a debilitating effect on performance. On the factual learning task, the intrusion of task-irrelevant responses was expected to interfere with both the learning and the recall of the material studied. Because of the limited exposure to the study passage, overlearning would be unlikely so that what was learned would be relatively unstable and unorganised and, as such, highly susceptible to interference resulting from anxiety. Even greater interference was expected on the reasoning task. The presence of task-irrelevant responses was expected to have a particularly disruptive effect on the application of the complex cognitive processes required for performance on this task as generalisations were made, inferences drawn and hypotheses formulated and tested.

On the basis of these considerations two hypotheses were examined.

HYPOTHESIS 1

In low ego-involvement conditions, anxiety has no influence on performance. With both tasks, there will be no difference in the performance of LA, MA and HA groups of subjects.

HYPOTHESIS 2

In high ego-involvement conditions, anxiety acts to disrupt performance in complex tasks. In performing both tasks, LA subjects will be superior to MA subjects and MA subjects will be superior to HA subjects.

Differences in performance for the various anxiety groups were also expected under the two ego-involvement conditions. For the factual learning task, ego-involvement was expected to facilitate the performance of LA and MA subjects. For these subjects the enhancing effects of the increased motivation induced by the high ego-involvement instructions were expected to outweigh any negative effects due to the intrusion of task-irrelevant responses associated with anxiety. Thus it was expected that their performance would be superior in the high ego-involvement condition. For the HA subjects, however, the facilitating effects of the increased motivation were expected to be completely counteracted by the interfering effects of anxiety.

With the more complex reasoning task, the interfering effects of anxiety were expected to be greater than for the factual learning task. Because of this, only the performance of LA subjects was expected to be superior in the high ego-involvement condition. For MA subjects similar levels of performance were expected for the two ego-involvement conditions. For HA subjects the interfering effects of anxiety in the high ego-involvement condition were expected to be substantially greater than any facilitating effects that might occur, so that their performance was predicted to be superior in the low ego-involvement condition.

On the basis of these expectations, two further hypotheses, concerned with difference in performance under the two ego-involvement conditions, were examined.

HYPOTHESIS 3

With the factual learning task, the performance of the LA and MA subjects will be superior when ego-involvement is high. However, HA subjects are expected to perform no better when ego-involvement is high than when it is low.

HYPOTHESIS 4

With the reasoning task, the performance of LA subjects will be superior when ego-involvement is high, the performance of MA subjects will be similar in the two conditions of ego-involvement and the performance of HA subjects will be superior when ego-involvement is low.

Method

The subjects of the study were 173 sixth form male high school students attending three metropolitan boys' high schools in Sydney.

The content of the study passage consisted of a description of life among the Trobriand Islanders of the South Pacific.* This content appeared to be particularly suitable, since it was closely related to content typically taught at the high school level and yet there was little chance of the subjects having had any prior experience with it. To

* An earlier version of the study passage and performance measures was used in a previous study (Sinclair[26]).

control the difficulty level of the vocabulary used in the passage, only words from the Thorndike-Lorge[24] lists which occur in reading materials with a frequency of six or more times per million words were included. Thorndike and Lorge state that words appearing with this frequency are suitable for use with students in third form and above. The passage contained 1,332 words and one illustration, and filled almost six quarto pages of typescript.

Two performance tests were constructed. One measure, the factual learning measure, consisted of 20 multiple-choice questions for which the correct answer was explicitly stated in the study passage. The second measure, for reasoning measure, contained 12 multiple-choice questions for which the correct answer was not explicitly stated in the study passage. In answering these questions the subject was required to make deductions, and to draw inferences and implications from the given information.

Three weeks prior to the test administration, the High School Form of the Test Anxiety Scale (Mandler and Cowen[25]), specially adapted for Australian conditions, was administered. A split-half reliability coefficient of 0·86 was obtained for this measure. Subjects scoring in the lower, middle and upper thirds of the anxiety distribution were designated as LA, MA and HA respectively. For each level of anxiety, the subjects were divided into two groups by use of a table of random numbers, one group being allocated randomly to the high ego-involvement condition and the other to the low ego-involvement condition.

To establish conditions of high ego-involvement,* the subjects were informed that the test was one of scholastic aptitude and that their results would be made available to their headmaster. When the testing was completed, they were informed as to the actual purpose of the test. To establish conditions of low ego-involvement the subjects were informed that the purpose of the test was to establish whether the study passage was a good one for sixth form students or whether the questions were too easy or too difficult.

Twenty-five minutes were allowed for study of the passage. Twenty minutes were provided in which to answer the twenty factual learning questions and a further twenty minutes were provided in which to answer the twelve reasoning questions. These time limits were sufficient to enable all subjects to complete both tests. So that performance on the reasoning measure would not be influenced by the subjects' ability to recall information from the passage necessary for answering the questions asked, they were instructed that they could use the study passage in answering these questions.

Results

The design of the study was a 2×3 factorial, involving 2 levels of ego-involvement (high and low) and 3 levels of anxiety (high, moderate

* The administration of the instruments in the high ego-involvement condition was carried out by the author in each school. The administration of the instruments in the low ego-involvement condition was carried out by T. Heys and W. J. Fenley whose assistance is gratefully acknowledged.

and low). This design was used for each of the two performance measures (factual learning and reasoning) with unequal numbers of subjects in each cell.

For the factual learning measure, the means of scores of the different anxiety groups are presented in Table 12.1. A reliability coefficient (K.R.20) of 0·59 was obtained for this measure.

TABLE 12.1

Mean Factual Learning Scores for LA, MA and HA Groups of Subjects in Two Conditions of Ego-involvement

	Low ego-involvement			High ego-involvement		
Anxiety level	N	$\bar{X}$	sd	N	$\bar{X}$	sd
LA	28	13·82	2·20	31	16·16	1·81
MA	28	14·32	1·94	29	14·62	2·58
HA	24	13·71	2·74	33	14·03	2·26

A summary of the results of the analysis of variance carried out on these data (Winer,[27] pp. 241-44) is presented in Table 12.2. Both main effects and the interaction were found to be significant. When individual group mean scores were examined by the Newman-Keuls procedure, it was observed that the performance of the LA group in the high ego-involvement condition had largely accounted for the significant results. As predicted, there were no significant differences found between the anxiety groups in the condition of low ego-involvement. In the high ego-involvement condition, as predicted, the performance of the LA subjects was superior to that of MA and HA subjects. The expected significant difference between the MA and HA groups did not emerge. Finally, again as hypothesised, the performance of the LA group in high ego-involvement conditions was superior to that of the LA group in low ego-involvement conditions while for the HA groups performance was similar in these two conditions. The expected superiority of the MA group in the high ego-involvement condition was not found.

TABLE 12.2

Summary of the Analysis of Variance for the Factual Learning Measure

Source	Sum of squares	df	Mean square	F
Ego-involvement	41·73	1	41·73	8·17**
Anxiety	36·02	2	18·01	3·53*
Interaction	39·20	2	19·60	3·84*
Error	853·16	167	5·11	

** $p < \cdot 01$
* $p < \cdot 05$

In sum, the hypothesised relationships for the LA and HA groups in the two conditions of ego-involvement were all confirmed. Those for the MA group were not confirmed, the performance of that group being no different from that of the HA group.

For the reasoning measure, the mean scores of the different anxiety groups are presented in Table 12.3. A reliability coefficient (K.R.20) of 0·68 was obtained for this measure.

TABLE 12.3
Mean Reasoning Scores for HA, MA and LA Groups of Subjects in Two Conditions of Ego-involvement

	Low ego-involvement			High ego-involvement		
Anxiety level	N	$\overline{X}$	sd	N	$\overline{X}$	sd
LA	28	8·00	1·89	31	8·48	2·06
MA	28	7·36	2·08	29	8·38	1·82
HA	24	6·88	2·58	33	7·76	2·05

A summary of the results of the analysis of variance carried out on these data is presented in Table 12.4. In this analysis only the mean square for level of ego-involvement was significant, indicating a general superiority in the high ego-involvement conditions. When pairs of means were analysed, again using the Newman-Keuls procedure, it was found that there were no differences between the anxiety groups in either ego-involvment condition. This was predicted for the low ego-involvement condition but for the high ego-involvement condition an inverse relationship between level of anxiety and performance had been predicted. All anxiety groups performed better in the high ego-involvement condition (although in no case did the difference reach an acceptable level of significance). This was predicted for the LA subjects but not for the MA and HA groups. In fact, for HA subjects superior performance had been predicted for the low ego-involvement condition.

TABLE 12.4
Summary of the Analysis of Variance for the Reasoning Measure

Source	Sum of squares	df	Mean square	F
Ego-involvement	27·16	1	27·16	6·28*
Anxiety	24·77	2	12·39	2·87
Interaction	2·23	2	1·11	—
Error	721·68	167	4·32	

* $p < \cdot 05$

Discussion

With respect to the factual learning task, the results obtained confirmed, in large measure, the hypotheses that were developed for testing. In test-like conditions, anxiety was observed to debilitate performance on that task. With respect to the reasoning task, however, few predicted relationships were supported. Despite the complexity of the task, anxiety did not appear to influence performance in the test-like condition. A possible reason for this latter result is to be found in the manner in which the reasoning test was administered. So that all subjects would have approximately equal access to the factual information upon which the reasoning items depended, the subjects were allowed to consult the study passage while answering the questions. This would make the reasoning task rather comparable to an open-book examination in which the student is able to consult certain reference material on answering the questions asked. This procedure, by providing a memory-support (Sieber[28]) in the performance situation, may well have had a reassuring, anxiety-reducing effect on the HA subjects so that interference to performance due to anxiety may have been minimal.

The results obtained provide a number of conclusions that bear directly on classroom practice and on the different theories that have been developed to explain the influence of anxiety on learning and performance. With respect to the factual learning task, the results support the conclusion that anxiety operates to debilitate performance when a complex task is to be performed in test-like conditions. This conclusion suggests that in important examinations, the HA student will be at a considerable disadvantage. When competing with other students for scholarships, university entrance, school prizes, employment opportunities or simply place in class, anxiety will act to interfere with and reduce the level of his performance.

The results also support the conclusion that while instructions designed to increase level of ego-involvement will raise the level of performance of LA students, it will not do so for MA and HA students. Sarason's theory suggests that for the MA and HA student, the positive motivational benefits deriving from the ego-involving instructions are cancelled out by the operation of task-irrelevant responses which are also elicited.

This conclusion suggests that the widely adopted practice in education of attempting to motivate students by placing strong emphasis upon the importance of examinations and the need to do well and avoid failure will be of value only to low test-anxious students. In the present study with respect to the performance of moderately and high test-anxious students on the factual learning task, little was achieved by increasing level of ego-involvement and, through this, anxiety. In fact, it may be that this emphasis, from a long term view, will have quite harmful effects. Since, at high levels, anxiety is such an unpleasant and exhausting experience, this emphasis may serve to engender a strong dislike of school which may eventually lead the student to drop out of school prematurely. Some support for this possibility is provided by Spielberger[29] who observed, in one study, that HA college students had a higher drop out rate than LA students of comparable ability.

In addition to the implications provided for educational practice, the results of the present study also provide implications for theory. The conclusion that in a test-like situation, anxiety will interfere with performance on a complex task is, as we have seen, consistent with the viewpoint of Sarason and his colleagues (Mandler and Sarason,[23] Sarason *et al.*[4]). It is also, however, consistent with the Spence-Taylor theory, although in this theory it is the drive function of anxiety that is emphasised rather than the cue function. Spence and Taylor (Spence and Spence[1]) conceive of anxiety as a drive which combines multiplicatively with the habit strengths of responses present in the individual's response hierarchy. When the desired response is not clearly dominant in the response hierarchy, as tends to be the case in complex performance situations, increase in drive (anxiety) serves to heighten competition among potential responses and in so doing disrupts performance.

The conclusion reached that increase in level of ego-involvement (stress) serves to raise the performance of LA individuals but not MA and HA individuals is, again, consistent with Sarason's theory. This conclusion, however, is not easily accounted for by the Spence-Taylor theory. Although, in the most recent statement of their position (Spence and Spence[1]), they give passing reference to the question of situational factors (such as ego-involving instructions) that serve to elicit anxiety, they have not considered this question in detail, nor attempted to manipulate such factors in their research studies.

A number of directions for future research are suggested by the results of the present study. In this study the subjects used were male and of above-average ability. There is a need, then, for research to be carried out to determine if the conclusions reached in this study also hold for females and students of average and below-average ability. It is important, too, that ways be found to control the interfering effects of anxiety in the classroom. In particular, ways need to be found by which the HA student may be challenged but his anxiety kept within non-debilitating limits. One suggestion that arises from the present study is the possibility of using open-book examinations where reasoning is the major objective of assessment. Being able to consult appropriate reference material in the examination situation reduces the strain of having to remember and recall large bodies of information and in so doing may serve to reduce anxiety and the interference to reasoning that results. Sieber[28] in an important recent article, provides further experimental evidence that the provision of memory supports will be a particular aid to HA students in counteracting the interfering effects of anxiety. In that article she also suggests a number of other ways by which the HA student may be helped to perform more effectively. In particular she discusses the benefits that may be derived from instruction in the use of verbal encoding skills, diagrams, mnemonic devices, notational systems and outlining systems for organising general ideas prior to the development of detail. There is a need for these suggestions to be followed up in classroom-oriented research.

References

[1] J. T. SPENCE and K. W. SPENCE, "The Motivational Components of Manifest Anxiety: Drive and Drive Stimuli", in C. D. Spielberger (Ed.), *Anxiety and Behavior*, Academic Press, New York, 1966, pp. 291-326.

[2] D. O. HEBB, "Drive and the C.N.S. (Conceptual Nervous System)". *Psychol. Rev.*, 1955, **62**, pp. 243-54.

[3] R. B. MALMO, "Activation: A Neuropsychological Dimension". *Psychol. Rev.*, 1959, **66**, pp. 367-86.

[4] S. B. SARASON, K. S. DAVIDSON, F. F. LIGHTHALL, R. R. WAITE and B. K. RUEBUSH, *Anxiety in Elementary School Children*, John Wiley & Sons, New York, 1960.

[5] J. A. TAYLOR, "The Relation of Anxiety to the Conditioned Eyelid Response". *J. exp. Psychol.*, 1951, **41**, pp. 81-92.

[6] K. W. SPENCE and J. A. TAYLOR, "Anxiety and Strength of the UCS as Determinants of the Amount of Eyelid Conditioning". *J. exp. Psychol.*, 1951, **42**, pp. 183-88.

[7] J. A. TAYLOR and K. W. SPENCE, "The Relationship of Anxiety Level to Performance in Serial Learning". *J. exp. Psychol.*, 1952, **44**, pp. 61-64.

[8] E. K. MONTAGUE, "The Role of Anxiety in Serial Rote Learning". *J. exp. Psychol.*, 1953, **45**, pp. 91-98.

[9] R. R. STANDISH and R. A. CHAMPION, "Task Difficulty and Drive in Verbal Learning". *J. exp. Psychol.*, 1960, **59**, pp. 361-65.

[10] J. D. LUCAS, "The Interactive Effects of Anxiety, Failure, and Intraserial Duplication". *Am. J. Psychol.*, 1952, **65**, pp. 59-66.

[11] J. DEESE, R. S. LAZARUS and J. KEENAN, "Anxiety, Anxiety Reduction and Stress in Learning". *J. exp. Psychol.*, 1953, **46**, pp. 55-60.

[12] I. G. SARASON, "The Effect of Anxiety and Two Kinds of Failure on Serial Learning". *J. Personality*, 1957, **25**, pp. 383-92.

[13] H. I. KALISH, N. GARMEZY, E. H. RODNICK and R. C. BLEKE, "The Effects of Anxiety and Experimentally Induced Stress on Verbal Learning". *J. gen. Psychol.*, 1958, **59**, pp. 87-95.

[14] W. M. NICHOLSON, "The Influence of Anxiety upon Learning: Interference or Drive Increment?" *J. Personality*, 1958, **26**, pp. 303-19.

[15] S. FESHBACH and A. LOEB, "A Further Experimental Study of a Response-interference versus a Drive-facilitation Theory of the Effect of Anxiety upon Learning". *J. Personality*, 1959, **27**, pp. 497-506.

[16] I. G. SARASON, "The Effect of Anxiety, Motivational Instructions and Failure on Serial Learning". *J. exp. Psychol.*, 1956, **51**, pp. 253-59.

[17] I. G. SARASON, "Effect of Anxiety and Two Kinds of Motivating Instructions on Verbal Learning". *J. abnorm. soc. Psychol.*, 1957, **54**, pp. 166-71.

[18] E. D. LONGNECKER, "Perceptual Recognition as a Function of Anxiety, Motivation, and the Testing Situation". *J. abnorm. soc. Psychol.*, 1962, **64**, pp. 215-21.

[19] B. W. HARLESTON, "Test Anxiety and Performance in Problem Solving Situations". *J. Personality*, 1962, **30**, pp. 557-73.

[20] L. S. WRIGHTSMAN, "The Effects of Anxiety, Achievement Motivation, and Task Importance upon Performance on an Intelligence Test". *J. educ. Psychol.*, 1962, **53**, pp. 150-56.

[21] G. L. PAUL and C. W. ERIKSEN, "Effects of Test Anxiety on 'Real-Life' Examinations". *J. Personality*, 1964, **32**, pp. 480-94.

[22] A. J. CARON, "Curiosity, Achievement, and Avoidant Motivation as Determinants of Epistemic Behaviour". *J. abnorm. soc. Psychol.*, 1963, **67**, pp. 535-49.

[23] G. MANDLER and S. B. SARASON, "A Study of Anxiety and Learning". *J. abnorm. soc. Psychol.*, 1952, **47**, pp. 166-73.

[24] E. L. THORNDIKE and I. LORGE, *The Teacher's Word Book of 30,000 Words*, Bureau of Publications, Teachers College Columbia University, New York, 1944.

[25] G. MANDLER and J. E. COWEN, "Test Anxiety Questionnaires". *J. consult. Psychol.*, 1958, **22**, p. 228.

[26] K. E. SINCLAIR, "The Influence of Anxiety and Level of Ego Involvement on Classroom Learning and Performance". Unpublished PhD dissertation, University of Illinois, 1965.

[27] B. J. WINER, *Statistical Principles in Experimental Design*, McGraw-Hill, New York, 1962.

[28] J. E. SIEBER, "A Paradigm for Experimental Modification of the Effects of Test Anxiety on Cognitive Processes". *Am. educ. Res. J.*, 1969, **6**, pp. 46-61.

[29] C. D. SPIELBERGER, "The Effects of Manifest Anxiety on the Academic Achievement of College Students". *Ment. Hyg.*, 1962, **46**, pp. 420-26.

Chapter 13

The Differential Effect of Anxiety on Performance in Progressive and Terminal School Examinations

ERIC GAUDRY and GEORGE D. BRADSHAW
Faculty of Education, University of Melbourne

Pupils in 14 secondary classes were given an intelligence test and the Test Anxiety Scale for Children (TASC) early in the school year. Marks in mathematics in both progressive and terminal examinations were collected and analysed as a function of anxiety, intelligence and method of examining. The experimental hypothesis was that high test-anxious children would perform relatively better under the less stressful conditions of progressive examining than under terminal examining when compared with low-anxious children in the same class. The anxiety/method-of-assessment interaction was significant and in the predicted direction. Implications for school examining practices are discussed.

The Test Anxiety Scale for Children (TASC) was developed as a measure of a specific anxiety: that which is experienced in test or test-like situations. In validating the scale, the authors (Sarason *et al.*[1]) hypothesised that the more "test-like" the situation, the more the interfering effects of anxiety are evidenced. They reported two validity studies in support of this hypothesis.

In the first study the performance of high- and low-anxious children was compared on two psychological tests, the Stroop and the Porteus Mazes, which, because of their different character, involved different levels of stress. The authors found a significant interaction between anxiety and task when the number of errors was considered, but not for overall attainment itself. For school performance, and achievement

From the *Australian Journal of Psychology*, 1970, **22**, pp. 1-4. Reprinted by permission of E. Gaudry and G. D. Bradshaw and the *Australian Journal of Psychology*.

examinations generally, the important factor is, in most instances, the actual attainment of the student rather than the number of errors he makes.

In the second study, in which attainment was used as the dependent variable, a significant interaction between anxiety and task was found, but again quite different tasks were used; performance on a battery of scholastic tests was compared with performance on a perceptual ability test.

The authors attribute the absence of a significant interaction for attainment in the first study to the fact that the type of performance required in the Porteus Mazes is different from that required in the Stroop Test. Since the tasks used in the second study were also dissimilar, the same issue arises and it is possible that the significant result obtained in that study might have been due to factors other than a difference in stress. Neither study involved a comparison of attainment on similar tasks given under varying conditions of stress, which would seem to be the most direct test of this hypothesis.

The present investigation was planned to provide more direct evidence, based on the assessment of school achievement under normal classroom conditions, in support of the hypothesis that the more "test-like" the situation, the more interfering are the effects of anxiety.

A common practice in Victorian schools is to assess students' progress by combining marks gained from progressive testing with those gained from terminal examinations. Typically the nature of these two testing situations varies in formality, progressive assessment being based on assignments and on short tests conducted in regular class periods in a rather informal manner, often without stringent time limits. Terminal examinations, on the other hand, are often taken in the school hall or other unfamiliar locations with strict time limits, physical separation from classmates, and furthermore, followed by written reporting of results to parents. From the Sarason *et al.* framework, it can be predicted that high-anxious children do relatively better under progressive assessment than under terminal assessment when compared with low-anxious children of similar ability.

Method

In each of 14 government schools in Melbourne, the following procedure was followed. A Grade 7 or 8 class, containing at least 24 pupils of one sex, was selected. Early in the year an intelligence test (A.C.E.R. Intermediate A) and the TASC, modified for use with junior secondary school pupils, were administered. The criteria, taken from the school records, were as follows:

1. The progressive mark was the mean for each pupil on at least three progressive assessments.
2. The terminal mark was the result on a formal examination held either at the end of the first term or at mid-year.

Within each class, the 24 or more pupils of the one sex were split at the median on both intelligence test raw score and on TASC score to form four groups. A table of random numbers was used to allocate *S*s to above or below the median when ties occurred.

For each class, the mean progressive and the terminal marks of the pupils were separately converted to normally distributed scores with a mean of 8·0 and a standard deviation of 3·5. For each of the four subgroups referred to in the previous paragraph, the normalised marks were combined to give a mean progressive mark and a mean terminal mark. In this way, each of the fourteen schools contributed a pair of mean scores to each of the four groups in the experiment.

Results

The main results are contained in Table 13.1.

TABLE 13.1

Effects of Anxiety, Intelligence and Assessment on Performance

Source	df	MS	F
A Anxiety	1	28·80	12·26**
B Intelligence	1	301·62	128·35**
A × B	1	0·08	
Error (a)	52	2·35	
C Assessment	1	0·03	
A × C	1	2·02	4·92*
B × C	1	0·15	
A × B × C	1	0·22	
Error (b)	52	0·41	

* $p < \cdot 05$
** $p < \cdot 01$

As expected, the high intelligence *S*s performed significantly better than the less able (9·67 *v.* 6·39 score points), the low-anxious performed significantly better than the high-anxious (8·54 *v.* 7·52) and the interaction between method of assessment and anxiety was significant.

The pattern of this interaction is shown in Table 13.2 where it can be seen that, although the low-anxious performed better under both methods of assessment than did the high-anxious, the difference was less under the progressive marking system than in the terminal system.

TABLE 13.2

Means for Anxiety × Assessment Interaction

Method of assessment	Anxiety Low	High
Progressive	8·39	7·64
Terminal	8·69	7·41

Discussion

This experiment was deliberately focused on within class comparisons so the findings on anxiety, for example, refer to the comparison of the performance of high-anxious children with that of low-anxious children in the same classes, not to high- and low-anxious scorers in any absolute sense. While a good case can be made for using absolute scores—and indeed most, if not all, experiments have used them—the organisation of school makes it likely that intraclassroom studies will be of value. For example, the effects of anxiety could well be more closely related to the intelligence level and the educational aspirations of classmates than to overall levels.

The main hypothesis of an interaction between anxiety and method of assessment was confirmed. That is, while both the high-anxious groups performed worse than their low-anxious counterparts, high anxiety had a less interfering effect under progressive examining than under terminal examining (Table 13.2). This supported the claims made by Sarason *et al.* concerning the effect of test anxiety on performance in situations varying in "test-like" characteristics.

There were two other significant effects (Table 13.1). One reflected the expected higher performance of the high intelligence group. The other indicated a significantly weaker performance overall for the high-anxious group. This finding was consistent with previous research (e.g., Sarason *et al.*,[1] p. 132) which indicated a negative relationship between TASC score and achievement. The absence of significant interactions involving intelligence would appear to preclude the possibility of explaining the interaction between anxiety and method of assessment as an artifact of the low negative relationship between intelligence and anxiety.

The main finding of this study, that of an interaction between anxiety and method of assessment, was a verification of the Sarason *et al.* hypothesis applied to a school learning situation. The implication for education is that a change in the conditions of examining affects high- and low-anxious pupils differently. An increase in emphasis on formal examining places high-anxious pupils at a disadvantage relative to the less anxious while the introduction of progressive assessment favours the high-anxious. However, the low-anxious performed better than the high-anxious under both terminal and progressive examining. The disadvantage suffered by the low-anxious under progressive examining is likely to be relative rather than absolute provided that the progressive assessment is based on tests and assignments where the constraints of good assessment practice are preserved.

Reference

[1] S. B. SARASON, K. S. DAVIDSON, F. F. LIGHTHALL, R. R. WAITE and B. K. RUEBUSH, *Anxiety in Elementary School Children*, John Wiley & Sons, New York, 1960.

Chapter 14

Test Anxiety and Achievement Behaviour Systems Related to Examination Performance in Children

F. N. COX
Department of Psychology, University of Melbourne

The purpose of this study was to investigate relations between measures of the achievement and test-anxiety behaviour systems and elementary school performance in arithmetic and reading. Both measures were administered to a sample of 262 children attending fourth and fifth grade elementary schools in Canberra. A theoretical analysis of both measures led to two hypotheses: that there would be a negative correlation between test anxiety and arithmetic, and a positive correlation between achievement behaviour and reading. Results were consistent with these expectations, and it was suggested that both measures may have predictive value for this population. It was also argued that these findings provide further evidence for the validity of both measures and some support for the hypothesis that these measures are tapping relatively discrete behaviour systems.

Two strategies have been adopted in attempts to establish the validity of measures of achievement motivation and general and test anxiety scales: experimentation with manipulation of the motivational measure (McClelland *et al.*,[1] Mandler and Sarason,[2] Sarason *et al.*,[3] Spence[4]) and correlational studies of the relations between these measures and quality of academic performance (Cox,[5] McCandless and Castaneda,[6] Morgan,[7] Riciuti,[8] Sarason *et al.*[3]). This article is concerned with the second approach. The main purpose is to investigate relations between measures of the achievement and test-anxiety behaviour systems and performance on two elementary school subjects — arithmetic and reading.

From *Child Development*, 1964, **35**, pp. 909-15. Reprinted by permission of F. N. Cox and *Child Development*.

Theoretical Considerations

Since the publication of *The Principles of Behavior* one of the critical questions in motivation theory has been the utility of Hull's conceptual distinction between associative and motivational tendencies in behaviour. This issue has been reviewed in several recent major publications on motivation (Bindra,[9] Brown,[10] Spence[11]), but most of the evidence discussed in these books has been obtained from simple, rigorously controlled experiments. Farber[12] and Wittenborn,[13] however, have argued that sharp differentiation between drive and habit variables can be extended to more complex personality measures, such as *n* Achievement and rating scales of a variety of personality characteristics.

The present writer (Cox[5, 14, 15]) has attempted to apply this drive/habit distinction to three motivational measures of child behaviour—the Yale General and Test Anxiety Scales and an index of the achievement behaviour system. Briefly, the argument has been that the Yale General Anxiety Scale can be regarded as a workable measure of generalised drive, while the Test Anxiety Scale (TAS) and the Index Achievement Behaviour (IAB) are assessing what Whiting and Child[16] have termed a "behaviour system", or complex combination of drive and habit variables. Evidence obtained from two studies (Cox[5, 14, 15]) of large samples of Australian fourth and fifth grade elementary school children has been consistent with these arguments. In these studies emphasis has been on attempting to classify these measures on the basis of their content, scoring and correlates, but the relation between TAS and IAB has not yet been discussed.

One way to approach this question is to consider the ways in which these two measures are likely to be associated with quality of performance on specified school subjects. The TAS, it will be recalled, consists of questions concerned with physiological concomitants and subjective experiences of anxiety in the classroom, and with quite specific, habitual ways of behaving. A high proportion of affirmative responses to these questions, a high "test-anxiety" score, seems likely to be associated with frequent evocation of response tendencies which seem likely to impair attention and concentration in the classroom situation. Consequently, it appears reasonable to predict that test anxiety will be negatively correlated with quality of performance on school subjects which demand close attention and sustained concentration in the school situation. Arithmetic would seem to afford an excellent example of such a subject. Clinical experience is certainly consistent with this prediction and few teachers would disagree with it.

With respect to the IAB, the prediction is for a positive correlation between scores on this measure and quality of performance in reading. High IAB scores are obtained when children's imaginary productions to selected TAT and Michigan Picture Test cards provide repeated evidence of acceptance of studying, either for its own sake or as a means to a culturally approved goal.* The assumption made in this

* The cards used in the study reported here were TAT Card 1, and Michigan Picture Test Cards 3, 8G, and 11G. The scoring system is described in detail elsewhere (Cox[15]).

study was that frequent production of stories of these kinds would be associated with wide reading experience.

Since there did not appear to be any *a priori* reasons for predicting the nature of the relations between TAS and reading, or IAB and arithmetic, the hypotheses were confined to the expectations of a negative correlation between TAS and arithmetic, and a positive correlation between IAB and reading.

Method

SAMPLE

Subjects in this study comprised 262 children* in fourth and fifth grade in two middle class Canberra schools. In both schools children were divided into "superior" and "inferior" subgrades on the basis of their academic records in the first three grades. Consequently, eight school classes were tested.

PREDICTOR MEASURES

The TAS and IAB were administered in November, 1960, to intact school grades in the ways described earlier (Cox[5, 15]). The Australian Council for Educational Research Junior B Intelligence Test was also administered at the same time. This test was designed to measure the general ability of Australian children from 8 to 12 years of age, as revealed by their performance on material of a verbal nature. There are 65 items in this test, and these are separated into 5 subtests covering vocabulary, logical reasoning, analogies, number series and arithmetical problems. A retest reliability coefficient of 0·88 has been obtained for a sample of 107 children after an interval of 12 months. With respect to validity, there is evidence that performance on the Junior B is correlated highly with other intelligence and standardised achievement tests. For example, for a sample of 152 children, scores on the Junior B correlated to the extent of $r = 0{\cdot}71$ with the A.C.E.R. Junior Non-Verbal test, $r = 0{\cdot}56$ with a Word Knowledge test, and $r = 0{\cdot}50$ with a Reading for Meaning achievement test.

Teachers were never present during the administration of these measures.

CRITERION MEASURES

After the measures had been scored examination marks for arithmetic and reading were collected. These examinations were conducted in December, 1960. It should be mentioned that, *within* grades, each school used the same examination to assess children who belonged to different subgrades. In both schools these examinations were marked by teachers who had not taught the children during that academic year.

* This sample was the same as that used in the earlier study (Cox[15]) of the effects of educational streaming on level of test anxiety, except that four children were absent from school examinations. The sample is described in detail in the earlier article.

Results

Table 14.1 lists means and standard deviations for the three predictor variables.

TABLE 14.1

Means and Standard Deviations of Scores on Three Predictor Measures ($N=262$)

Measure	Mean	SD
Achievement Behaviour System (IAB)	6·2	2·1
Intelligence Quotient (ACER Junior B)	106·3	13·4
Text Anxiety Scale (TAS)	14·9	5·2

Note: The Junior B Intelligence test was constructed to yield a mean IQ of 100, with an SD of 15. This sample, however, was drawn from two middle class schools situated in a residential suburb of a non-industrialised city.

Since it had already been shown (Cox[14, 15]) that scores on the TAS, IAB, and Junior Intelligence tests were correlated quite highly with level of subgrade, it was decided to restrict this analysis to performance *within* subgrades. Initially, data from each subgrade were analysed separately. Scores on all variables were intercorrelated,* and it was found that, for children of a given subgrade level, distributions of scores and patterns of relations were similar for both grades and both schools. Consequently, it was decided to attempt to combine results for all children from a given subgrade level.†

It was established that, for both "superior" and "inferior" streams, the correlation coefficients obtained from two different grades and two different schools could be regarded as having been randomly drawn from a common population (Edwards,[17] p. 135), so average correlations were computed.‡

Results are presented in terms of the hypotheses listed earlier.

HYPOTHESIS I

As the data in Table 14.2 show, for both educational streams there is a highly significant negative correlation between TAS and arithmetic examination marks, and these findings are consistent with the hypothesis.

It is of interest to note that the correlations between TAS and reading, while not significant, are positive for both streams. The negative correlation between TAS and intelligence, while not significant, is consistent with those reported by other writers (McCandless and Castaneda,[6] Sarason,[18] Sarason *et al.*[3]) in this field. The lack of significance in *this* study has to be considered in relation to the method of analysis: namely, computing correlations *within* subgrades. This procedure of dividing the sample into two fairly homogeneous intellectual groups is also responsible for the size of the correlations between intelligence and arithmetic and reading. It will be recalled (Cox[15]) that scores on this intelligence test correlated $r = 0 \cdot 51$ with level of subgrades, and subgrade placement

* All correlations reported in this study are product-moment coefficients, and all were computed by SILLIAC (ILLIAC at Sydney University).

† Sex differences were found to be small and inconsistent so they were ignored in the study.

‡ Individual correlation coefficients were transformed to Fisher's z, weighted according to the number in each subgrade, and averaged.

was determined on the basis of examination performance in the first three grades of school.

TABLE 14.2

Average Intercorrelations between Test Anxiety, Intelligence, Arithmetic and Reading (N=262)

	"Superior" Stream (N=140)			"Inferior" Stream (N=122)		
	Intelligence	Arithmetic	Reading	Intelligence	Arithmetic	Reading
TAS	−·14	−·43*	·08	−·13	−·41*	·10
Intelligence	..	·10	·14	..	·11	·15

* Significant at the ·01 level

HYPOTHESIS 2

The prediction of a positive correlation between scores on the IAB and reading marks is strongly supported by the data in Table 14.3.

TABLE 14.3

Average Intercorrelations between Achievement Behaviour, Intelligence, Arithmetic and Reading (N=262)

	"Superior" Stream (N=140)			"Inferior" Stream (N=122)		
	Intelligence	Arithmetic	Reading	Intelligence	Arithmetic	Reading
IAB	·13	·10	·49*	·15	·08	·46*
Intelligence	..	·10	·14	..	·11	·15

* Significant at the ·01 level

It should also be mentioned that the correlations between IAB scores and arithmetic marks, while positive for both streams, are not significant.

In general, considering the restricted nature of the samples studied, and the consistency of findings in the two educational streams, the patterns of correlations presented above provide fairly substantial support for the two hypotheses.

Discussion

The negative correlations obtained between test anxiety and arithmetic are consistent with similar findings reported by several other writers (McCandless and Castaneda,[6] Sarason,[18] Sarason *et al.*[3]) who have examined educational correlates of self-report measures of anxiety. It is possible, of course, to interpret this finding in several ways: in terms of hypothetical personality characteristics of anxious individuals (Sarason *et al.*[3]); in terms of the alleged effects of hypothetical task-irrelevant responses (Mandler and Sarason[2]); in terms of the alleged effects of a high level of motivation or arousal (Bindra,[9] Hebb[19]); or in terms of an assumed increase in generalised drive leading to the evocation of a relatively large number of responses, only one of which will be correct for a given task (Spence[4, 11]).

In the opinion of the present writer, the kind of evidence reported in this study cannot be used to decide between these various theoretical formulations. A more productive alternative would seem to be to restrict hypotheses to particular measures and, perhaps, to specified populations. With these qualifications in mind, it is suggested that the negative correlation between test anxiety and arithmetic can be explained in terms of the evocation of response tendencies which seem likely to impair attention and concentration in the classroom situation. A high level of test anxiety in elementary school children is assumed to be associated with *both* a high level of drive and with the evocation of specific response tendencies. Such an interpretation, while clearly by no means the only one that could be offered to explain the present findings, has the merit of being able to account for other findings (Cox[5, 14]) with the Yale Test Anxiety Scales for Children.

The small, positive correlations between test anxiety and reading seem worthy of mention in view of Lynn's[20] report of a significant positive correlation between anxiety and reading in a sample of English children. At the present time, however, it seems premature to offer interpretations of a finding which requires replication before it can be accepted with confidence.

The positive correlations between the index of achievement behaviour and reading examination performance are consistent with those reported by some writers (McClelland *et al.*,[1] Morgan,[7] Riciuti[8]) who have used McClelland's measure of achievement motivation. Following Farber's[12] suggestion, the present writer favours an associative rather than a motivational interpretation of this finding: the suggestion being that high scores on the IAB (and, perhaps, *n*-Achievement) are associated with wide reading experience. The finding that IAB correlates more highly with reading than with arithmetic is consistent with this argument.

Perhaps the most interesting finding in this study is that arithmetic and reading have different non-intellectual correlates. This is consistent with Haggard's[21] conclusions from his longitudinal study of personality correlates of various achievement groups. From the point of view of the predictor variables used in the present study, this finding suggests that it may be profitable to combine the Index of Achievement Behaviour and the Yale Test Anxiety Scale to predict academic performance in elementary school children. While further research is required to examine the predictive value of both measures, the present findings certainly do provide further support for their validity and some evidence for the hypothesis that they are tapping relatively discrete behaviour systems.

References

[1] D. C. McClelland, J. W. Atkinson, R. A. Clark and E. L. Lowell, *The Achievement Motive*, Appleton-Century-Crofts, New York, 1953.

[2] G. Mandler and S. B. Sarason, "A Study of Anxiety and Learning". *J. abnorm. soc. Psychol.*, 1952, **47**, pp. 155-73.

[3] S. B. Sarason, K. S. Davidson, F. F. Lighthall, R. R. Waite and B. K. Ruebush, *Anxiety in Elementary School Children*, John Wiley & Sons, New York, 1960.

[4] K. W. Spence, "A Theory of Emotionally Based Drive (D) and its Relation to Performance in Simple Learning Situations". *Am. Psychologist*, 1958, **13**, pp. 131-41.

[5] F. N. Cox, "Correlates of General and Test Anxiety in Children". *Aust. J. Psychol.*, 1960, **12**, pp. 169-77.

[6] B. R. McCandless and A. Castaneda, "Anxiety in Children, School Achievement, and Intelligence". *Child Dev.*, 1956, **27**, pp. 379-82.

[7] H. H. Morgan, "A Psychometric Comparison of Achieving and Non-achieving College Students of High Ability". *J. consult. Psychol.*, 1952, **16**, 292-98.

[8] H. N. Riciuti, *The Prediction of Academic Grades with a Projective Test of Achievement Motivation: 1. Initial Validation Studies,* Educational Testing Service, Princeton, New Jersey, 1954.

[9] D. Bindra, *Motivation: A Systematic Reinterpretation*, Ronald Press, New York, 1959.

[10] J. S. Brown, *The Motivation of Behavior*, McGraw-Hill, New York, 1959.

[11] K. W. Spence, *Behavior Theory and Learning*, Prentice-Hall, Englewood Cliffs, N.J., 1960.

[12] I. E. Farber, Comments on Professor Atkinson's paper, in M. R. Jones (Ed.), *Nebraska Symposium on Motivation*, University of Nebraska Press, 1954.

[13] J. R. Wittenborn, "Inferring the Strength of Drive", in M. R. Jones (Ed.), *Nebraska Symposium on Motivation*, Nebraska University Press, 1957.

[14] F. N. Cox, "Educational Streaming and General and Test Anxiety". *Child Dev.*, 1962, **33**, pp. 381-90.

[15] F. N. Cox, "An Assessment of the Achievement Behavior System in Children". *Child Dev.*, 1962, **33**, pp. 907-16.

[16] J. W. Whiting and I. L. Child, *Child Training and Personality*, Yale University Press, New Haven, Conn., 1953.

[17] A. L. Edwards, *Experimental Design in Psychological Research*, Holt Rinehart and Winston, New York, 1950.

[18] I. G. Sarason, "Test Anxiety and the Intellectual Performance of College Students". *J. educ. Psychol.*, 1961, **52**, pp. 201-06.

[19] D. O. Hebb, "Drives and the C.N.S. (Conceptual Nervous System)". *Psychol. Rev.*, 1955, **62**, pp. 242-54.

[20] R. Lynn, "Temperamental Characteristics Related to Disparity of Attainment in Reading and Arithmetic". *Br. J. educ. Psychol.*, 1967, **27**, pp. 62-67.

[21] E. A. Haggard, "Socialization, Personality, and Achievement in Gifted Children". *Sch. Rev.*, 1957, **64**, pp. 318-414.

Chapter 15

The Effects of Manifest Anxiety on the Academic Achievement of College Students

CHARLES D. SPIELBERGER
Duke University, Durham, North Carolina

Acute shortages of trained professional and technical manpower have caused the academic mortality rate for college students to be a subject of considerable general concern to our society (Iffort[1]).

There is a growing appreciation of the important role mental health and emotional factors play in the academic adjustment of college students.

Even apparently well-adjusted students have their share of emotional difficulties. Heath and Gregory[2]—in a study of male college sophomores chosen on the basis of good health, satisfactory academic status, and overtly good social adjustment—reported that 90 per cent of their subjects raised questions or presented problems which were judged by the investigating staff as requiring professional aid for solution.

Rust and Davie[3]—in assessing the nature, frequency, and severity of the personal problems of undergraduate college students—found that nearly 80 per cent of those who responded to their questionnaire reported that they had at least one personal problem during the current school year which bothered them "very often" or "fairly often"; 35 per

A paper based, in part, on the data of this investigation was read at the Annual Meeting of the South-eastern Psychological Association, held in Gatlinburg, Tenn., in April, 1961.

This investigation was supported, in part, by a grant from the U.S. Public Health Service. The grant to Dr. Spielberger and Dr. Henry Weitz covered research project OM-362 titled "A Proposed Demonstration Project for Improving the Academic Adjustment of College Freshmen".

From *Mental Hygiene*, 1962, **46**, pp. 420-26. Reprinted by permission of C. D. Spielberger and *Mental Hygiene*.

cent of their sample indicated specifically that they had been troubled often by "nervousness".

These findings are consistent with general observations that late adolescence in the American culture is a time of "storm and stress" and a period of unusual difficulty in adjustment (Farnham[4]).

Several recent studies (McKeachie,[5] McKeachie, Pollie and Speisman[6]) have demonstrated impressively that anxiety is manifested by college students in conventional classroom test situations to such an extent that the general level of academic performance is impaired. Strong motivations to achieve high grades appear to contribute directly to the adjustment difficulties of many students whose anxiety about failure is intensified by the academic situation.

Thus, it is apparent that college life is characterised by conditions and expectations which may heighten anxieties already present in students or may induce new anxieties. It would seem reasonable to expect that the stresses of college life are likely to have most serious effects upon those students who have developed pronounced tendencies to respond to threatening situations with anxiety and conflict.

But when investigations of the relationship between measures of student neuroticism or emotional adjustment and academic achievement are examined, the findings are equivocal and inconsistent.

For example, Thurstone[7] has reported that less well-adjusted students tended to achieve higher grades, while Stagner[8] has found that unstable and maladjusted students did less well than their more stable contemporaries. Other studies have reported no difference in the emotional adjustment scores of academic underachievers and overachievers (Rust and Ryan[9]). Such inconsistencies have been attributed to inadequacies in the variety of personality tests which have been used, differences between the student populations which have been studied, and varying criteria of academic success (Harris[10]).

Also, it has been noted that methods of data analysis have frequently not taken into account the possibility that a given personality variable may have different effects for persons with differing intellectual endowments (Spielberger and Katzenmeyer[11]).

To this point Berger and Sutker[12] investigated the combined effects of emotional adjustment and scholastic aptitude on the academic achievement of college students. Their measure of emotional adjustment did not by itself differentiate between academic successes and failures, but when used in combination with measures of ability, a larger number of the most able students with high conflict scores were academic failures than were students with equal ability but low conflict scores.

The purpose of the present study was to investigate the relationship between anxiety level and academic performance for college students when the student's ability is taken into account.

It was expected that college students with high anxiety would be more likely to perform less adequately throughout their college careers than would non-anxious students. Specifically, it was hypothesised that anxious students would obtain poorer grades and would be more likely to drop out of school because of academic failure than would non-anxious students.

Method

The measure of anxiety employed in the present study was the Taylor Manifest Anxiety Scale (MAS). This scale (Taylor[13]) consists of 50 items from the Minnesota Multiphasic Personality Inventory (MMPI) which were judged by clinical psychologists to be consistent with Cameron's[14] description of anxiety as manifested in chronic anxiety reactions.

The MAS was administered to all students enrolled in Introductory Psychology courses at Duke University at the beginning of each of six consecutive semesters from September, 1954, through June, 1957. The A.C.E. Psychological Examination for College Freshmen (1949 edition), which had been routinely administered as part of a battery of placement tests to all students entering the University as freshmen, served as the measure of scholastic ability.

Grade point averages (GPAs) for the *single* semester during which each student took the MAS served as one criterion of academic achievement. These were obtained from official University records. The student's GPA is the weighted average of his academic performance in course work where 4 points are credited for each hour of A, 3 points for B, 2 points for C, 1 point for D, and 0 for F.

Only male students were included in the present study, since it had been found previously that MAS scores for male and female college students may not have the same intellectual correlates (Spielberger[15]). Eight students who obtained scores of 7 or higher on the Lie Scale of the MMPI were eliminated from the study.

Those male students scoring in the upper and lower twenty per cent of the MAS score distribution (raw scores of 19 and above and 7 and below) were designated as HA and LA respectively. After the data for the six semester subsamples were pooled, MAS scores, ACE scores and GPAs were available for a total of 140 HA students and 144 LA students whose Lie scores were below 7.

The long-term effects of anxiety on academic performance were evaluated in a follow-up study in which the graduation status of each of the HA and LA students was determined three years subsequent to the time the original data collection was completed.

For those students who had not graduated from the University by June, 1960, and who were no longer enrolled, their reasons for leaving and their cumulative GPAs at the time they departed were obtained from official University records.

Academic failure was defined for the purpose of the present study as: (1) having been dismissed by the University because of poor academic performance, and/or (2) having left the University with a grade point average below 1·75 (a GPA of 1·90 is required to graduate).

Both criteria were deemed necessary in that students who performed unsatisfactorily were often allowed to leave school for "personal reasons" so that the stigma of "academic failure" would not deter their acceptance at other institutions. Seventeen students, eleven HA and six LA, were either still enrolled in the University or had left with averages above 1·75. In evaluating the relationship between anxiety and drop-outs resulting from academic failure, these students were eliminated from the sample; for this analysis there were 129 HA students and 138 LA students.

Results

The students were subdivided into five levels of scholastic ability, on the basis of their ACE total scores. Each level consisted of approximately 20 per cent of the total sample. The lowest level of ability was designated I; the highest was designated V. The ACE score ranges for levels I through V were 62-102; 103-116; 117-126; 127-137 and 138-174, respectively.

The GPAs of the HA and LA students were then compared for these ability levels. The relationship between manifest anxiety and grades for students of different levels of scholastic ability is depicted in Figure 15.1, where it may be noted that in the broad middle range of ability, the HA students obtained poorer grades than did the LA students. There appeared to be no differences between the HA and LA students at the extremes of ability.

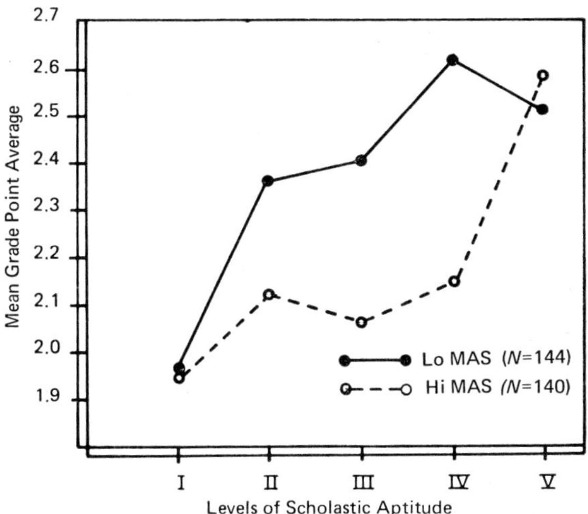

Fig. 15.1 Mean grade point averages for high and low anxiety college students at five levels of scholastic ability.

These data were subjected to an analysis of variance (Lindquist,[16] factorial design). The hypothesised main effect of anxiety was statistically significant ($F = 5{\cdot}48$; $df = 1/274$; $p < 0{\cdot}025$). The expected relationship between scholastic ability and GPA was also highly significant ($F = 5{\cdot}60$; $df = 4/274$; $p < 0{\cdot}001$).

Although the effects of anxiety and scholastic ability on grades appear to be interactive, i.e., the effect of anxiety depends on the student's level of ability, the statistical test of this interaction was not significant ($F = 1{\cdot}36$; $df = 4/274$; $p > 0{\cdot}20$).

It may be noted in Fig. 15.1, however, that the *observed* interaction is heterogeneous; failure to obtain a statistically significant interaction may result from the fact that analysis of variance tends to provide a relatively insensitive test of such interactions (Lindquist[16]).

When the relationship between anxiety and dropout rate resulting from academic failure is examined, 8 of 138 LA students and 26 of 129 HA students were classified as academic failures, according to the previously stated criteria. The total number of students in the HA and LA groups at each level of ability and the number who dropped out of school because of academic failure are reported in Table 15.1. More than 20 per cent of the HA students failed, as compared to fewer than 6 per cent of the LA students. When students in Group I, the lowest ability group, are excluded from consideration, nearly 18 per cent of the relatively able HA students are found to have left the University because of academic failure, as compared to only 4.5 per cent of the relatively able LA students.

TABLE 15.1

High- and Low-anxious Students at Five Levels of Scholastic Ability Who Dropped Out of School Classified as Academic Failures

Scholastic ability	High-anxious students No.	No. fail	% fail	Low-anxious students No.	No. fail	% fail
I	33	9	27·3	22	3	13·6
II	22	3	13·6	26	1	3·8
III	31	7	22·6	23	1	4·4
IV	21	5	23·8	37	0	0·0
V	22	2	9·1	30	3	10·0
Total	129	26	20·2	138	8	5·8

Discussion

The findings of the present study provide evidence of the detrimental effects of anxiety on college grades and dropout rates resulting from academic failure. The effect of anxiety on grades resulted from the fact that HA students in the middle ranges of ability did poorer than LA students of comparable ability (see Figure 15.1).

Although the obtained relationship was based on academic performance during a single semester, the data on dropouts indicated that the effects of anxiety on academic performance are not limited to a single semester. A larger percentage of the HA students were academic failures at all levels of ability, except the highest.

Moreover, when only the relatively able students are considered (those at ability levels II, III, IV and V), the percentage of HA students who failed was nearly four times as great as the percentage of LA academic failures. It is apparent that the loss to society of the creative abilities of potentially able students through underachievement and/or academic failure constitutes an important mental health problem in education.

The grades of low-aptitude students were uniformly low, irrespective of their anxiety level; poor academic performance presumably resulted from their limited ability. However, since the dropout rate resulting from academic failure was approximately twice as high for the HA students at ability level I as for the LA students at this level, the combination of high anxiety and limited ability appears to have a more detrimental effect upon the performance of HA students over a period of time.

For the superior students, grades were high and apparently independent of anxiety level. It would seem reasonable to assume that college work was relatively easy for such students; their superior intellectual endowment made it possible for them to obtain good grades, irrespective of their anxiety level.

A more detailed analysis of the performance of students who scored in the highest level of academic ability suggests, however, that high anxiety may actually facilitate the performance of the most able students. For such students anxiety may provide increased motivation (Spence[17]) which stimulates greater effort in their academic work.

For the purpose of examining this possibility, the GPAs for only those students in the highest ability group whose ACE scores were 150 or above were considered. The mean GPA for the very superior HA students ($N = 9$) was 3·01 as compared to a mean GPA of 2·70 for LA students of comparable ability ($N = 12$). This difference, however, did not reach a satisfactory level of statistical significance ($t = 0{\cdot}90$; $df = 13$; $p > 0{\cdot}05$).

Perhaps the most important implication of the findings of the present study is that it appears possible to identify members of the college population who, because of emotional problems, are not likely, under general conditions, to function at levels commensurate with their intellectual potential.

By identifying such students at the earliest possible time and offering them therapeutic opportunities, the academic mortality among able students who fail because of difficulties in their emotional adjustment could be reduced.

Ideally, such students should be identified at the beginning of their freshman year. The effects of anxiety on the academic performance of college freshmen might be expected to be more detrimental than for students in the present sample (predominantly sophomores and juniors).

The college freshman must adjust to demands for academic achievement under conditions of increased complexity of subject matter and heightened competition from his peers.

In addition, he is confronted with establishing a new set of social relationships in a strange environment. To the extent that freshmen with heightened anxieties can be identified early and offered therapeutic assistance, it is possible that academic casualties and, in some cases, emotional disorders can be prevented.

Summary

In order to assess the effects of manifest anxiety on academic performance, the grades achieved by anxious and non-anxious college students for a single semester's work were examined.

The long-term effects of anxiety on academic performance were evaluated by determining—three years subsequent to the initial data collection—the number of anxious and non-anxious students who either had graduated or had left the University, classified as academic failures.

It was found that anxious students in the middle ranges of ability obtained lower grades and a higher percentage of academic failures than non-anxious students of comparable ability. Students of low ability earned poor grades irrespective of their anxiety level; however, a higher percentage of these students, with high anxiety, were academic failures than were the non-anxious students of limited ability.

For the very superior students (those with ACE scores above 150), it appeared that anxiety may have actually facilitated academic performance. To the extent that anxious students—likely to be underachievers or academic failures—can be identified early and offered effective therapeutic assistance, academic mortality rates resulting from emotional factors can be reduced.

References

[1] R. E. IFFERT, "Retention and Withdrawal of College Students", Office of Education, U.S. Department of Health, Education and Welfare, Washington, D.C., Bulletin No. 1.

[2] C. W. HEATH and L. W. GREGORY, "Problems of Normal College Students and their Families". *Sch. Soc.*, 1946, **63**, pp. 355-58.

[3] R. M. RUST and J. S. DAVIE, "The Personal Problems of College Students". *Ment. Hyg.*, 1961, **45**, pp. 247-57.

[4] M. L. FARNHAM, *The Adolescent*, Harper & Bros., New York, 1951.

[5] W. J. MCKEACHIE, "Anxiety in the College Classroom". *J. educ. Res.*, 1951, **45**, pp. 153-60.

[6] W. J. MCKEACHIE, D. POLLIE and J. SPEISMAN, "Relieving Anxiety in Classroom Examinations". *J. abnorm. soc. Psychol.*, 1955, **50**, pp. 93-98.

[7] L. L. THURSTONE and THELMA G. THURSTONE, "A Neurotic Inventory". *J. abnorm. soc. Psychol.*, 1930, **1**, pp. 3-30.

[8] R. STAGNER, "The Relation of Personality to Academic Aptitude and Achievement". *J. educ. Res.*, 1953, **26**, pp. 648-60.

[9] R. M. RUST and F. J. RYAN, "The Relationship of some Rorschach Variables to Academic Behavior". *J. Personality*, 1953, **21**, pp. 441-56.

[10] D. HARRIS, "Factors Affecting College Grades: A Review of the Literature, 1930-1937". *Psychol. Bull.*, 1940, **37**, pp. 125-66.

[11] C. D. SPIELBERGER and W. G. KATZENMEYER, "Manifest Anxiety, Intelligence, and College Grades". *J. consult. Psychol.*, 1959, **23**, p. 278.

[12] I. L. BERGER and A. R. SUTKER, "The Relationship of Emotional Adjustment and Intellectual Capacity to the Academic Achievement of College Students". *Ment. Hyg.*, 1956, **40**, pp. 65-77.

[13] JANET A. TAYLOR, "A Personality Scale of Manifest Anxiety". *J. abnorm. soc. Psychol.*, 1953, **48**, pp. 285-90.

[14] N. CAMERON, *The Psychology of Behavior Disorders: A Bio-Social Interpretation*, Houghton-Mifflin, Boston, 1947.

[15] C. D. SPIELBERGER, "On the Relationship between Manifest Anxiety and Intelligence". *J. consult. Psychol.*, 1958, **22**, pp. 220-24.

[16] E. F. LINDQUIST, *Design and Analysis of Experiments in Psychology and Education*, Houghton-Mifflin, Boston, 1953.

[17] K. W. SPENCE, "A Theory of Emotionally Based Drive (D) and its Relation to Performance in Simple Learning Situations". *Am. Psychologist*, 1958, **13**, pp. 131-41.

ACKNOWLEDGEMENT

The author wishes to express his appreciation to W. G. Katzenmeyer, J. B. Grier and Edna Bissette for their assistance in the collection and analysis of these data.

Chapter 16

Educational Streaming and Anxiety in Children

F. N. COX and S. B. HAMMOND
University of Melbourne

In recent years several educational psychologists (Cox,[1] Hallworth,[2] Sarnoff *et al.*,[3] Sarnoff *et al.*[4]) have examined the relations of various educational streaming practices with general and with test anxiety among primary and secondary school children. These investigators have compared the anxiety levels of American and English primary school children, of English secondary school students attending Grammar and Secondary Modern schools, and of Australian primary school children. A noteworthy outcome of most of these studies is the remarkable similarity of reported findings. This consistency, and the likelihood that these findings would be of interest to Australian educationists prompted the present writers to summarise this evidence and to report a similar study of their own of Melbourne secondary school children.

Comparison of American and English Primary School Children

Sarnoff and his colleagues[3, 4] preface their comparisons of the general and test anxiety levels of American and English school children with an analysis of current educational policies and practices in the two countries. They point out that the "Eleven-plus" examinations in England form part of a centralised, well-established educational policy; that at, or near, the completion of fifth grade, all pupils who attend State primary schools are obliged to undergo a series of national examinations if they want to be eligible for further government support for secondary schooling leading up to university entrance. In general, performance at these examinations determines the educational and, hence, the vocational

From the *Australian Journal of Education*, 1964, **8**, pp. 85-90. Reprinted by permission of F. N. Cox and S. B. Hammond and the *Australian Journal of Education.*

career of most English school children: successful performance leads to enrolment at "Grammar" schools, which offer an academic curriculum of pre-university standard, and failure leads to enrolment at "Secondary Modern" schools, the curriculum of which is not directed towards university entrance.

In 1958 Sarnoff and his colleagues emphasised that there was, at that time, no comparable national system in the United States, that American educational policy was decentralised, and that each local school system adopted practices to its own liking. Thus, while some American primary schools used some kind of homogeneous grouping of children, many others did not. Further, where it existed, "homogeneous grouping in the American primary school (to the extent one can say 'the' American primary school) has tended to become subject-matter-oriented rather than classroom-oriented. That is, the practice of dividing the second grade classes, for example, into the 'slow' and the 'rapid' learners has tended to give way to grouping *within* classes on the basis of different learning areas, e.g., reading or arithmetic" (Sarason *et al.*[5]).

On the basis of these arguments Sarnoff and his team predicted that test anxiety would be higher in English than in American primary school children, and they proceeded to test this hypothesis by administering to large samples of such children questionnaires designed to measure "test" and "general" anxiety.

Before discussing their findings, it is important to consider the nature of these two measures. The Yale Test Anxiety Scale (Sarason *et al.*,[6] Cox and Leaper[7]) comprises 30 simple questions about the anxiety reactions of children before, during, and after testing—"testing" being explicitly defined as *any* situation in which a teacher attempts to assess how much the pupils know. There is other evidence (Sarason *et al.*,[8] Cox[9]) of its reliability and validity. The Yale General Anxiety Scale (Sarason *et al.*,[10] Cox and Leaper[7]), by contrast, comprises 45 simple questions about the anxiety and fear reactions of children in a wide variety of situations. Thus it gives a measure of the general emotionality of the student. Sarnoff and his colleagues predicted that test anxiety would be higher in English than in American primary school children, but they did not anticipate that the two groups would differ in *general* anxiety scores. To test the first hypothesis, both measures were administered to samples of 597 American children, drawn from grades 1 to 4 of six New England schools, and to 533 English pupils from the same grades of two schools near London. From these large samples a subsample of 160 subjects from each country was drawn so as to be matched on grade level, sex and social class. That is, an attempt was made to make the groups sociologically as equivalent as possible so that differences in test anxiety would not be due to these other variables.

Results were in accordance with expectations: the mean test anxiety score for English children was 10·0, for American children 7·5—the difference being significant beyond the 0·001 level. Sarnoff and his colleagues argue that this mean difference reflects the influence of many variables, such as national differences in educational policy, classroom atmospheres, teacher attitudes towards school work success, and the reactions of students towards school.

As predicted, American and English primary school children did not differ in general anxiety scores: the difference between the two groups was confined to anxiety about being tested and evaluated by teachers. This evidence, then, is consistent with the argument that differences in anxiety level between American and English children are the result of, among other things, different educational policies and practices, that they are not the result of more general national temperamental differences.

Anxiety in Secondary Modern and Grammar School English Children

In view of these findings and in the light of the great debate over the wisdom of the "Eleven-plus" examinations, it is surprising that there has not been a series of studies to assess the effects of this examination on the anxiety level of secondary school pupils. Hallworth[2] has recently reported results from a study of 896 children who were attending either Secondary Modern or Grammar schools near Birmingham, but he concentrated on measures of general rather than test anxiety. He found that pupils at Secondary Modern Schools obtained higher mean scores on the Children's Form of the Manifest Anxiety Scale (Castaneda, McCandless and Palermo[11]), a scale of Separation Anxiety (Hallworth[12]), and an adaptation of the Pintner Scale of Emotional Instability (Pintner *et al.*[13]) than Grammar School children, and in each case the difference was significant beyond the 0·001 level. Hallworth suggests that his findings cast considerable doubt upon the validity of the commonly held point of view (Davis,[14] Davis and Havighurst[15]) that anxiety level is higher in the middle than in the lower social class, and his results and those of Sarason and his colleagues[16] are certainly at variance with Davis' arguments.

With respect to the alleged effects of the "Eleven-plus" examinations on anxiety level, this study is not particularly convincing. It is possible that Hallworth's two groups may have differed in anxiety level before they undertook this examination. Again, his complete reliance upon measures of *general* anxiety makes it difficult to attribute his mean differences to relatively specific educational experiences. It is difficult to believe that differing educational experiences alone could produce differences in level of general anxiety. What is required is longitudinal studies of general and test anxiety in English school children, so that both kinds of anxiety can be related systematically to relevant sociological, family and school correlates over an extended period of time.

Educational Streaming in Australian Primary School Children

The evidence obtained by Sarnoff and his colleagues prompted Cox[1] to investigate relationships between educational streaming practices and levels of general and test anxiety in a sample of primary school children in Canberra.

Two government schools located in middle class, residential suburbs were selected for this study so that differences between streaming groups would not be likely to be due to social class sociological variables. In each school streaming practices were instituted at the beginning of fourth grade: division into "superior" and "inferior" streams being determined on the basis of the children's scholastic performance in the first three grades. While attempts were made to disguise streaming differences by labelling forms by reference to teachers' names, there was evidence that children were aware of the real basis of the division. It seemed probable that most of their parents knew whether their children were in the "high" or "low" stream. It also seemed likely that this awareness would affect parental attitudes towards their children because the city is still small, with very restricted employment possibilities for school leavers who are unable to qualify for Public Service or University entrance. Consequently, it was predicted that *test* anxiety scores would be higher in children who were in the "inferior" educational streams.

Results from the analysis of the scores of a sample of 200 fourth and fifth grade children supported this hypothesis: the mean difference in test anxiety scores was significant beyond the 0·001 level. Further, level of test anxiety increased significantly from fourth to fifth grade, which suggests increasing concern with academic performance as entry to secondary school came closer. Scores on the *general* anxiety scale, however, were found to be quite unrelated to streaming, confirming Sarnoff's finding that educational streaming practices have specific rather than generalised effects on the anxiety level of primary school children.

The consistency of these findings led the present writers to investigate levels of test anxiety in a wide range of Melbourne secondary school students who were attending third or fourth form.

TABLE 16.1

Description of Sample of Melbourne Secondary School Children

Type of school	Form III	Form IV	N
Non-State Girls'	two forms	two forms	128
Non-State Boys'	one higher, one lower	one higher, one lower	164
High School A	one upper boys, one lower girls	one upper girls, one lower boys	144
High School B	one upper mixed, one lower mixed	one upper boys, one upper girls	141
Technical College	—	one upper boys, one lower boys	41
		18 forms	618

Note: The Non-State school for girls did not employ streaming. In all the other schools, each form is divided into a "higher" and "lower" stream.

Educational Streaming in Melbourne Secondary School Children

Since the Child Form of the Yale Test Anxiety Scale was unsuitable for secondary school students, it was decided to adapt the College Form

(Mandler and Sarason[17]) of that Scale for this study. This measure is designed to elicit information about the reactions of subjects before, during and after testing—"testing" in this case being explicitly defined in terms of individual and group intelligence tests and course examinations.

This test-anxiety scale was administered to the sample of secondary school students described in Table 16.1.

In order to test the effects of streaming practices on test anxiety, the authors chose seven instances from Table 16.1 in which it seemed legitimate to compare two groups that differed only as regards streaming. In High School B this meant treating separately boys and girls in Form III. In High School A, where there is a crossover confounding of sex, form and streaming, the significance of streaming was established by analysis of variance, and the streaming comparisons within forms are derived by making adjustments for sex differences.

In the third form streaming is associated with an increase in test anxiety in only one of the four groups, whereas a significant increase in the lower stream occurs in all three comparisons in the fourth (Intermediate) form. It seems that the imminence of a public examination has led to a relative increase in anxiety about examinations by students in the inferior stream.

TABLE 16.2

The Effect of Streaming in Forms III and IV: Average Test Anxiety Scores

Type of school	Higher stream	Lower stream	Difference
	Form III		
Non-State Boys'	18·7	18·4	−0·3
State High A Mixed	15·8	18·7	2·9*
State High B Boys'	13·9	14·6	0·7
State High B Girls'	21·6	21·7	0·1
	Form IV		
Non-State Boys'	15·2	18·9	3·7
State High A Mixed	14·1	17·9	3·8
Technical Boys'	16·8	18·2	1·4

* Adjusted for sex difference

These students were also tested with a measure of general anxiety, but only trivial differences were found between the pairs of streamed groups in the above tables. The Melbourne results are thus consistent with the other studies in showing streaming effects on test anxiety but not on more general measures of anxiety.

The non-State girls' school did not practise streaming. The mean scores for the four forms listetd in this school ranged from 18·7 to 21·6. These values fall neatly between the means for two streamed groups of girls at High School A (Higher IV, 17·9; Lower III, 22·5), and rather below those of girls at High School B. It is possible that the effect of streaming is to offer about as much reassurance to the higher stream as it offers threat to the lower stream. This possibility seems worth investigating, and any general conclusions about the relations of streaming practices to test anxiety must ultimately include the effects on the higher as well as the lower streams. At present, all that can be stated is that streaming practices tend to be associated with relatively higher *test* anxiety in the *lower* streams.

References

[1] F. N. Cox, "Educational Streaming and General Text Anxiety". *Child Dev.*, 1962, **33**, pp. 381-90.

[2] H. J. Hallworth, "Anxiety in Secondary Modern and Grammar School Children". *Br. J. educ. Psychol.*, 1961, **31**, pp. 281-91.

[3] I. Sarnoff, F. F. Lighthall, R. R. Waite, K. S. Davidson, and S. B. Sarason, "A Cross-cultural Study of Anxiety Amongst American and English School Children". *J. educ. Psychol.*, 1958, **49**, pp. 129-36.

[4] I. Sarnoff, S. B. Sarason, F. F. Lighthall and K. S. Davidson, "Test Anxiety and the 'Eleven-plus' Examinations". *Br. J. educ. Psychol.*, 1959, **29**, pp. 9-16.

[5] S. B. Sarason, K. S. Davidson, F. F. Lighthall, R. R. Waite and B. K. Ruebush, *Anxiety in Elementary School Children*, John Wiley & Sons, New York, 1960.

[6] S. B. Sarason *et al.*, op. cit., pp. 86-89.

[7] F. N. Cox and Patricia M. Leaper, "General and Test Anxiety Scales for Children". *Aust. J. Psychol.*, 1959, **11**, pp. 70-80.

[8] S. B. Sarason *et al.*, op. cit., pp. 125-58.

[9] F. N. Cox, "Correlates of General and Test Anxiety in Children". *Aust. J. Psychol.*, 1960, **12**, pp. 169-77.

[10] S. B. Sarason *et al.*, op. cit., pp. 92-94.

[11] A. Castaneda, B. R. McCandless and D. S. Palermo, "The Children's Form of the Manifest Anxiety Scale". *Child Dev.*, 1956, **27**, pp. 317-26.

[12] H. J. Hallworth, op. cit., p. 285.

[13] R. Pintner, J. J. Loftus, G. Forlano and B. Alster, *Aspects of Personality*, World Books, New York, 1938.

[14] A. Davis, "Socialization and Adolescent Personality", in *Adolescence, 43rd Year Book, Part 1*, National Society for the Study of Education, Chicago, 1944, Chap. 11, pp. 198-216.

[15] A. Davis and R. J. Havighurst, "Social Class and Color Differences in Child-rearing". *Am. Soc. Rev.*, 1946, **11**, pp. 698-710.

[16] S. B. Sarason *et al.*, op. cit., p. 208.

[17] The writers wish to thank Professors Sarason and Mandler for making this Form available to them. The measure is described in G. Mandler and S. B. Sarason, "A Study of Anxiety Learning". *J. abnorm. soc. Psychol.*, 1952, **47**, pp. 166-73. The adapted form will be made available on request for research purposes in Australia.

Chapter 17

The Effect of a Single Experience of Success or Failure on Test Anxiety

GEORGE D. BRADSHAW and ERIC GAUDRY
School of Education, University of Melbourne

Junior high school pupils classified by sex, socio-economic area of school and attainment in English were assigned at random to 1 of 2 treatments. One group was given a difficult vocabulary test which they were likely to fail while the second group was given an easy vocabulary test. The failing group scored significantly higher than the successful group in the TASC which was administered immediately after the treatments. Significant differences were also found for level of attainment, for sex and for the interaction of treatment with level of attainment. The results are discussed in relation to earlier research findings that streaming practices in schools tend to be associated with higher test anxiety in the lower streams.

In a comparative study of British and American primary school children, Sarnoff *et al.*[1] found a higher level of test anxiety in British children for each of the grades 1-4. In the subsequent report, *Anxiety in Elementary School Children*, Sarason *et al.*[2] suggested that one of the important factors contributing to higher test anxiety in British primary school children may be the practice of streaming on attainment, which, they state, takes place usually at the end of the second or third grade of primary school (p. 152). This hypothesis was not supported by data published in either reference. In fact, an examination of the data of Sarnoff *et al.*[1] (Table 1, p. 133) shows that the mean difference in test anxiety between English and American children for grades 1 and 2 combined was 11·3 compared with a mean difference of 10·9 for grades 3 and 4 combined. It is clear that, as the difference for the two lower grades cannot have resulted from streaming, other explanations

From *Australian Journal of Psychology*, 1968, **20**, pp. 219-23. Reprinted by permission of G. D. Bradshaw and E. Gaudry and the *Australian Journal of Psychology*.

must be sought. In discussing factors which were not controlled in his matching procedure, Sarnoff commented that English children are exposed to formal education with emphasis on attainment at an earlier age than are American children. This may well have contributed to the observed differences in test anxiety between the English and the American children, but other cultural differences in educational practices and in child-rearing would have to be considered.

Two recent studies, one at the primary level (Cox[3]), and the other at the junior secondary level (Cox and Hammond[4]), have provided some evidence that "streaming practices tend to be associated with relatively higher test anxiety in the lower streams". It does not necessarily follow from this evidence that streaming has caused a higher level of test anxiety in the lower stream.

It seems reasonable to believe that an important cause of test anxiety is the continued experience of failure in test situations. From this, it follows that, if children are grouped by attainment, those placed in the lower stream would tend to have a higher level of test anxiety because of their more frequent experiences of failure in the past.

The situation in most schools will be complex and a series of studies is needed to establish factors which raise or lower the level of test anxiety. The primary purpose of this investigation was to examine the basic question whether an experience of failure increases test anxiety. The plan followed was to give one group of students an experience of success, and a second group of students an experience of failure, on a vocabulary test, each group then being given the Test Anxiety Scale for Children (TASC).

The experimental hypothesis was that the mean score on the TASC for the students given an experience of failure would be higher than for those given an experience of success.

Attainment was included in the design as a factor with two levels. A low but significant negative correlation between attainment and test anxiety has been found by Sarason *et al.*[2] (p. 132). A significant main effect for level of attainment could therefore be expected, with a consequential reduction in the size of the within groups error term in the analysis. The design also allows for the possibility of an interaction between the experimental treatment and the level of attainment.

For similar reasons sex was included as a factor in the design. It was expected on Sarason's findings, that girls would be more test-anxious than boys, and again, an interaction between treatment and sex was possible.

Method

SUBJECTS

The subjects were Grade 9 secondary pupils pursuing an academic programme in ten government co-educational high schools. Five of the schools were drawn from industrial areas while the other five were taken from "white collar" areas. One class of pupils was included from each school. The names of the pupils in each class were placed in order of merit on marks gained in English at a recent term examination. This list was then divided into an upper and lower half. Where two or more pupils tied at the cutting point, a table of random numbers was used to determine which was to be placed in the upper group and which in the lower.

The pupils in each class were then sorted into four groups on the two dichotomies, sex and attainment in English. From each of these four groups six cases were selected at random. Using a table of random numbers each group of six was split into two groups of three, one group of three being assigned to the "success" treatment and the others to the "failure" treatment. In four cases, due to sex imbalance in the class, two pupils only, instead of three, were included in each of the eight cells.

Those in each class who were not included in the experimental treatments formed a "placebo" group.

TEST MATERIALS

Three multiple-choice vocabulary tests of forty items were prepared, a difficult form for the Failure group, an easy form for the Success group and a form of intermediate difficulty for the "placebo" group. The first three items were common to all forms. The form for the Failure group contained words such as *equivocal*, *eschew*, *flaunt*, and *chimerical*, while the form for the Success group contained words such as *civil, vex, instrument*, and *fender*. The intermediate form contained a mixture of words from the easy and difficult forms.

In a preliminary trial of the easy and hard forms on the best academic Grade 9 class in a Melbourne high school, it was established that no child of this ability level was likely to score higher than 20 on the hard form or less than 35 on the easy form.

Some minor modifications were made to the TASC to make it more appropriate for Australian children in lower secondary grades.

PROCEDURE

All testing was carried out during one week in the middle of the school year. A seating arrangement was planned so that the Success group (S) was physically separated from the Failure group (F) by placing the "placebo" group down the centre of the room.

When the three groups were seated according to the pre-arranged plan, and the appropriate vocabulary tests had been distributed, the experimenter said, "The first test is a test of your knowledge of words. There are 40 questions in the test. You will have five minutes. When you have finished it we will mark it before we do the next test. When you know your mark, you will be able to tell from the board how well you did. A mark of over 30 is very good, a mark between 20 and 30 is satisfactory, a mark below 20 is poor." These divisions were then written prominently on the blackboard. While the pupils were working, answer keys were distributed. As the three forms had been prepared so that the same numbered answer was correct for each of the three sets of 40 items, only one type of answer key was necessary. At the end of the five minutes, each pupil marked his own paper.

Allowing no time for children to compare results, the TASC was distributed and administered in the manner recommended by Sarason *et al.*

After collecting the forms the experimenter explained to the class that they had taken part in an experiment in which some were given more difficult words to answer than others, the important issue being to reassure pupils who may have been worried about their low scores.

RESULTS

In schools with three cases per cell, one case was dropped at random so that for each school in the analysis there were two cases per cell. The mean score of these two cases was used as the basic observation so the analysis then became a 2 × 2 × 2 × 2 factorial design with five observations per cell. The analysis is reported in Table 17.1.

TABLE 17.1
Analysis of Variance of TASC Scores Following a Single Experience of Success or Failure

Source	df	Mean square	F
Treatment	1	281·3	5·14*
Level	1	423·2	7·73**
Sex	1	312·1	5·70*
Area	1	72·2	1·32
T × L	1	273·8	5·00*
T × S	1	140·5	2·57
T × A	1	192·2	3·51
L × S	1	7·2	—
L × A	1	42·1	—
S × A	1	125·0	2·28
T × L × S	1	96·8	1·77
T × L × A	1	11·3	—
T × S × A	1	115·2	2·10
L × S × A	1	18·1	—
T × L × S × A	1	2·5	—
Within	64	54·8	

* $p < \cdot 05$
** $p < \cdot 01$

Treatment, level, sex and socio-economic area are all fixed effects so that the within groups estimate of variance provided the appropriate error term for all comparisons.

It can be seen from Table 17.1 that three of the main effects and one interaction were significant at the 5 per cent level. Those who experienced failure scored significantly higher on the subsequent test anxiety scale than those who experienced success (the mean scores were 13·23 *v.* 11·35); females scored significantly higher than males (13·28 *v.* 11·30); children from the lower half of the class scored significantly higher than children from the upper half (13·44 *v.* 11·14); the interaction between treatment and level in class was significant. No other effect reached an acceptable significance level.

Discussion

The hypothesis was that a group given a single experience of failure would score significantly higher on the TASC than a group given a single experience of success. This treatment effect was significant, but no simple conclusion can be drawn without considering the significant interaction between treatment and level of attainment. The pattern of this interaction can be seen in Table 17.2 which shows the four relevant means.

TABLE 17.2

Mean Scores on TASC

Level of attainment	Treatment		Mean
	Failure	Success	
Upper	11·15	11·13	11·14
Lower	15·30	11·58	13·44
Mean	13·23	11·35	12·29

It would appear from this table that the differential treatment had no effect on the upper half of the classes but a marked effect on the lower half. It is not possible on these data alone to decide whether the difference is due to the effect in the lower group of the single instance of failure, or to the effect of the single instance of success, or to both. The last alternative seems the most probable of the three. But all alternatives support the hypothesis. The investigation has established that, under certain conditions, the level of anxiety is affected differentially by a single experience of success or failure.

It would seem reasonable therefore to conclude that the cumulative effects of such success and failure will lead to the negative correlation between attainment and test anxiety referred to above and to conclude that the level of anxiety can be affected by changes in the relative frequency of success and failure.

When children are streamed on the basis of attainment into separate classes, the immediate result will be that the children in the lower streams will have a higher average level of test anxiety than children in the upper streams, the situation observed by Cox and Hammond.[4]

If these children were then given a programme of work appropriate to their level of attainment with correspondingly easier examinations, one would expect to find a drop in test anxiety. A higher level of test anxiety should not then be found in the lower stream, a result which would appear to be inconsistent with the evidence of Cox and Hammond.[4] A possible explanation of this apparent inconsistency is that a special programme of work and examinations was not provided for the lower streams in the schools studied by Cox and Hammond.[4] Even where provision is made, a high level of test anxiety might continue if the children in the lower stream have high educational and vocational aspirations at variance with their level of attainment. The reverse situation may also be found. A drop in test anxiety might occur where a child ceases to be interested in educational success so that he no longer treats a low examination mark as a failure in relation to his own aspirations.

In essence, the results of this study suggest that the association of test anxiety with streaming is not due to streaming *per se*, but with the past history of success and failure which has led to placement in an upper or lower stream.

Any change in educational practice which decreases the relative frequency of failure in the lower stream, such as differential teaching and examining, should lead to a drop in test anxiety. Whether such a drop would actually occur would probably depend on other factors such as changes in level of aspiration, reporting practices and parental pressures.

References

[1] I. Sarnoff, F. F Lighthall, R. R. Waite, K. S. Davidson and S. B. Sarason, "A Cross-cultural Study of Anxiety amongst American and English School Children". *Educ. Psychol.*, 1958, **49**, pp. 129-36.

[2] S. B. Sarason, K. S. Davidson, F. F. Lighthall, R. R. Waite and B. K. Ruebush, *Anxiety in Elementary School Children*, John Wiley & Sons, New York, 1960.

[3] F. N. Cox, "General and Test Anxiety Scales for Children". *Aust. J. Psychol.*, 1960, **12**, pp. 169-77.

[4] F. N. Cox and S. B. Hammond, "Educational Streaming and Anxiety in Children". *Aust. J. Educ.*, 1964, **8**, pp. 85-90.

Chapter 18

Relation of Achievement Motivation and Test Anxiety to Performance in Programmed Instruction

HOWARD R. KIGHT
State University of New York, Buffalo
JULIUS M. SASSENRATH
University of California, Davis

The purpose of this study was to investigate the influence of achievement motivation and test anxiety on performance in programmed instruction. A quasi-projective measure of achievement imagery, a test-anxiety questionnaire, and an achievement pretest were administered to 139 undergraduate pupils and related to their performance on programmed instruction. Performance was analysed using three criteria: (*a*) *time needed to complete the material,* (*b*) *number of incorrect responses, and* (*c*) *a short-term retention test. The high-achievement-motivated students performed better on all three criteria and hence learned more efficiently with programmed instruction than low-achievement-motivated students. High-test-anxiety students also worked faster and made fewer errors than low-anxiety students, but failed to exhibit higher retention scores.*

Considerable attention has been given in recent years to the study of achievement motivation and its concomitant effect upon classroom learning. McClelland[1] and his followers have spurred much of this interest by providing ways to measure or identify achievement motivation objectively. Yet the research up to this point has not produced any clear-cut agreement with regard to the influence of achievement motivation within the classroom.

From the *Journal of Educational Psychology*, 1966, **57**, pp. 14-17. Reprinted by permission of H. R. Kight and J. M. Sassenrath and the *Journal of Educational Psychology*.

When grade-point averages (GPAs) are employed, as they often are, to represent scholastic achievement, the disparity becomes even clearer. Studies, for example, by McClelland *et al.*[2] and by Weiss, Wertheimer, and Groesbeck[3] have reported moderate correlations of 0·51 and 0·34, respectively, between achievement motivation and GPAs of subjects (*S*s), using college students as *S*s. Other studies by Lowell[4] and Parrish and Rethlingshafer,[5] for example, have been unable to show any significant relationship between grades and achievement motivation. Admitting that GPAs represent a rather general estimate of academic achievement, it could easily be argued that some other means of assessing achievement is needed.

Frequently some type of paper-and-pencil task has been employed as a measure of achievement—ranging from simple code substitution to highly complex arithmetic problems. The results generally have shown that *S*s with high achievement motivation tend to exhibit higher performance scores than do low-achievement-motivated *S*s, especially on the simpler tasks (French[6]). And although paper-and-pencil tasks may afford a more reliable index of achievement, they do not usually represent actual class material. If the influence of achievement motivation is to be fully understood, particularly at the college level, it would seem highly desirable to have the tasks represent actual course material.

One technique which seems valuable in this regard is programmed instruction. Not only is a student's rate of performance easily recorded, but also the difficulty of all items (tasks) is kept intentionally low. High-achievement-motivated students thus have an opportunity to work faster and to show higher overall proficiency than do *S*s with low achievement motivation. One of the two major purposes of this study, then, is to verify the hypothesis that high-achievement-motivated *S*s will exhibit higher performance on programmed instruction than will *S*s with low achievement motivation.

A second major purpose of this study is to investigate the relationship of a second, equally important motivation variable—test anxiety—to performance on programmed instruction. Although the research interest in test anxiety seems to be increasing, its influence upon performance within the classroom, particularly on programmed instruction, has not been sufficiently studied.

The results have generally shown that low-anxious *S*s perform better than high-anxious *S*s when the task involves either complex tasks or stress-motivating instructions (Lucas,[7] Nicholson,[8] Sarason, Mandler and Craighill[9]). Considerably less attention has been devoted to ascertain situations whereby high-anxious *S*s would actually excel in performance. One of the few studies to approach this problem was by Grimes and Allinsmith[10] in which it was found that highly anxious children worked best in highly structured situations. Since programmed instruction does represent a fairly well-structured, non-stressful situation as a rule, it would seem plausible to expect the high-test-anxious *S*s to work faster and show greater proficiency than low-test-anxious *S*s on this type of task. This, then, represents the second major hypothesis to be verified by this investigation.

Method

The *S*s for this study included 139 undergraduate students in Educational Psychology at Indiana University. Before beginning the programmed-instruction phase of the course, all *S*s were administered the following three instruments:

1. IOWA PICTURE INTERPRETATION TEST (Form RK).

This test, developed by Hedlund,[11] consists of four alternative responses to each of 24 Thematic Apperception Test (TAT) pictures. *S* is instructed to rank order each set of four alternatives on the basis of how well he describes what is happening in the picture. *S*'s achievement motivation, labelled his "achievement imagery" score, is derived by summing the ranks assigned by him to each alternative previously designated as an AI choice.

2. TEST ANXIETY QUESTIONNAIRE (TAQ).

Mandler and Sarason[12] developed this instrument to assess a person's feelings and attitudes about a variety of testing situations, for example, achievement, aptitude, etc. The strength of a person's subjective response is marked along a 0-15 point continuum and a total score obtained by summing for all 35 items.

3. ACHIEVEMENT PRETEST

This test, consisting of objective-type questions, was designed to serve as a preliminary measure of *S*'s skill and knowledge of basic principles related to test construction and evaluation. The questions closely paralleled but did not duplicate statements appearing on the programmed-instruction material.

During the three weeks which followed, approximately two hours each week, *S*s were given a series of three linear-type programmed booklets, dealing with the construction and analysis of classroom achievement tests.* Special care was taken at the outset to explain the main purposes and advantages underlying this type of instruction and to stress the relevance of the material being presented. Each booklet contained about 50 supply-type frames to which *S* responded on a specially prepared answer sheet. A record was kept of the number of correct responses for each *S* as well as the number of minutes spent. Mimeographed reading material, unrelated to the programmed material, was handed to each *S* as he completed each unit so that all *S*s began a unit at the same time and spent the same number of class periods. The experimenter supervised all aspects of the programmed instruction.

Design

On both the achievement-motivation and text-anxiety scales, *S*s were categorised as being either High (above the median) or Low. *S*s were

* The authors are indebted to John Krumboltz of Stanford University for providing most of the programmed-instruction material.

also classified as High (above the median) or Low on the basis of their pretests so that within each level of achievement motivation and test anxiety *S*s could be matched according to their pretest ability. This produced a $2 \times 2 \times 2$ factorial design and permitted the application of a three-way analysis of variance on each of several performance measures.

To adequately represent *S*s' performances on the programmed instruction, three separate measures were obtained. These included: (a) length of time each *S* took to complete the material, (b) number of frames answered incorrectly, and (c) *S*'s proficiency on an achievement test,* administered at the conclusion of the programmed instruction.

Results

Table 18.1 presents a comparison of means on the three performance measures for *S*s classified as High or Low in achievement motivation and High or Low in test anxiety.

In order to statistically test the two hypotheses—namely, that a higher degree of motivation, either achievement motivation or test anxiety, would produce better performance on the programmed instruction—an analysis of variance was performed on each of the three performance measures.†

On the first performance measure—minutes taken to complete the programmed material—all three main effects were significant and in the predicted direction. *S*s who were high in achievement motivation, test anxiety, or who scored high on the pretest tended to work through the program at a faster rate (Fs $= 11{\cdot}20$, $5{\cdot}08$, $7{\cdot}10$, respectively; $df = 1/131$). It should be noted, however, that a significant interaction occurred between achievement motivation and test anxiety ($F = 4{\cdot}16$; $df = 1/131$).

TABLE 18.1

Mean Scores on Three Measures of Performance in Programmed Instruction

Groups	Time	Errors	Retention
Low AM–Low TA	125·2	26·5	20·1
Low AM–High TA	124·6	19·9	20·6
High AM–Low TA	107·6	20·2	24·1
High AM–High TA	100·0	13·8	27·0

Note: AM: Achievement Motivation. TA: Test Anxiety

On the second performance measure—number of incorrect responses on the programmed material—two main effects were significant. *S*s high in achievement motivation or test anxiety tended to commit fewer errors (Fs $= 9{\cdot}25$, $5{\cdot}18$, respectively; $df = 1/131$). There was also a

* The achievement test was constructed as a parallel form of the pretest. Both tests were found by a previous analysis to have internal consistency reliabilities above 0·75 and to intercorrelate 0·81 with each other.

† These and succeeding calculations were performed on the IBM 709 data processing system at the Indiana University Computing Center. Grateful acknowledgement is made to Dale Hall who made computer time available for this study.

significant interaction effect between test anxiety and pretest ability ($F = 4 \cdot 08$; $df = 1/131$).

As a third measure of *S*s' performance on the programmed instruction, scores on the short-term retention test were analysed. Two main effects of achievement motivation and pretest ability were significant. Thus, *S*s high on either of these two variables scored reliably higher on the retention test than did *S*s low on the same variable (Fs $= 8 \cdot 00$, $37 \cdot 50$, respectively; $df = 1/130$).

Conclusions

The results of the present investigation substantially confirm both hypotheses. Specifically, it has been demonstrated that groups with high achievement motivation or high test anxiety (a) required less time to complete the programmed learning material, (b) made fewer overt errors on the material, and (c) received higher scores on a short-term retention test than did low-achievement-motivated or low-test-anxiety groups. These findings are in accord with some of the reported research, though it is hazardous at this point to make any direct comparisons. The occurrence of several significant interactions adds further scepticism and doubt regarding the overall effects of any one motive.

One important conclusion which has stemmed from the analysis of both Time and Errors scores is that on well-structured but relatively easy material such as programmed instruction, the highly motivated *S*s work much more efficiently than the less-motivated *S*s. In summary, the high-achievement-motivated and high-test-anxiety groups work faster and make fewer errors than those who are low on either variable. One possible explanation for this is that the highly motivated *S*s are able to derive greater benefit from the immediate knowledge of results, characteristic of programmed instruction.

References

[1] D. C. McClelland, *Personality*, Sloane, New York, 1951.

[2] D. C. McClelland, J. W. Atkinson, R. A. Clark and E. L. Lowell, *The Achievement Motive*, Appleton-Century-Crofts, New York, 1953.

[3] P. Weiss, M. Wertheimer and B. Groesbeck, "Achievement Motivation, Academic Aptitude and College Grades". *Educ. Psychol. Measur.*, 1959, **19**, pp. 663-65.

[4] E. L. Lowell, "The Effect of Need for Achievement on Learning and Speed of Performance". *J. Psychol.*, 1952, **33**, pp. 31-40.

[5] J. Parrish and Dorothy Rethlingshafer, "A Study of the Need to Achieve in College Achievers and Non-achievers". *J. genet. Psychol.*, 1954, **50**, pp. 209-26.

[6] E. G. French, "Some Characteristics of Achievement Motivation". *J. exp. Psychol.*, 1955, **50**, pp. 232-36.

[7] J. D. Lucas, "The Interactive Effects of Anxiety, Failure, and Intra-serial Duplication". *Am. J. Psychol.*, 1952, **65**, pp. 59-66.

[8] W. M. Nicholson, "The Influence of Anxiety upon Learning". *J. Personality*, 1958, **26**, pp. 303-19.

[9] S. B. Sarason, G. Mandler and P. G. Craighill, "The Effect of Differential Instructions on Anxiety and Learning". *J. abnorm. soc. Psychol.*, 1952, **47**, pp. 561-65.

[10] J. W. Grimes and W. Allinsmith, "Compulsivity, Anxiety, and School Achievement". *Merrill-Palmer Quart.*, 1961, **7**, pp. 247-69.

[11] J. L. Hedlund, "Construction and Evaluation of an Objective Test of Achievement Imaginery". Unpublished doctoral dissertation, University of Iowa, 1953.

Chapter 19

Effects of State Anxiety and Task Difficulty on Computer-Assisted Learning

HAROLD F. O'NEIL, Jr., CHARLES D. SPIELBERGER, and DUNCAN N. HANSEN
Florida State University

Performance on a computer-assisted learning task and changes in state anxiety (A-state) were investigated for 29 college students. An IBM 1440 system presented the learning materials and recorded responses. The measures of anxiety were scores on the A-state scale of the State-Trait Anxiety Inventory (STAI) and changes in systolic blood pressure. STAI A-state scores and blood pressure both increased while students worked on difficult learning materials and decreased when they responded to easy materials. Students with high A-state scores made more errors on difficult materials and fewer errors on easy materials than low A-state Ss. *The results were discussed in terms of Spence-Taylor Drive Theory and Spielberger's Trait-State Anxiety Theory.*

Most studies concerning the effects of anxiety on learning have originated either in artificial laboratory settings or realistic but poorly controlled natural settings. Computer-Assisted Instruction (CAI) systems provide a convenient natural setting in which it is possible to evaluate the learning process under carefully controlled conditions with materials that are relevant to the real-life needs of *S*. In the present study, the

The authors wish to express their appreciation to Harve E. Rawson who helped conduct this experiment, and to John B. Keats who developed the CAI mathematics materials. This research was supported in part by grants to the second author from The Florida State University Research Council (31-034) and to the third author from the United States Office of Education, Title B (No. 16-989). A paper based on this research was presented at the 1968 American Educational Research Association meetings, Chicago, Illinois.

From the *Journal of Educational Psychology*, 1969, **60**, pp. 343-50. Reprinted by permission of H. F. O'Neil, C. D. Spielberger and D. N. Hansen and the *Journal of Educational Psychology*.

effects of anxiety on the learning process were investigated in a CAI setting.

Research on anxiety has suffered from ambiguity with regard to the status of anxiety as a theoretical concept. Spielberger[1] has recently emphasised the need to distinguish between anxiety conceptualised as a transitory state or condition of the organism and as a relatively stable personality trait. State anxiety (A-State) consists of feelings of apprehension and heightened autonomic nervous system activity that vary in intensity and fluctuate over time. Trait anxiety (A-Trait) refers to individual differences in anxiety proneness, that is, to differential tendencies among individuals to respond with different levels of A-State in situations that are perceived as threatening. Persons high in A-Trait are also more disposed to see certain types of situations as more dangerous, particularly situations that involve failure or some threat to the individual's self-esteem (Spielberger and Smith[2]).

To study the effects of anxiety on learning, a theory of learning is needed that specifies the complex relationship between anxiety and behaviour. According to the drive theory proposed by Spence[3] and Taylor,[4] the performance of high-anxious students would be inferior to that of low-anxious students on complex or difficult tasks in which competing error tendencies were stronger than correct responses, and superior on tasks in which correct responses were dominant relative to incorrect response tendencies. Empirical support for the Spence-Taylor Drive Theory has been reported by Spence[5] in eyelid conditioning, Taylor,[4] and Spence and Spence[6] in serial learning and paired-associate learning, and many others (e.g., Denny,[7] Lucas,[8] Spielberger and Smith[2]).

The present study investigated the relationship between A-State and performance in learning difficult and easy mathematics concepts by CAI. It was hypothesised that A-State measures would increase during the learning of difficult CAI materials and decrease for easy materials. With respect to the relationship between A-State and performance, it was hypothesised that *S*s who were high in A-State would make more errors than low A-State *S*s on the difficult CAI task, and that this relationship would be reversed on the easy task. A unique feature of this study was that measures of A-State were obtained while *S*s performed on the learning task.

Method

SUBJECTS

The *S*s were 29 undergraduate students (16 males, 13 females) who were enrolled in the Introductory Psychology course at Florida State University. In order to satisfy the balanced design criterion for statistical evaluation with biomedical computer programs (Dixon[9]), three male *S*s were dropped from the data analyses.*

* The two male *S*s with the highest A-Trait scores were dropped so that the mean A-Trait scores for males and females would be more comparable. A third male *S* was eliminated because of his inability to perform satisfactorily on the easy CAI task. For this task, his error rate was five standard deviations above the mean for the total group.

ANXIETY MEASURES

The State-Trait Anxiety Inventory (STAI; Spielberger, Gorsuch, and Lushene[10]) was used to assess A-Trait and the phenomenological aspects of A-State. The 20-item STAI A-Trait scale required *S*s to indicate how they generally feel; the 20-item STAI A-State scale required them to indicate "how you feel *right now*". Measures of systolic blood pressure (SBP) were obtained as indicants of the physiological aspects of A-State. Blood pressure was measured by means of a desk model Baumanometer, Model 300.

APPARATUS AND LEARNING MATERIALS

A CAI typewriter terminal controlled by an IBM 1440 system (IBM[11]) presented the learning materials and recorded *S*s' responses. The CAI program was written in a linear format using COURSEWRITER I (IBM[11]), an author-programmer language. This program was composed of two main parts: a difficult section that required *S*s to prove the mathematical field properties of complex numbers, and an easy section that consisted of problems on compound fractions. The programming logic required *S* to solve each succeeding problem correctly before he could attempt the next one. After the first five correct problems in each section, a short anxiety scale consisting of four STAI items was presented.

Step 1: There are two ways that this computer can write the fractional number three-fourths. One way is $\frac{3}{4}$. The other way is 3/4. In this program, all fractional numbers will be written like this – 3/4. You are going to need a little practice.

Step 2: Type two thirds.

Step 3: (Answer) 2/3.

Step 4: You should have typed 2/3. Try again.

Fig. 19.1 The easy CAI materials format.

The format for the easy materials is presented in Fig. 19.1. The computer first typed the problem context as indicated in Step 1. It then typed the specific problem to which *S* was expected to respond (Step 2). If *S* typed the correct answer (Step 3), the computer responded "good" and proceeded to the next question. If *S* responded incorrectly, Step 4 was presented. The *S* continued to respond until he gave the correct answer.

For the difficult materials, the computer first presented the student with a series of definitions and examples concerning the field properties of complex numbers, for example, substitution of terms, commutivity with respect to addition, associativity with respect to addition, etc. The problem was then presented in the format indicated in Fig. 19.2. The problem itself is presented Step 1, followed by a proof statement (Step 2), as in the proof of a geometric theorem. From a sheet listing the field properties of complex numbers, *S* selected a validating property and typed his answer (Step 3). If he typed in the correct answer, in this case "S" (substitution), the computer would respond "correct" and the next problem would be presented. However, if *S* responded incorrectly, he would be given another example of the correct validating property (Step 4) and told to try again. The *S* was required to respond to each item until he gave the correct answer.

Step 1: We will show, for all pairs of elements in C, that their sum is also an element of C. To do this, we will select two arbitrary elements Z1 = (a,b) and Z2 = (c,d) and show that Z1 + Z2 is an element of C.

Step 2: Z1 + Z2 = (a,b) + (c,d) (Type the abbreviation to justify this step.)

Step 3: The subject types "S" to indicate that the answer is SUBSTITUTION.

Step 4: Make sure that you are using the correct abbreviation. If R = 8 and S = 7, then 8 + 7 may be written in place of R + S. Try again.

Fig. 19.2 Difficult CAI materials format.

EXPERIMENTAL DESIGN

The study was conducted by two *E*s who supervised as many as eight *S*s at the same time. The experimental procedures, which were the same for all *S*s, were divided into four periods: the pretask period, two performance periods (difficult and easy), and the post-task period. During the performance periods, *S* first progressed through the difficult learning materials, and then the easy materials. The two A-State measures, SBP and the STAI A-state scale, were taken at the end of each period. Measurement of SBP always preceded the administration of the STAI except during the pretask period when SBP followed the STAI. The design of the study minimised the possibility of any systematic *E* bias since all anxiety measures were taken blind and neither *E* took a complete series of anxiety measures on any single *S*.

PROCEDURE

The *S*s were seated at a CAI terminal which was located in a sound-deadened, air-conditioned room. The *S* remained in the experimental room for the entire experiment; *E* entered the room only to read instructions, administer the anxiety scales, and take blood pressure.

In the pretask period, each *S* was asked to read an introductory booklet that contained instructions designed to induce mild stress, and directions for operating the terminal. The instructions were:

> It has been found that success in this program does not require mathematical or quantitative ability . . . it requires instead, the ability to make the same kinds of abstractions and generalisations that you are expected to make in many college courses.

After reading these instructions, *S* pressed a buzzer to summon *E* who administered, first, the STAI A-Trait scale and then the STAI A-State scale. To emphasise the state and trait instructions, *E* read them aloud. Upon completion of the STAI, *S*'s blood pressure was taken four to eight times until it had stabilised (two SBP readings in a row, not differing by more than 2 millimetres of mercury). The blood pressure cuff was removed after each series of readings so *S*s could operate the terminal.

After the SBP measure was obtained in the pretask period, *S*s were immediately given the difficult materials. After *S* had responded correctly to the first five proof statements, a brief (four-item) anxiety scale was presented by the computer.* The *S* was instructed to respond to this scale according to "how you felt while working on the complex numbers". Upon completing the brief anxiety scale, *S* continued through the remaining items of the difficult section. After this section was completed, SBP was taken and the STAI A-State scale was given with the following instructions:

> Fine. Now I want you to fill out this questionnaire again. This time I want you to circle the appropriate number to indicate how you felt while you were working on the complex numbers program. Read each item carefully and check it according to how you *felt* while working on this program.

After the difficult CAI task was completed, the easy task was presented. Immediately following the first five items of the easy CAI task, another brief four-item A-State scale was administered by the computer. The *S* then continued until the easy CAI task was finished. At this point, *S*'s SBP was taken and the STAI A-State scale was given with the following retrospective instructions:

> Good. Now I want you to circle the appropriate number to indicate how you felt while working through the compound fractions program. Remember, respond to each item according to how you felt while you were working on the fractions.

Post-task period. After a 3-minute waiting period, a final measure of SBP was taken and the 20-item STAI A-State scale was given (for the fourth time) with standard instructions. Each *S* was then assured that he had performed satisfactorily and thanked for his participation in the experiment.

Results

The dependent variables in this study were STAI A-State scores, SBP measures, and errors on the difficult and easy CAI tasks. In evaluating the effects of experimental conditions on each of these measures, task

* The four-item A-State scale administered by the computer during the learning task consisted of items from the 20-item STAI A-State scale that had shown the highest item-remainder correlation coefficients in previous research (C. D. Spielberger and R. L. Gorsuch. *The Development of the State-Trait Anxiety Inventory*. Final report to United States Public Health Service for Grants No. MH 7229, MH 7446, and HD 947, entitled *Mediating Processes in Verbal Conditioning*, available from C. D. Spielberger, Department of Psychology, Florida State University, Tallahassee, Florida 32306). These items were: (a) "I feel pleasant", (b) "I feel regretful", (c) "I find myself worrying about something", (d) "I am calm". The *S* responded to each item by rating himself on the following 4-point scale: (a) "Not at all", (b) "Somewhat", (c) "Moderately so", (d) "Very much so".

periods and sex were the independent variables in a two-factor analysis of variance with repeated measures. Errors were further examined as a function of STAI A-State scores.

STAI A-STATE

The mean STAI A-State scores for the pretask period, the two performance periods, and the post-task period are presented in Fig. 19.3. It may be noted that A-State scores increased from the pretask period to the difficult task period, decreased in the easy task period, and showed no change from the easy task period to the post-task period. When these data were statistically evaluated, only the periods main effect was significant, $F = 13 \cdot 448$, $df = 3/72$, $p < 0 \cdot 001$. Thus, STAI A-State scores differed significantly in the four periods, but there were no differences in the A-State scores of men and women. Individual *t* tests revealed that A-State scores were significantly higher in the difficult task period than in any of the other periods, and that A-State scores in the easy period were significantly lower than in either the pretask period or the difficult task period.

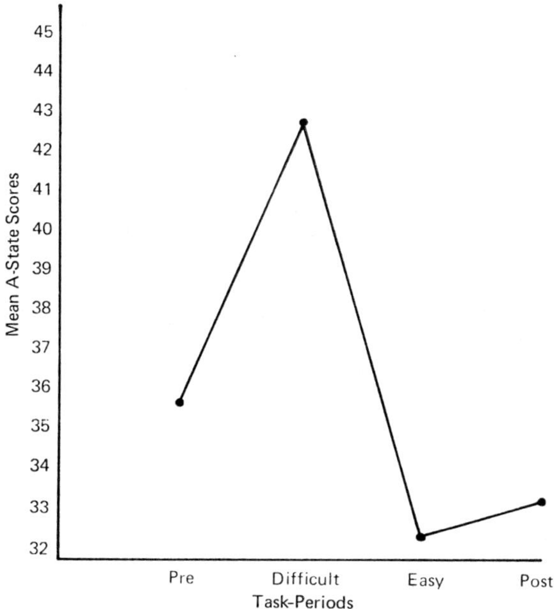

Fig. 19.3 Mean STAI A-State scores across task-periods.

SYSTOLIC BLOOD PRESSURE

The mean SBP values, corresponding to the periods for which STAI A-State measures were available, are presented in Fig. 19.4. It may be noted that SBP increased during the difficult task period, decreased during the easy task period, and showed little change from the easy task period to the post-task period. In the analysis of variance for these data, the main effects for sex, $F = 11 \cdot 44$, $df = 1/24$, and task-periods, $F = 8 \cdot 54$, $df = 3/72$, were statistically significant at the $0 \cdot 01$ level. These results indicated (a) that SBP for males was much higher than for females; and (b) that SBP showed changes over task-periods similar to those obtained for the STAI A-State scores, as may be noted by comparing Figs 19.3 and 19.4. Differences between mean SBP scores across periods were further evaluated by a series of *t* tests. For both men and women, the SBP measures taken immediately after *S*s performed on the difficult task were significantly higher than in any other period.

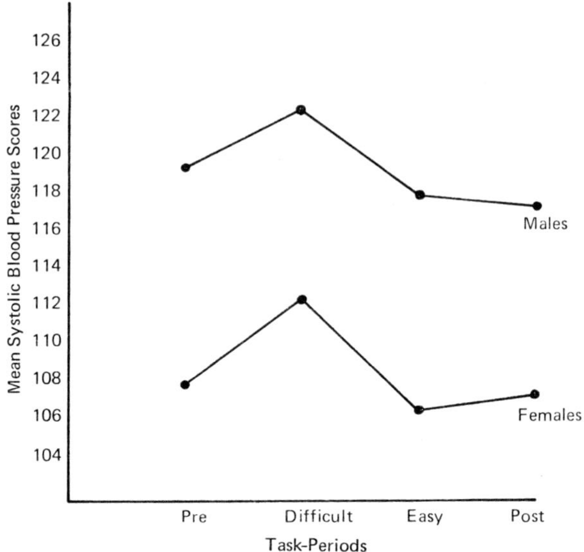

Fig. 19.4 Mean systolic blood pressure for males and females across task-periods.

ERRORS ON THE CAI TASKS

In the analysis of the error data for the difficult and the easy CAI tasks, each task was divided into two sections. For the difficult task, the first section consisted of the 5 proof statements, Diff/(1-5), and the second section consisted of the remaining 12 proof statements, Diff/(6-17). Similarly, for the easy task, the two sections corresponded to the first 5 items, Easy/(1-5), and the remaining 11 items, Easy/(6-16). (Brief A-State scales were given immediately after the first section of each task.) The mean number of errors per correct response for the first and second sections of the difficult and easy tasks are presented in Fig. 19.5. It may be noted that the Diff/(1-5) section produced the most errors, the Diff/(6-17) section produced an intermediate number of errors, and that errors fell almost to zero for both sections of the easy task. These data were evaluated in an analysis of variance in which sex was the between-*S* variable and tasks was the within-*S* variable. A significant *F* ratio for tasks was obtained, $F = 20 \cdot 71$, $df = 3/72$, $p < 0 \cdot 001$, indicating that the mean number of errors declined across the four performance periods. There were no differences in the mean number of errors for men and women.

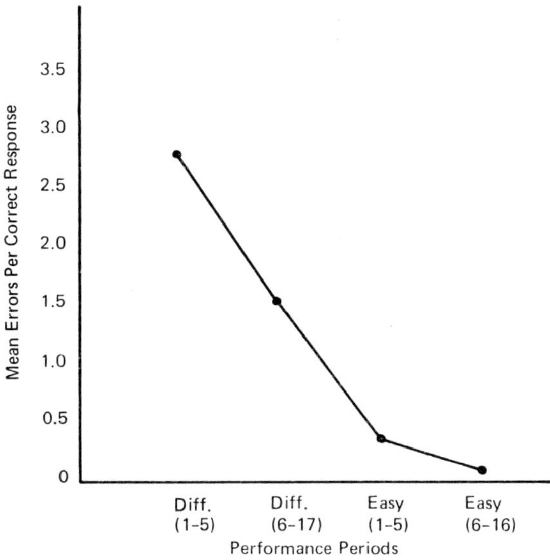

Fig. 19.5 Mean errors per correct response for the two sections of the difficult and easy task.

RELATION BETWEEN A-STATE AND ERRORS ON THE CAI TASKS

Since there were no significant sex differences in the previous analyses for either STAI A-State scores or errors, the data for both sexes were combined in evaluating the relationship between these measures. However, separate analyses were carried out for the difficult and easy tasks because there were significant differences between them in the mean number of errors and there were very few errors on the easy task. For these analyses, *S*s were divided at the STAI A-State median that was obtained on each task. The *S*s whose scores were above the median were designated the high-A-State group and those below the median were designated the low-A-State group.

The median STAI A-State score for the difficult task was 43. Two *S*s whose scores fell at the median were dropped from this analysis. The number of errors made by the high- and low-A-State groups on the two sections of the difficult task are indicated in Fig. 19.6. The high-A-State *S*s made nearly twice as many errors on the Diff/(1-5) section than did the low-A-State *S*s. In contrast, the high-A-State *S*s made fewer errors on the Diff/(6-17) section than did the low-A-State *S*s. An analysis of variance for these data yielded a significant A-State $\times$ Tasks interaction, $F = 5 \cdot 08$, $df = 1/24$, $p < 0 \cdot 05$, and a main effect of Tasks, $F = 6 \cdot 59$, $df = 1/22$, $p < 0 \cdot 05$.

A similar analysis was carried out for the easy task. The median STAI A-State score on this task was 32 and four *S*s whose scores fell at the median were dropped from the analysis. No statistically significant

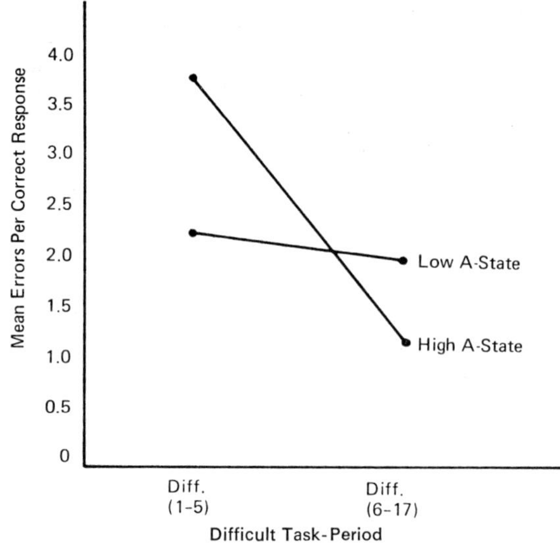

Fig. 19.6 Mean errors per correct response for high-A-State and low-A-State *S*s for the two sections of the difficult task.

F ratios were obtained in the analysis of the data for the easy task, indicating that differences in A-State were unrelated to performance. However, as may be noted in Fig. 19.5, there were so few errors on the easy task that it would be difficult for any personality variable to influence error rate.

Discussion

In this study, state anxiety increased when *S*s worked on difficult CAI materials and decreased while *S*s performed on easy CAI materials. This pattern of change in A-State was observed for the 20-item STAI A-State scales, the SBP measures, and the brief anxiety scales that were embedded in the learning materials. The adjusted means for the four-item, computer-presented anxiety scales were 41·80 for the difficult section and 32·20 for the easy section, as compared to means of 43 and 32·31 for the corresponding full scale STAI A-State measures.

While there were no differences in the STAI A-State scores for men and women, the SBP scores for males were significantly higher than for females. The most parsimonious explanation of this difference is that SBP is dependent upon physical characteristics, such as height, weight, and body build (Gregg[12]). The males, on the average, were taller, heavier, and more muscular than the females and higher levels of SBP would be expected on the basis of these physical differences. Since changes in SBP for the males were parallel to those observed for the females, the data for males and females may be regarded as replications of the experimental findings in samples with different population parameters.

Since there were so few errors on the easy task, only the analyses of the data for the difficult task provided meaningful information regarding the relationship between level of anxiety (A-State) and errors. For the difficult task there were actually two levels of difficulty, corresponding to the first 5 proof statements and the remaining 12 proofs. The mean number of errors for Diff/(1-5) was 2·76, and for Diff/(6-17) it was 1·58; the difference between these means was statistically significant.

For Diff/(1-5), the high-A-State *S*s made more errors than *S*s who were low in A-State, whereas low-A-State *S*s made more errors than high-A-State *S*s on Diff/(6-17). On the assumption that A-State reflects drive level, the finding that performance on the CAI task was an interactive function of level of A-State and task difficulty is consistent with drive theory (Spence and Spence[6]), which predicts that the effects of anxiety on learning will depend upon the relative strength of correct responses and competing error tendencies. In the present study, A-State apparently influenced performance by activating error-tendencies on the more difficult section of the CAI task on which error rate was relatively high, and by activating correct responses on the easier section of this task for which error rate was lower. It should also be noted that the CAI mode of presentation of the learning materials provided an effective method for the concurrent manipulation of level of A-State and the difficulty of the learning task.

In contrast to the complex interactive relationship obtained between A-State, task difficulty, and errors, no significant differences were found as a function of A-Trait. There was, however, a strong relationship between A-Trait and A-State. The Pearson product-moment correlation between A-Trait and A-State scores on the Diff/(1-5) task was 0·50. But despite this moderately strong relationship, the small number of *S*s whose A-State scores were inconsistent with their A-Trait scores contributed so much variability that the analysis of errors on the learning task as a function of A-Trait failed to yield any statistically significant *F* ratios. It is interesting to note that the performance of these inconsistent *S*s was determined more by their A-State scores than by their A-Trait scores.

These results support Spielberger's[1] contention that it is important to distinguish between A-Trait and A-State in research on anxiety and learning. Although individuals high in A-Trait are more likely to manifest higher levels of A-State in learning relatively difficult materials, particularly where there is some threat to self-esteem, specific situational and task factors may also produce high levels of A-State in some *S*s who are low in A-Trait. It is also probable that some *S*s who are high in A-Trait may not respond with high levels of A-State because a particular task is not threatening to them. Therefore, there would seem to be no meaningful alternative to the actual measurement of A-State as *S*s perform on a learning task, but this is rarely done in investigations of anxiety and learning.

References

[1] C. D. SPIELBERGER, "Theory and Research on Anxiety", in C. D. Spielberger (Ed.), *Anxiety and Behavior*, Academic Press, New York, 1966.

[2] C. D. SPIELBERGER and L. H. SMITH, "Anxiety (Drive), Stress, and Serial-position Effects in Serial-verbal Learning". *J. exp. Psychol.*, 1966, **72**, pp. 589-95.

[3] K. W. SPENCE, "A Theory of Emotionally Based Drive (D) and its Relation to Performance in Simple Learning Situations". *Am. Psychologist*, 1958, **13**, pp. 131-41.

[4] J. A. TAYLOR, "Drive Theory and Manifest Anxiety". *Psychol. Bull.*, 1956, **53**, pp. 303-20.

[5] K. W. SPENCE, "Anxiety (Drive) Level and Performance in Eyelid Conditioning". *Psychol. Bull.*, 1964, **61**, pp. 129-39.

[6] K. W. SPENCE and J. SPENCE, "The Motivational Components of Manifest Anxiety: Drive and Drive Stimuli", in C. D. Spielberger (Ed.), *Anxiety and Behavior*, Academic Press, New York, 1966.

[7] J. P. DENNY, "The Effects of Anxiety and Intelligence on Concept Formation". *J. exp. Psychol.*, 1966, **72**, pp. 596-602.

[8] J. D. LUCAS, "The Interactive Effects of Anxiety, Failure, and Intra-serial Duplication". *Am. J. Psychol.*, 1952, **65**, pp. 59-66.

[9] W. J. DIXON (Ed.), *Biomedical Computer Programs*, University of California Press, Los Angeles, 1967.

[10] C. D. SPIELBERGER, R. GORSUCH and R. LUSHENE, *State-Trait Anxiety Inventory, Preliminary Test Manual*. Consulting Psychologists Press, Palo Alto, Calif., 1969.

[11] INTERNATIONAL BUSINESS MACHINES CORPORATION, *IBM 1401, 1440 or 1460 Operating System: Computer Assisted Instruction*. Endscott, New York, 1965.

[12] D. E. GREGG, "The Regulation of Pressure and Flow in Systemic and Pulmonary Circulation", in C. H. Best and N. B. Taylor (Eds), *The Physiological Basis of Medical Practice*, Williams and Wilkins, Baltimore, 1961.

Chapter 20

Test Anxiety, Intelligence and Academic Achievement

ERIC GAUDRY and DONALD FITZGERALD
School of Education, University of Melbourne

School marks at the half-yearly examination were collected in English, Mathematics, History, Geography, French and Science. Using a multivariate analysis, the performance of children in twelve Grade 7 schools was examined as a function of anxiety and intelligence. Considerable support was found for the experimental hypothesis that high anxiety would tend to facilitate the performance of the most able children while lowering that of the remainder when compared with their low anxiety counterparts. High anxiety was found to be associated with the greatest performance deficit at the second highest of the five levels of ability. A possible explanation for this result was advanced.

The theory of emotionally based drive proposed by Spence and Taylor (Spence,[1] Taylor[2]) has stimulated many researchers to investigate the relationship between anxiety and academic achievement. This theory states that the effect of anxiety or drive level on performance in a learning task depends upon the relative strength of the correct and competing responses. On simple tasks in which correct response tendencies are stronger than competing responses, high drive (D) facilitates performance; on complex or difficult tasks in which competing response tendencies may be stronger than the correct responses, high D interferes with performance, at least in the initial stages of learning.

A recent extension of Drive Theory, to encompass intelligence, takes into account the possibility that individual differences in intelligence and anxiety may have different effects on learning that depend on the difficulty of the task and the stage of learning. The fundamental assumption in this extension of Drive Theory, first explicated by Spielberger,[3] is that the relative strengths of the correct and competing response-tendencies are determined in part by the subjects' level of intelligence.

In very simple tasks where few error-tendencies are evoked in either high- or low-IQ *S*s, high anxiety (HA) is expected to facilitate performance. Tasks of intermediate difficulty may be expected to be relatively easy for high-IQ *S*s in whom fewer competing error tendencies are evoked and for whom the strength of correct response tendencies is stronger. In contrast, such tasks may be quite difficult for low-IQ *S*s in whom numerous error tendencies are generated and the strength of correct response tendencies is relatively weak. On such tasks, HA should facilitate the performance of *S*s with high IQ while leading to decrements in *S*s with low IQ. However, as learning progresses and the habit strength of correct responses increases relative to that of error tendencies, HA should begin to facilitate performance even for the low ability *S*s.

With tasks that are very difficult even for the most able subjects, the prediction is that low-anxious (LA) *S*s will initially show superior performance. As the task becomes easier with repeated trials, high anxiety should begin to facilitate the performance for high-IQ *S*s and lower that of low-IQ *S*s. The possibility of high-anxious, low-IQ *S*s finally surpassing the performance of the low-anxious, low-IQ *S*s would depend on whether the task could be mastered by the low-IQ *S*s.

Evidence supporting this extension is scarce because of the traditional reluctance of experimental psychologists to come to grips with individual differences. However, there are four studies, two concerned with laboratory tasks and two with academic achievement which directly tested this extension of Drive Theory. Denny,[4] using an ingenious concept formation task designed to give a good range of scores, found anxiety and intelligence to be interactive. High anxiety was associated with high performance for high-IQ *S*s but with low performance for low-IQ *S*s when compared with their low-anxious counterparts. Katahn[5] found a strikingly similar result using a serial learning task.

Spielberger[6] subdivided introductory psychology students into five levels of ability. He found that high anxiety was associated with poorer performance than was low anxiety at the four lower levels but with slightly better performance at the very highest level of ability. Katahn[5] found the same pattern of results at Vanderbilt.

The Yale Test Anxiety Scales (TAS) prepared by Sarason and his colleagues have also been used to investigate the relationship between anxiety and academic achievement. Many investigators (e.g., Atkinson and Litwin,[7] Caplehorn and Sutton,[8] Cox,[9] Sarason[10]) have reported negative correlations between scores on the TAS and various measures of academic achievement. While the TAS was not developed as a measure of generalised drive as was the MAS, it is possible to interpret these negative correlations in this framework (for discussion of this point see Cox[9]).

This raises the possibility that the relationship between test anxiety scores and academic achievement may be being obscured by an anxiety by intelligence interaction. Accordingly, it was decided to analyse the performance of junior high-school pupils on a variety of school subjects as a function of anxiety and intelligence. Sex was included as an independent variable to see if this interaction might differ for males and females.

Method

SUBJECTS

The subjects were pupils from twelve Grade 7 secondary schools in Victoria. Seven classes were located in the Melbourne metropolitan area and five in rural areas.

PROCEDURE

The Test Anxiety Scale for Children (TASC), with minor modifications to make it appropriate for Australian children in lower secondary grades, and the Australian Council for Educational Research Intermediate Test D, a measure of intelligence, were given to all *S*s before the half-yearly examination. School marks for this examination were collected for English, Mathematics, History, Geography, French and Science. These marks were standardised to yield distributions with a mean of 50 and a standard deviation of 10. This was done within each class, as the investigation was concerned with performance within class settings.

The TASC was factor-analysed, using Alpha analysis (Kaiser and Caffrey[11]). The Varimax rotated solutions produced four meaningful factors. Factor scores on the first factor which was uncorrelated with intelligence and which accounted for most variance, were used as the independent variable of anxiety. The three questions having the highest loadings on this factor were items 25, 7 and 19. These items are reproduced below:

25. When the teacher says that he is going to give the class a test, do you become afraid that you will do poorly? (Loading 0·68).
7. When the teacher is teaching you mathematics, do you feel that other children in the class understand better than you? (Loading 0·65).
19. Are you afraid of school tests? (Loading 0·59).

Other questions with high loadings were 1, 12, 20 and 15. (All above 0·50). All those items are also concerned with worry and apprehension about performing poorly in test situations.

The data were analysed by a multivariate analysis of variance which provided estimates not only for each school subject, but also a pooled estimate for the six subject-areas combined. Because the prediction was that only the most able would find school examinations easy, the pupils within each class were divided into five levels of intelligence. The contrast examined was between the top fifth and the bottom four-fifths of each class. However, other orthogonal contrasts allowed for an examination of the performance of the four levels within the lower section.

Thus, within each class, the pupils were separated by sex, then divided into high- and low-anxiety groups by splitting at the median, and further subdivided into five levels of intelligence to form a sex by anxiety by intelligence design. For each class, cell means were computed and used as the units of measurement in the various analyses.

Results

The main results are shown in Tables 20.1-20.7.

TABLE 20.1
Multivariate Analysis of School Marks for Intelligence

Variable	Mean square	F	p
English	2732·9	73·5	<0·001
Mathematics	3614·5	92·7	<0·001
History	1552·4	34·4	<0·001
Geography	2541·1	56·7	<0·001
French	2363·0	48·1	<0·001
Science	3567·5	87·5	<0·001

As expected, the very able students performed significantly better than the bottom four-fifths in all subject areas.

The probability of the multivariate contrast for the highest level of intelligence versus the other four levels is less than 0·001.

The corresponding analysis for anxiety is shown in Table 20.2.

TABLE 20.2
Multivariate Analysis of School Marks for Anxiety

Variable	Mean square	F	p
English	124·1	3·34	<0·07
Mathematics	338·4	8·68	<0·005
History	34·9	0·77	<0·38
Geography	57·9	1·29	<0·26
French	107·2	2·18	<0·14
Science	60·4	1·48	<0·23

In all subjects, the direction of the difference in performance favoured the LA *S*s over the HA *S*s. However, this difference was significant beyond the 0·05 level only in mathematics. The probability for the multivariate contrast is less than 0·18.

The analysis for sex is shown in Table 20.3.

TABLE 20.3
Multivariate Analysis of School Marks for Sex

Variable	Mean square	F	p
English	298·6	8·03	<0·005
Mathematics	23·2	0·60	<0·441
History	0·1	0·00	<0·960
Geography	80·5	1·80	<0·182
French	102·3	2·08	<0·151
Science	51·8	1·27	<0·261

The mean performance of the girls was higher than the boys in English, French and History, whereas the mean performance of the boys was slightly higher in Science, Mathematics and Geography. Only the English result was significant beyond the 0·05 level. Overall, the girls displayed significantly superior performance (< 0·001).

The anxiety by intelligence interactions are shown in Table 20.4.

TABLE 20.4
Multivariate Analysis of School Marks for Anxiety by Intelligence Interaction

Variable	Mean square	F	p
English	6·62	0·18	$<0·67$
Mathematics	100·22	2·57	$<0·11$
History	88·85	2·00	$<0·16$
Geography	214·45	4·79	$<0·03$
French	10·23	0·21	$<0·65$
Science	11·33	0·28	$<0·60$

Although the multivariate contrast yielded a probability level of less than 0·245 and therefore the null hypothesis cannot be rejected, the pattern of the relationship that appeared will be reported as they are, in our opinion, suggestive for future research. The interaction was significant beyond the 0·05 level for Geography and approached that level of significance in Mathematics and History. The pattern of the interactions for the multivariate contrast showed that at levels 1, 2, 3 and 4, LA *S*s performed better than HA *S*s (48·8 *v.* 46·3) while at level 5, HA *S*s were insignificantly different from LA *S*s (56·8 *v.* 56·5). As the anxiety by intelligence contrast was the primary concern in this investigation, the pattern of the interactions is shown in Table 20.5.

TABLE 20.5
Means for Intelligence by Anxiety Interaction

	English		Maths		History		Geography		French		Science	
Anxiety	IQ level		IQ level		IQ level		IQ level		IQ level		IQ level	
	1234	5	1234	5	1234	5	1234	5	1234	5	1234	5
High	46·4	56·4	45·1	56·4	47·0	56·0	46·3	58·1	46·8	56·2	46·4	57·7
Low	49·1	57·3	49·3	57·6	49·4	54·3	49·7	55·3	49·3	56·8	48·6	58·0

In History and Geography, the HA, high-IQ group performed better than the LA, high-IQ *S*s while HA was associated with lower performance at the lower ability levels. In the other four subjects, the pattern of interaction was similar to that found in History and Geography, with the effect of anxiety being produced only in the lower ability groups.

In order to detect which ability levels were being most affected by high anxiety, the scores of all six subjects were combined at each of five levels of ability. These means are shown in Table 20.6.

TABLE 20.6
Means for the Ability Groups for the Six Subjects Combined

Anxiety	Intelligence level				
	1	2	3	4	5
High	40·5	46·9	49·0	49·4	56·8
Low	42·8	47·6	49·0	54·8	56·5

High anxiety had a detrimental effect on performance at the two lowest and the second highest levels whereas the direct of the effect was reversed at the highest level of ability. There were no anxiety by sex effects, or anxiety by sex by intelligence which reached an acceptable level of significance.

A *post-hoc* comparison of the performance of the *S*s at levels 4 and 5 is reported in Tables 20.7, 20.8 and 20.9. (See the section headed Discussion for a justification for this analysis.)

TABLE 20.7
Multivariate Analysis of School Marks for Anxiety—Intelligence Levels 4 and 5

Variable	Mean square	F	p
English	124·15	3·34	$<0·07$
Mathematics	338·36	8·68	$<0·004$
History	34·87	0·77	$<0·38$
Geography	57·87	1·29	$<0·26$
French	107·22	2·18	$<0·14$
Science	60·39	1·48	$<0·22$

While the LA group did perform significantly better than the HA group only in Mathematics (55·9 *v.* 53·1; $< 0·05$), a similar effect was found in English ($< 0·07$).

These main effects of anxiety have to be interpreted in terms of the anxiety by intelligence interactions shown in Table 20.8.

TABLE 20.8
Multivariate Analysis of School Marks for Intelligence by Anxiety—Intelligence Levels 4 and 5

Variable	Mean square	F	p
English	57·00	1·53	$<0·22$
Mathematics	136·54	3·50	$<0·06$
History	261·72	5·79	$<0·02$
Geography	328·03	7·33	$<0·007$
French	205·69	4·19	$<0·04$
Science	57·54	1·41	$<0·24$

In this table, the interactions were significant beyond the 0·05 level in Mathematics, History, Geography and French with the probability for the multivariate contrast being less than 0·063. The pattern of these interactions is shown in Table 20.9.

TABLE 20.9
Means for Intelligence by Anxiety for Levels 4 and 5

	English		Maths		History		Geography		French		Science	
Anxiety	IQ level		IQ level		IQ level		IQ level		IQ level		IQ level	
	4	5	4	5	4	5	4	5	4	5	4	5
High	49·8	56·4	49·1	56·4	48·8	56·0	49·6	58·1	48·8	56·2	50·5	57·7
Low	54·2	57·3	54·2	57·6	54·3	54·3	56·0	55·3	56·0	56·8	54·1	58·0

In all cases, the interactions are in the predicted direction. The only other effects reaching the 0·05 level were a sex effect in English ($p < 0·005$) and an intelligence effect for all subject areas.

Discussion

The experimental hypothesis was that high anxiety would facilitate the performance of the most able group and lower the performance of the remainder when compared with the comparable low-anxious groups. While the multivariate analysis (Table 20.4) yielded a probability figure of less than 0·25 reaching the 0·05 level only in Geography, and therefore the hypothesis received no support, the data are generally suggestive of the predicted trends. The results shown in Table 20.5 show that the means were in the expected direction in each of the six subject areas. The mean scores presented in Table 20.6 present a clear picture of the trend of these interactions. That is, while high anxiety was associated with slightly higher performance for the most able children, it was associated with lower performance at all other levels except the centre group where the mean scores were identical.

One aspect of these means merits further comment. This was the large score difference between the LA and HA groups at level 4 (5·4 score units). This is more than double that of any other difference between the LA and HA subgroups. While the tests of the significance of difference between means (Tables 20.7, 20.8 and 20.9) for levels 4 and 5 cannot be justified in terms of the hypothesis being tested, it should be remembered that the theory was developed within a very narrow frame of reference.

Extrapolation to the very complex field of academic achievement is likely to involve variables which do not affect the learning of laboratory tasks such as a list of paired-associates. It is in this exploratory phase that subsidiary hypotheses can be derived and tested by further studies.

Remembering that all the contrasts reported in this paper are concerned with the comparisons of one group's performance with the performance of other groups *within the same class*, a feasible explanation immediately presents itself. The pupils at level 4 are above average in ability but are performing at a level below that of the pupils at level 5. If the pupils at level 4 have high academic and vocational aspirations and are perhaps under strong parental pressure to succeed, then this is the very group on which high anxiety might be expected to have the most interfering effect. In terms of Spielberger and Lushene's[12] distinction between State and Trait anxiety, the pupils at level 4, while at the same level of Trait anxiety as those at level 5, may respond to examination stress with a very high amount of State anxiety. Finding the examination situation somewhat difficult, this high level of anxiety would interfere with performance. On the other hand, even if the HA children at level 5 responded with high State anxiety, this would facilitate performance as the task is for them a relatively easy one. Consequently, the anxiety by intelligence interaction should be most marked in the comparison of the performance of the two upper levels. This is clearly evident in Tables 20.8 and 20.9.

This *post-hoc* analysis should be treated with caution and requires independent validation. However, it should be noted that the children in the two top levels of ability would be of approximately the same ability level as those on which the anxiety by ability interactions were reported by Spielberger[6] and Katahn[5] at first year college level at Vanderbilt and Duke Universities.

Of the other effects, little needs to be said. As expected, intelligence was highly related to performance, the overall means rising regularly with increasing ability. The sex contrast showed females to have higher scores in the more verbal subjects of English, French and History, and the males to be slightly superior in the more technical subjects (Science, Mathematics and Geography).

References

1 K. W. Spence, "A Theory of Emotionally Based Drive (D) and its Relation to Performance in Simple Learning Situations". *Am. Psychologist,* 1958, **13**, pp. 131-41.

2 J. A. Taylor, "Drive Theory and Manifest Anxiety". *Psychol. Bull.*, 1956, **53**, pp. 303-20.

3 C. D. Spielberger (Ed.), *Anxiety and Behavior*, Academic Press, New York, 1966.

4 J. P. Denny, "Effects of Anxiety and Intelligence on Concept Formation". *J. exp. Psychol.*, 1966, **72**, pp. 596-602.

5 M. Katahn, "Interaction of Task Difficulty and Ability in Complex Learning Situations". *J. pers. soc. Psychol.*, 1966, **3**, pp. 475-79.

6 C. D. Spielberger, "The Effects of Manifest Anxiety on the Academic Achievement of College Students". *Ment. Hyg., N.Y.*, 1962, **46**, pp. 420-26.

7 J. W. Atkinson and G. H. Litwin, "Achievement Motive and Test Anxiety as Motives to Approach Success and Avoid Failure". *J. abnorm. soc. Psychol.*, 1960, **60**, pp. 52-63.

8 W. F. Caplehorn and A. J. Sutton, "Need Achievement and its Relation to School Performance, Anxiety and Intelligence". *Aust. J. Psychol.*, 1965, **17**, pp. 44-51.

9 F. N. Cox, "Test Anxiety and Achievement Behaviour Systems related to Examination Performance in Children". *Child Dev.*, 1964, **35**, pp. 909-15.

10 S. B. Sarason, K. S. Davidson, F. F. Lighthall, R. R. Waite and B. K. Ruebush, *Anxiety in Elementary School Children*, John Wiley & Sons, New York, 1960.

11 H. F. Kaiser and J. Caffrey, "Alpha Factor Analysis", *Psychometrika*, 1966, **30**, pp. 1-14.

12 C. D. Spielberger and R. E. Lushene, "Theory and Measurement of Anxiety States", in R. B. Cattell (Ed.), *Handbook of Modern Personality Theory*, Aldine, Chicago, Ch. 10, 1969.

Chapter 21

Digit Span: An Indicant of Trait or State Anxiety?

WILLIAM F. HODGES
University of Colorado

CHARLES D. SPIELBERGER
Florida State University

Clinical psychologists generally interpret lower scores on Digit Span (DS) relative to other Wechsler subtests as indicating anxiety. However, research findings on this topic are inconsistent and difficult to interpret because of ambiguity with regard to the concept of anxiety. To clarify this ambiguity, Spielberger has proposed a conception of anxiety that elaborates on the distinction, initially proposed by Cattell and Scheirer, between anxiety as a transitory state (A-state) and as a relatively stable personality trait (A-trait). The present study evaluated the relationship between DS performance and measures of A-trait (Taylor Manifest Anxiety scale) and A-state (Zuckerman Adjective Checklist) for 72 male undergraduates. The Ss *reporting high levels of A-state showed significant decrements in DS performance. There was no difference in the DS performance of high- and low-A-trait* Ss.

For many years clinical psychologists have interpreted the pattern of scores obtained on subtests of the Wechsler Intelligence Scale as reflecting important personality characteristics of individuals taking the test. One of the most frequent inferences is that a low score on the Digit Span (DS) test, as contrasted with scores on other subscales, indicates the presence of anxiety (Rapaport, Gill and Schafer,[1] Rapaport, Schafer and Gill,[2] Wechsler[3]).

The research summarised in this report was based on data obtained while the authors were associated with the Department of Psychology at Vanderbilt University. It was supported in part by a United States Public Health Service Fellowship (5-F1-MH-28,537) from the National Institute of Mental Health to the first author and by a research grant (HD 947) to the second author from the National Institute of Child Health and Human Development, United States Public Health Service.

From *Journal of Consulting and Clinical Psychology*, 1969, **33**, pp. 430-34. Reprinted by permission of W. F. Hodges and C. D. Spielberger and the *Journal of Consulting and Clinical Psychology*.

While clinicians tend to agree that DS performance is lowered by "anxiety", the meaning and conceptual status of anxiety is ambiguous. Cattell and Scheier[4] have noted that the term "anxiety" has been used to refer both to a transitory state or condition of the organism and to a relatively stable personality trait. Although variables that loaded differentially on their State and Trait anxiety factors have been identified by Cattell and Scheier, they have not specified the nature of the relationship between these two anxiety concepts.

Spielberger has recently proposed a theoretical conception of anxiety that specifies the relationship between the concepts of State and Trait anxiety (Spielberger,[5] Spielberger and Lushene[6]). Building on the work of Freud,[7, 8] Cattell and Scheier,[4] and Spence,[9] Spielberger defines State anxiety (A-State) as consisting of subjective feelings of apprehension and concern and heightened autonomic nervous system activity; whereas Trait anxiety (A-Trait) refers to anxiety proneness, that is, to individual differences in the disposition to respond with high levels of A-State under stressful circumstances.

The failure in most investigations of DS and anxiety to distinguish between A-State and A-Trait has made the literature in this area difficult to interpret. Anxiety (presumably A-State) was induced in two studies by telling *S*s they were doing poorly on a test of ability (Griffiths,[10] Moldawsky and Moldawsky[11]). For *S*s exposed to this stressful experimental condition, significant decrements in DS performance were obtained as compared to non-stress control groups. In two other studies in which the anxiety measures could be reasonably interpreted as indicants of A-State, decrements in DS performance were also found to be associated with increases in A-State (Pyke and Agnew,[12] Walker and Spence[13]).

The results have been inconsistent and contradictory in investigations of the relationship between DS and presumed measures of A-Trait, such as the Taylor Manifest Anxiety (*MA*) scale, the IPAT Anxiety scale, and the Welsh *A* scale. Three studies have reported no relationship between DS performance and A-Trait measures (Jackson and Bloomberg,[14] Matarazzo,[15] Walker and Spence[13]), one study found a positive relationship (Jurjevich[16]), and one reported a negative relationship (Calvin *et al.*[17]). The results have also been equivocal in studies in which clinical diagnosis was used as the criterion of A-Trait (Lewinski,[18] Merril and Heathers,[19] Warner[20]).

The present study was designed to evaluate the relationship between DS performance and measures of State and Trait anxiety. The *S*s who differed in A-Trait were required to perform on a DS task under failure and control conditions.* In accordance with Trait-State Anxiety Theory (Spielberger and Lushene[6]), high-A-Trait *S*s were expected to respond with higher levels of A-State than low-A-Trait *S*s in the failure condition, but not in the non-threatening control condition. It was further expected that performance decrements in DS would be inversely related to level

* An additional condition involving the threat of shock was also used, but these data were not relevant to the hypotheses of the present study and are reported elsewhere (Hodges[22]).

of A-State but not necessarily to A-Trait, since anxiety must be aroused in order for it to interfere with behaviour.

Method

The *S*s were 72 male undergraduates enrolled in the Introductory Psychology course at Vanderbilt University who volunteered for an experiment on "numbers". The Taylor[21] *MA* scale served as the measure of A-Trait. The *S*s with *MA* scale scores of 18 or greater were designated the high-A-Trait group; those with scores of 11 or lower were designated the low-A-Trait group. These cutoff points approximated the upper and lower quartiles of the *MA* scale distribution for males, after *S*s with Lie scale scores of 8 or higher had been eliminated from the *S* pool.

Prior to the experiment, each *S* was assigned either to the Failure (stress) Condition or the Control (non-stress) Condition. The *S*s were tested individually. At the beginning of the experiment, there was an 8-minute rest period during which *S* was required to complete the Zuckerman[23] Affect Adjective Check List (AACL) by checking adjectives that described "how you feel at this moment". The AACL served as the measure of the phenomenological component of A-State.

Since Wechsler[3] considered performance on Digits Backwards (DB) to be particularly sensitive to anxiety level, a special DB task was constructed for this study. After *S* completed the AACL, he was given DB from the WAIS (Wechsler,[24] p. 41) in accordance with standard instructions to determine his limit, that is, the level at which he twice failed to repeat a series of a specified number of DB. He was then given two practice series, each one digit less than his limit, followed immediately by six more series of digits of the same length. The number of series correctly reproduced by *S* out of the six that were given to him was his Performance score.

After the Performance score was obtained, each *S* in the Failure Condition was told that, although he was not doing too badly, he could do better and that other *S*s seemed to be doing better then he was. In the Control Condition, *S* was told that he was doing fine and that the next set of DBs were to be "just as easy as the ones he had just completed". Six more series of digits of the same length were then given to obtain a Test score for each *S*. Following the test series, *S* was required to fill out the AACL again, according to how he felt "while repeating the last few series of digits".

Results

The effects of experimental conditions and level of A-Trait on DS performance are presented in Fig. 21.1. It may be noted that the failure instructions produced decrements in DS performance. In an analysis of variance of these data, in which Conditions and A-Trait level were the between-*S*s variables and Time Periods the within-*S*s variable, only the Conditions main effect ($F = 4{\cdot}97$, $df = 1/68$, $p < 0{\cdot}05$) and the Conditions $\times$ Time Periods interaction effect ($F = 6{\cdot}73$,

$df = 2/68$, $p < 0{\cdot}01$) were significant. The absence of any statistically significant effects involving the A-Trait variable confirmed the impression gained from Fig. 21.1 that DS Performance was unrelated to A-Trait.

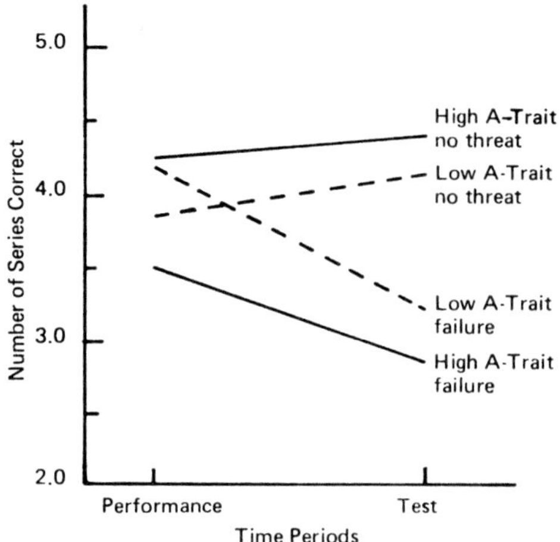

Fig. 21.1 The effects of failure and no-threat instructions and level of A-Trait on Digits Backwards during the Performance and Test Periods ($N = 18$ per group).

Next, the effects of experimental conditions and level of A-Trait on intensity of A-State during the Test Period were evaluated. An examination of the distribution of A-State scores obtained during the Test Period indicated that the median AACL score was 12. The data for 14 *S*s whose AACL scores fell at the median were eliminated; *S*s with scores above and below the median were designated the high- and low-A-State groups, respectively. In order to provide an equal number of *S*s in the high- and low-A-State groups, four *S*s with AACL scores below the median were randomly eliminated.

As may be noted in Table 21.1, all of the high-A-Trait *S*s in the Failure group were classified as high A-State, and all but one of the low A-Trait *S*s in the Control group were classified as low A-State. A statistical analysis of these data yielded a significant chi-square ($\chi^2 = 24{\cdot}78$, $df = 3$, $p < 0{\cdot}01$), indicating that the effect of experimental conditions on A-State was influenced by level of A-Trait.

TABLE 21.1

Frequency of High-A-Trait and Low-A-Trait Subjects in the Failure and Control Conditions Who Were Classified as High or Low in A-State under Stress

Conditions	Groups	N	Low A-State	High A-State
Control	Low A-Trait	14	13	1
Control	High A-Trait	13	6	7
Failure	Low A-Trait	13	8	5
Failure	High A-Trait	14	0	14
Totals		54	27	27

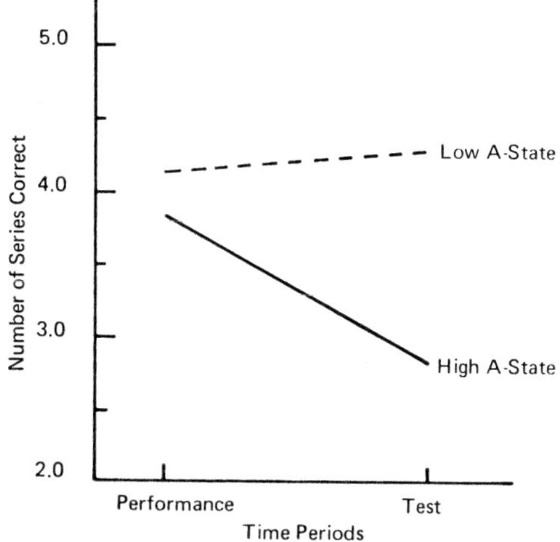

Fig. 21.2 The effects of low-A-State and high-A-State levels on Digits Backwards during the Performance and Test Periods ($N = 27$ per group).

The next step in the analysis of the data involved an evaluation of the effects of A-State on DS Performance. For this analysis, the data for the Failure and Control Conditions were combined. The mean DB scores obtained in the Performance and Test Periods by *S*s in the high- and low-A-State groups are presented in Fig. 21.2. These data were evaluated in an analysis of variance in which the most important finding was the significant A-State $\times$ Time Periods interaction ($F = 6{\cdot}52$, $df = 1/52$, $p < 0{\cdot}01$). The main effects of A-State ($F = 5{\cdot}50$, $df = 1/52$, $p < 0{\cdot}05$) and Time Periods ($F = 4{\cdot}90$, $df = 1/52$, $p < 0{\cdot}05$) were also statistically significant. In order to evaluate further the effects of A-State on DB Performance, the data for each Time Period were separately analysed by a Neuman-Keuls test (Winer[25]), which indicated that the high- and low-A-State groups did not differ in the Performance Period ($F = 0{\cdot}49$, $df = 1/52$) but that the DS Performance of the high-A-State group was significantly lower than that of the low-A-State group during the Test Period ($F = 11{\cdot}05$, $df = 1/52$, $p < 0{\cdot}01$).

Discussion

In the present study, the failure to find a relationship between DS Performance and scores on the Taylor *MA* scale provides further evidence that decrements in DS are unrelated to measures of A-Trait (Jackson and Bloomberg,[14] Matarazzo,[15] Walker and Spence[13]). The finding that *S*s in the Failure Condition showed a significant decrement in DS performance was consistent with the results of previous investigations in which some form of stress was used to induce anxiety (Griffiths,[10] Moldawsky and Moldawsky,[11] Pyke and Agnew,[12] Walker and Spence[13]), and suggests that decrements in DS performance are associated with elevations in A-State.

Evaluating the effects of experimental conditions on level of A-State, it may be noted in Table 21.1 that high-A-Trait *S*s were particularly disposed to manifest high levels of A-State under conditions of failure-stress. It may also be noted that over half of the high-A-Trait *S*s responded with high levels of A-State in the Control Condition, even though they were told that they were doing well. In contrast, less than half of the low-A-Trait *S*s responded with high A-State in the Failure Condition and only one low-A-Trait *S* responded with high A-State in the Control Condition. These results support the hypothesis that high-A-Trait *S*s tend to respond with high levels of A-State to situations that involve threats to self-esteem such as failure or threat of failure (Spielberger and Lushene[6]).

The finding of greatest theoretical importance in this study was the statistically significant decrement in DS performance for *S*s who reported a high level of A-State. The fact that high-A-State *S*s had lower DS scores than low-A-State *S*s in the Test Period but not in the Performance Period is consistent with the interpretation that decrements in DS Performance are produced by elevations in A-State. This finding is also consistent with Trait-State Anxiety Theory (Spielberger and Lushene[6]), which posits that performance decrements on learning and memory tasks are produced by differential levels of A-State rather than differences in A-Trait. According to this view, it would be expected that DS Performance will be related to A-Trait *only* when differential levels of A-State are induced (by environmental circumstances or stressful experimental conditions) in *S*s who differ in A-Trait.

An alternative explanation for the decrements in DS performance that were observed in the present study is that *S*s who did more poorly on the DS task experienced an increase in A-State in response to their deteriorating performance. This interpretation argues that the failure instructions in some way influenced performance without altering anxiety level, and that changes in A-State subsequently resulted from *S*'s reaction to his poor performance. Although the experimental design in the present study does not permit a definitive choice between these alternative explanations of the findings, the first interpretation, which emphasises the impact of anxiety level on performance rather than the reverse, would appear to be more consistent with the clinical literature.

References

[1] D. Rapaport, N. N. Gill and R. Schafer, *Diagnostic Psychological Testing*, Year Book Publishers, Chicago, 1945, Vol. 1. (Republished: Revised edition, International Universities Press, New York, 1968.)

[2] D. Rapaport, R. Schafer and M. Gill, *Manual of Diagnostic Psychological Testing. I: Diagnostic Testing of Intelligence and Concept Formation*, Josiah Macy, Jr. Foundation, New York, 1944.

[3] D. Wechsler, *The Measurement and Appraisal of Adult Intelligence*, Williams and Wilkins, Baltimore, 1958.

[4] R. B. Cattell and I. H. Scheier, *The Meaning and Measurement of Neuroticism and Anxiety*, Ronald Press, New York, 1961.

[5] C. D. Spielberger, "Theory and Research on Anxiety", in C. D. Spielberger (Ed.) *Anxiety and Behavior*, Academic Press, New York, 1966.

[6] C. D. Spielberger and R. E. Lushene, "Theory and Measurement of Anxiety States", in R. B. Cattell (Ed.), *Handbook of Modern Personality Theory*, Aldine, Chicago, in press, 1971.

[7] S. Freud, *New Introductory Lectures in Psychoanalysis*, Norton, New York, 1933.

[8] S. Freud, *The Problem of Anxiety*, Norton, New York, 1936.

[9] K. W. Spence, "Anxiety (Drive) Level and Performance in Eyelid Conditioning", *Psychol. Bull.*, 1964, **61**, pp. 129-39.

[10] J. S. Griffiths, "The Effect of Experimentally Induced Anxiety on Certain Subtests of the Wechsler-Bellevue". Unpublished doctoral dissertation, University of Kentucky, 1958.

[11] S. Moldawsky and P. C. Moldawsky, "Digit Span as an Anxiety Indicator". *J. consult. Psychol.*, 1952, **16**, pp. 115-18.

[12] S. Pyke and N. Agnew, "Digit Span Performance as a Function of Noxious Stimulation". *J. consult. Psychol.*, 1963, **27**, p. 281.

[13] R. E. Walker and J. T. Spence, "Relationship between Digit Span and Anxiety". *J. consult. Psychol.*, 1964, **28**, pp. 220-23.

[14] D. N. Jackson and R. Bloomberg, "Anxiety: Unitas or Multiplex?" *J. consult. Psychol.*, 1958, **22**, pp. 225-27.

[15] R. G. Matarazzo, "The Relationship of Manifest Anxiety to Wechsler-Bellevue Subtest Performance". *J. consult. Psychol.*, 1955, **19**, p. 218.

[16] R. M. Jurjevich, "Interrelationships of Anxiety Indices of Wechsler Intelligence Scales and MMPI Scales". *J. gen. Psychol.*, 1963, **69**, pp. 135-42.

[17] A. D. Calvin, P. B. Koons Jr., J. C. Bingham and H. H. Fink, "A Further Investigation of the Relationship between Manifest Anxiety and Intelligence". *J. consult. Psychol.*, 1955, **19**, pp. 280-82.

[18] R. J. Lewinski, "The Psychometric Pattern: I. Anxiety Neurosis". *J. clin. Psychol.*, 1945, **1**, pp. 214-21.

[19] R. M. Merril and L. B. Heathers, "Deviations of Wechsler-Bellevue Subtest Scores from Vocabulary Level in University Counseling-center Clients". *J. consult. Psychol.*, 1952, **16**, pp. 469-72.

[20] S. J. Warner, "The Wechsler-Bellevue Psychometric Pattern in Anxiety Neurosis". *J. consult. Psychol.*, 1950, **14**, pp. 297-304.

[21] J. A. Taylor, "A Personality Scale of Manifest Anxiety". *J. abnorm. soc. Psychol.*, 1953, **48**, pp. 285-90.

[22] W. F. Hodges, "Effects of Ego Threat and Threat of Pain on State Anxiety". *J. personal. soc. Psychol.*, 1968, **8**, pp. 364-72.

[23] M. Zuckerman, "The Development of an Affect Adjective Check List for the Measurement of Anxiety". *J. consult. Psychol.*, 1960, **24**, pp. 457-62.

[24] D. Wechsler, *Manual for the Wechsler Adult Intelligence Scale*, Psychological Corporation, New York, 1955.

[25] B. J. Winer, *Statistical Principles in Experimental Design*, McGraw-Hill, New York, 1962.

Subject Index

Author Index